ACLS History E-Book

Reprint Series

The ACLS History E-Book Project (www.historyebook.org) collaborates with constituent societies of the American Council of Learned Societies, publishers, librarians and historians to create an electronic collection of works of high quality in the field of history. This volume is produced from digital images created for the Project by the Scholarly Publishing Office and the Digital Library Production Service at the University of Michigan, Ann Arbor. The digital reformatting process results in an electronic version of the text that can be both accessed online and used to create new print copies. This book and hundreds of others are available online in the History E-Book Project through subscription.

Many of the works in the History E-Book Project are available in print and can be ordered either directly from their publishers or as part of this series. For information refer to the online Title Record page for each book. Inquiries regarding this series can be directed to info@hebook.org.

ACLS
HISTORY E-BOOK

http://www.historyebook.org

OXFORD STUDIES IN AFRICAN AFFAIRS

TRADE AND POLITICS
IN THE NIGER DELTA
1830–1885

TRADE AND POLITICS
IN THE NIGER DELTA
1830-1885

AN INTRODUCTION TO THE
ECONOMIC AND POLITICAL HISTORY
OF NIGERIA

BY

K. ONWUKA DIKE

OXFORD
AT THE CLARENDON PRESS

Oxford University Press, Ely House, London W.1

GLASGOW NEW YORK TORONTO MELBOURNE WELLINGTON
CAPE TOWN SALISBURY IBADAN NAIROBI LUSAKA ADDIS ABABA
BOMBAY CALCUTTA MADRAS KARACHI LAHORE DACCA
KUALA LUMPUR HONG KONG

FIRST PUBLISHED 1956

REPRINTED LITHOGRAPHICALLY IN GREAT BRITAIN
AT THE UNIVERSITY PRESS, OXFORD
FROM CORRECTED SHEETS OF THE FIRST EDITION
1959, 1962, 1965, 1966

PREFACE

THE history of the Niger Delta in the period under survey is to some extent an introduction to the economic and political history of Nigeria. This region became from the sixteenth century the main centre of the African trade with Europeans in the Gulf of Guinea. During the seventeenth and eighteenth centuries the Delta was one of the most important, if not the leading, slave mart in West Africa. In the first thirty years of the nineteenth century when the trade in palm oil had begun to displace the trade in men it exported more oil than the rest of West Africa put together. When in 1830 the Landers proved that the Delta was the mouth of the River Niger, a succession of British commercial expeditions sought to penetrate the hinterland through the Niger waterway. In the nineteenth century, therefore, this river, like the more famous Congo, became one of the highways of imperialism in Africa. The Royal Niger Company—the chief instrument by which Britain won her Nigerian empire—based its activities in the Delta and the Niger valley. British ascendancy in this important trading area justified her claim to supremacy in the Niger territories during the Berlin West African Conference of 1885.

This study analyses the detailed process by which the existing native governments were gradually supplanted by British consular power and following it the Crown Colony administration. For West Africa the period under survey was essentially an epoch of change and revolution. With the suppression of the traffic in men and the rise of 'legitimate commerce' the pattern of the earlier trade soon disappeared. The ramifications of the revolution which accompanied this economic change in the social and political planes are discussed in the introductory chapter.

This work is not, in the main, concerned with topics such as the suppression of the slave trade, the work of the Navy, or with the personalities and policies of the various Foreign and Colonial Secretaries. The British end is dealt with only in so far as it helps to explain events in West Africa. Two types of sources, British and African, have been used in the preparation of this book. As a rule British sources are cited in the footnotes, but from the nature of some of the African material it has not always been easy to indicate every source. There is, however, a note on the sources at the end of the book.

My thanks are due to Professor Vincent T. Harlow, now Beit Professor of the History of the British Empire, Oxford, and Professor Gerald S. Graham, Rhodes Professor of Imperial History, King's College, London, who supervised my doctoral dissertation and were always most helpful. The former rendered great assistance in arranging for the publication of this book. My friend and former teacher, Professor Jack Simmons of University College, Leicester, who called my attention to the importance of the subject of this study, very kindly read most of the chapters, and made valuable suggestions. Without the generous leave granted me by Professor W. Hamilton Whyte, first Director of the West African Institute of Social and Economic Research, in the academic year of 1952/3, this work would not have been ready for publication. Miss M. F. F. Etherton aided me tirelessly with the labour of checking and typing the manuscript. The staffs of the Public Record Office and of the British Museum, London, were always most courteous and helpful.

K. O. D.

Department of History,
University College,
Ibadan, Nigeria.

This book grew out of my thesis for the degree of Doctor of Philosophy (History) in the University of London. It is dedicated to the Old Boys of my Alma Mater, the Dennis Memorial Grammar School, Onitsha.

CONTENTS

MAP

CHAPTER I

The Pattern of West African Trade and Politics, 1481–1830

THE history of modern West Africa is largely the history of five centuries of trade with European nations; commerce was the fundamental relationship that bound Africa to Europe.[1] This long period of trade divides conveniently into two sections. The first opened with the Portuguese advent and ended with the prohibition of the slave trade in 1807. The second section covers the years 1807–85. A review of the former will soon show its essential characteristics and the more permanent elements in its organization. It is important to emphasize the pattern of trade during these 400 years in order to appreciate the depth and intensity of the revolution which occurred in it during the nineteenth century.

This trade fluctuated in accordance with European policies and demands. In the fifteenth and sixteenth centuries gold constituted the main quest.[2] During the seventeenth and eighteenth centuries the slave trade predominated. It must be admitted, however, that the total value of Portuguese trade with West Africa does not compare well with that of Asiatic commerce. A report included in the Cottonian MSS. of the British Museum shows that towards the end of the sixteenth century, whereas the eastern trade yielded an annual revenue of two million cruzados, the value to the Portuguese Crown of the entire trade of Guinea was only 280,000 cruzados.[3] But the

---

[1] Compare with the statement by J. Simmons in *Parish and Empire* (London, 1952). 'The British Empire was founded first of all upon trade. .. It was trade, first and foremost, that took Englishmen to the West Indies, to Africa, to India and Malaya and the Far East. This is a fact, not open to dispute, and it is in my view very foolish of English men to feel in any way ashamed of it.'

[2] From all accounts this early trade paid handsomely. Azurara records that the highest returns were registered between 1450 and 1458. Pachecco estimates that 170,000 dobras of pure gold were carried annually to Portugal from Guinea after 1481. 'There are indications, in the correspondence of King John II of Portugal that the Crown came to depend upon a regular supply of gold from Mina.' The quotation is from Almeida, *Historia de Portugal*, iii. 554, as cited by J. W. Blake in *European Beginnings in West Africa* (London, 1937), pp. 82–84.

[3] J. W. Blake, *European Beginnings*, pp. 96–98.

golden age of the Guinea traffic so far as Portugal was concerned ended about 1530. The report quoted above dealt with the trade of Portugal when her monopoly was on the wane. The discovery of the Cape route to India, therefore, did not mean the extinction of the African trade. The richer and vaster Asiatic commerce naturally demanded greater attention, but the West African trade did not die.

From 1510 Africans ceased to be mere curiosities in Portugal. At Lisbon in that year the first considerable number of African slaves for the West Indies were bought and exported. By 1539 the Portuguese were estimated to have been exporting between 10,000 and 12,000 annually. As is well known, this enforced movement of West Africans to the New World was accelerated by the European colonization of the Americas and Indies. In 1609 the English occupied Bermuda and by 1623 Barbados, the Leeward Islands, Nevis, Antigua, and Mont- · serrat were considered English possessions. The French and English also settled at St. Christopher in that year. In 1635 the French colonized Guadeloupe and Martinique, and Marie Galante in 1648. St. Lucia and Grenada were occupied in the fifties. The Dutch, in their turn, settled at Curaçao, St. Eustatius, and Tobago around the 1630's. The Danes, who were late arrivals, acquired the small island of St. Thomas in 1671. As the European colonization of the West Indies gained momentum so the exploitation of the Caribbean region increased the demand for African labour. In none of these islands did the slave trade assume importance until the introduction and development of the plantation method of sugar cultivation in the years 1640–50. This not only created a demand for labour greater than the system of indenture could supply, but also gave the planter a commodity—sugar—profits from the sale of which paid for the coveted Negroes. Meanwhile the position in Africa itself was changing. Portuguese monopoly of West African commerce collapsed when challenged in the sixteenth and seventeenth centuries because her military and naval defences were very weak. They could not withstand the naval might of England, Holland, and France. Henceforth West Africa from Cape Verde to the Bight of Biafra became the scene of European enterprise and rivalry. In the scramble for African slaves even small nations such as Denmark, Sweden, and Brandenburg fought for a share of the spoils.

During these two centuries none of the old staples of trade—gold, ivory, malaguetta, and Benin pepper—proved as permanent or profitable as the traffic in Africans themselves. This traffic in men was the principal item of African commerce and became important to the economies of the chief European nations engaged in it. It has been estimated that between 1450 and 1850 ten million West Africans—five to six million seem nearer the mark—crossed the Atlantic Ocean. This export of populations was at its height in the eighteenth century and averaged something between 70,000 and 80,000 a year.[1] The part played by African colonists in the building of the New World is now being acknowledged. In the eighteenth century economists reckoned that the wealth of the Indies was one of the main supports of the contemporary British empire. This wealth was largely the product of African labour. It is now known that the triangular trade —that is the trade between Britain, West Africa, and the West Indies —provided one of the many streams from whence emerged the capital that financed the industrial revolution.[2] No aspect of West African history has received fuller treatment, and justifiably so, than the iniquitous transatlantic slave trade. Sir Reginald Coupland stated, with scarcely any exaggeration, that the treatment of Africa by Christian Europe in the period of the slave trade constituted 'the greatest crime in history'.[3] This judgement has been endorsed openly or by implication by students of the trade from Clarkson, Bryan Edwards, Bandinel, and Palmerston to W. E. B. Dubois, U. B. Phillips, Donnan, Gaston-Martin, L. J. Ragatz, and many others. As Professor Blake pointed out, the student, like the abolitionist, has concentrated on the magnitude and organization of the trade, the rigours of the 'middle passage', the destination of the enslaved, and the winning of emancipation. Voluminous literature exists on every aspect of the trade and most of it offers graphic proof of the in- humanity and devastation wrought by that terrible traffic.[4]

[1] W. E. B. Dubois, *The Suppression of the African Slave Trade to the U.S.A. 1638–1870* (New York, 1904), and *Black Folk: Then and Now* (New York, 1939), p. 151; E. Donnan, *Documents Illustrative of the History of the Slave Trade to America* (Washington, D.C., 1930–5), see introduction; also C. Lloyd, *The Navy and the Slave Trade* (London, 1944), ch. iii. Figures quoted with regard to slavery are often based on conjecture, as research on this important subject is long overdue.

[2] W. E. Williams, 'Africa and the Rise of Capitalism' (Howard University Library unpublished manuscript, 1938); C. L. R. James, *The Black Jacobins* (London, 1938); Eric Williams, *Capitalism and Slavery* (Chapel Hill, U.S.A., 1944); also G. R. Mellor, *British Imperial Trusteeship, 1783–1850* (London, 1951).

[3] *The British Anti-Slavery Movement* (London, 1933), p. 35.

[4] Donnan, op. cit., Dubois, op. cit., Eric Williams, op. cit., H. A. Wyndham, *The Atlantic and Slavery* (London, 1935), pp. 4–7; U. B. Phillips, *American Negro Slavery* (New York, 1936); Gaston-Martin, *Nantes au XVIIIe siècle* (Paris, 1931);

In West African history the concentration of students on external factors[1] such as the suppression of the slave trade, the work of the Navy, the era of the explorers, the forts and settlements along the coast, the policies and personalities of the various Foreign and Colonial Secretaries, has tended to submerge the history of the indigenous peoples and to bestow undue prominence on the activities of the invaders. As yet no comprehensive assessment of the African middlemen's position in the Atlantic slave trade exists; few if any studies have displayed the real magnitude of the revolution brought about by the prohibition of the traffic from 1807 or the full effects of abolition on the existing native governments. As an instance, a major thread in West African history—the character of the association of the coastal kingdoms with the European traders—is treated, if at all, as merely incidental to the subject; yet without knowledge of this association the position of power occupied by the African middlemen in the period of the slave trade cannot be appreciated.[2]

British prohibition of this trade, a movement which in West Africa precipitated a radical change in the economic sphere—the trade was the economic mainstay of all the coastal principalities—soon wrought corresponding changes in the social and political planes. It is, of course, a truism that up to a point a profound change in the economy of any given community tends to bring about an unsettlement of and a readjustment in the social organization. Such a change did occur in nineteenth-century West Africa; in comparison with the three

and P. Rinchon, *Le Trafic négrier d'après les livres de commerce du capitaine gantois Pierre-Ignac-Lievrin van Alstein* (Brussels, 1938).

[1] Blake, in *Transactions of the Royal Historical Society*, 4th series, xxxii, points out that Dr. S. E. Crowe, in her *Berlin West African Conference, 1884–1885* (London, 1942), makes very little reference to the effects of Partition on the African peoples. He also calls attention to Sir Alan Burns's *History of Nigeria* (London, 1942), in which the author devotes 5 out of 25 chapters to population and physical features, 17 to the history of the country since 1851, and only 3 to the period 1481–1850. 'His sixth chapter on "the period of unrestricted slave trade, 1481–1807" exemplifies the submergence of the main pattern of African history by the concentration on the transatlantic slave trade.' The Gold Coast has been lucky in its historians. From Carl Reindorf, *History of the Gold Coast and Asante* to R. S. Rattray, *Tribes of the Ashanti Hinterland*, W. W. Claridge, *A History of the Gold Coast and Ashanti*, A. B. Ellis, *A History of the Gold Coast of West Africa*, and W. E. F. Ward, *A History of the Gold Coast*, due attention has always been given to the history of the indigenous inhabitants.

[2] So far as we know only a handful of scholars have touched on this aspect. See especially Wyndham, op. cit., pp. 3–7; also chs. ii and iii; E. C. Martin, *The British West African Settlements, 1750–1821* (London, 1927), pp. 48–49; also Blake, *R.H.S.*, 4th series, xxxii.

centuries that preceded them, the fifty years between 1830 and 1885 were an epoch of change and revolution; it was essentially a period of transition from a predominantly slave-trading economy to one based on trade in the raw materials of the West African forest. A cursory glance at the pattern of the early trade (1481–1807), is necessary not only for an understanding of its essential characteristics but even more for an appreciation of the depth and intensity of the revolution which swept away the old order in the nineteenth century.

The buying and selling of commodities is almost always accompanied by the contact of cultures, the exchange of ideas, the mingling of peoples, and has led not infrequently to political complications and wars. Trade with the Arabs, by way of the Saharan caravans, brought medieval West Africa into touch with the world of Islam; and with Islam came Arab culture and civilization. Nothing comparable to this occurred on the coasts of Guinea. While the earlier trade of the western Sudan brought Arab celebrities to West Africa, and men such as the renowned architect Es Sahili came from Moorish Spain to introduce stone buildings in the land of the Negroes, and the austere missionary and teacher of Tuat, Muhammad Abd el Kerim el Maghili, toured a vast area and was evidently at Kano and Katsina,[1] the native chiefs on the Atlantic seaboard barred the European traders from their hinterland. Men who eagerly participated in the Atlantic trade adopted a strictly abstentionist attitude in matters of culture and politics.

This attitude, which was evident from the first, remained in force till the nineteenth century. King John II's claim in 1486 to have created and maintained by force a West African empire and his assumption of the title 'Lord of Guinea' were not in keeping with the facts and were largely pretensions designed to keep out interlopers and rivals. Portuguese rule, or whatever there was of it, was strictly limited to their fortified trading posts on the coasts or on the adjacent islands. Their four bases were Arguim (an island situated in the bay formed by the arm of Cabo Blanco and the African mainland); Santiago Island (the largest island in the Cape Verde archipelago); São Jorge da Mina ('Mina' was a term vaguely used for the Gold Coast) and São Thomé Island, the base for the trade in the bights of Benin and Biafra. All these were founded before or about 1500.

[1] E. W. Bovill, *Caravans of the Old Sahara* (London, 1933); F. L. Shaw (Lady Lugard), *A Tropical Dependency* (London, 1905); and Es Sadi, *Tarikh es-Sudan.*

They were never designed for launching expeditions into the vast interior, an impossible undertaking considering the multitude of Africans and the handful of Portuguese, the extensive coastline, and the limited and inadequate material equipment at the disposal of the merchant-adventurers. Whatever the original intentions of the Portuguese might have been, West African peoples and conditions confined their activities to trade and diplomacy and allowed them little scope for conquest and empire.

The forts and settlements occupied commercially strategic areas. The Arguim base, for instance, was placed in a suitable position to divert towards the western coast the desert trade which for centuries had passed northwards by caravan across the Sahara to the ports of North Africa. São Jorge da Mina, their most important base in Guinea, defended the gold trade of Mina and its neighbourhood. That the Europeans came to think almost exclusively in terms of trade is evidenced by the fact that sections of the coast came to be known by the commodities they produced. Hence the Gum Coast, the Malaguetta or Grain Coast, the Tooth or Ivory Coast, the Gold Coast, and the Slave Coast.

One factor militating against their penetration of the interior was the African attitude to land. In strict West African customary law tribal land was corporatively owned.[1] The chiefs—protectors of the tribal heritage—could not sign away lands of which in reality they were merely trustees. This being the case the alienation of land to foreigners was out of the question and tribal leaders were in duty bound to oppose any encroachment on their preserves. That this practice was recognized even in the early stages of Portuguese trade is borne out by the fact that the ground on which their most important base in West Africa was built—the Castle of São Jorge da Mina —was 'leased' from the Fetu and Comani peoples. The African chief, Caramansa, who negotiated this 'concession', suspicious of Portuguese motives for desiring to build a fort, left the white invaders in no doubt of the outcome of duplicity on their side.[2]

To maintain the safety of their settlement the Portuguese courted the favour of the Fetu and Comani people; customary 'presents' were made to the rulers of the tribe and even interior potentates received their share of the 'gifts' in order to encourage the flow of

[1] T. O. Elias, *Nigerian Land Law and Custom* (London, 1950), pp. 6–7; also ch. v.
[2] J. W. Blake, in *R.H.S.*, 4th series, xxxii, pp. 49–69.

trade between the hinterland and the coast. To hold their own against the vast superiority of the natives the Portuguese, when it suited them, exploited inter-tribal jealousies, and only in extreme cases did they resort to armed intervention. Other methods such as conversion to Christianity, inter-marriage, and treaties of friendship were used to maintain good relations.

The situation in West Africa bore a striking resemblance to the pattern of British enterprise in contemporary India. Until the middle of the eighteenth century the East India Company was a purely trading body owning no Indian soil but the few square miles on which its main factories stood. British territorial conquest of the Indian sub-continent only gained momentum when the wars associated with the name of Dupleix and the Seven Years War gave her control over the Carnatic, the province surrounding Madras, and the rich state of Bengal.

There is little in the records to suggest that this arrangement altered in any essential particular from the fifteenth to the eighteenth centuries. The forts and settlements with their attendant native towns were no more than the vehicles through which the Atlantic trade was carried on. Economically this arrangement suited the African middle-men of the coast trade. They became the influential and wealthy agents between the African producers of the interior and European merchants on the seaboard. It was to their interest and to the dis-advantage of the foreigner that this arrangement should be main-tained. Even more than the African attitude to land it was the opposition of these coast chiefs that excluded the white man from the hinterland during 400 years of trade. European authorities on the coast repeatedly emphasized the opposition of the seaboard states to white penetration. Archibald Dalzel, Governor of Cape Coast in 1793, when African exploration was engaging the attention of Europe, declared that the 'principal impediment to the improvement of the geography of Africa' arose rather 'from the jealousy of the inhabitants of the sea coasts, in permitting white men to travel through their country, than from the danger or difficulty attending the penetration'. This jealousy he attributed to the middlemen's fear 'that the advantages of their trade with Europe should be lessened' and 'transferred from them to their neighbours; or that the inland kingdoms by obtaining European arms' would prove dangerous rivals. 'There are many instances in former writers', he concluded, 'of their care and cunning, in concealing from travellers the names and nature of the adjacent countries', and even at the end of the eighteenth century this attitude persisted.[1]

In the literature of the time this policy of abstention is confirmed and amplified. In 1734 Captain Snelgrave warned his countrymen that if white men dared ask questions about the interior 'the natives would have destroyed them, out of jealousy that they designed to make discoveries to their prejudice'.[2] But as the present study will reveal, even as late as 1854 when quinine mitigated the menace of malaria and the steam-engine facilitated river navigation, the opposition of the Delta states still barred the way to the hinterland kingdoms.[3]

It became a recognized fact that the sovereignty of the African states was unimpaired by the presence of Europeans. On the whole the political power of the African states reigned supreme over aliens and natives, for the strong and despotic governments provided by the coastal principalities suited the semi-military society of the time. Under these governments the slave trade throve amazingly. Moreover, through their administration of the forts the European governments had come to learn of the dissipation of energy and capital consequent on territorial responsibility and regularly warned their subjects to keep to trade and avoid entanglement in African politics. It followed, therefore, that so long as the existing indigenous governments served their trade interests well, white men were prepared to work through them and to endure whatever hazards and inconveniences this entailed. In recognition of this fact European governments deprecated activities other than trading, such, for instance, as developing gardens and plantations, on the grounds that the land occupied by the European was only leased from the natives.[4] In 1752 the Board of Trade forbade the Committee of the Company of Merchants to introduce cultivation in the Gold Coast on the plea that 'in Africa we were only tenants of the soil which we hold at the goodwill of the natives'.[5] Writing from Gambia in 1678 the local chief agent of the Royal African Company recommended that all trading should be conducted from sloops, 'for a factor once settled ashore is absolutely under the command of the king of the country where he lives, and is liable for the least displeasure to lose all the

[1] A. Dalzel, *The History of Dahomey* (London, 1793), pp. xxi–xxiii.
[2] W. Snelgrave, *A New Account of Some Parts of Guinea, and the Slave Trade* (London, 1734); see introduction.   [3] See Chapter IX.
[4] Wyndham, op. cit., pp. 4–7.   [5] Martin, op. cit., pp. 48–49.

goods he has in his possession, with danger also to his life'.[1] When in 1799 the Governor of Sekondi, going one evening to visit a neighbouring Dutch governor, was seized, stripped, and beaten by the natives, the Council of Cape Coast Castle merely commented that he had no business to be paying a call so late![2]

On the slave coasts this abstentionist policy was most pronounced. Here European forts such as those on the Gold Coast were not tolerated. At Whydah, a 'free port for all Europeans', the king disallowed the erection of anything stronger than a mud fort at the safe distance of three miles from the shore.[3] In the Niger Delta the merchant-adventurers made their sailing ships their home and with the exception of the baracoons (warehouses erected on the shore for slaves and barter goods), they had no foothold on African territory. These characteristics were commonplaces at the time and were emphasized by the most reliable of contemporary writers. 'There is no small number of Men in Europe', wrote William Bosman of the Gold Coast in 1721, 'who believe that the Gold Mines are in our power; that we, like the Spaniards in the West Indies, have no more to do but to work them by our Slaves: though you perfectly know that we have no means of access to these Treasures.'[4]

Adam Smith approved the maintenance of fortified trading posts in West Africa, but this approval did not contain any imperial intentions. Along with British ministers and consuls in foreign parts, he viewed them as 'public works' designed 'to facilitate commerce'. Their function was to protect the 'ordinary store or counting house' from interference by natives. 'Territorial ambitions *per se* were not involved in these considerations.'[5]

He showed that although Europeans possessed 'numerous and thriving colonies' in the West Indies and America, in Africa 'it was more difficult to displace the natives, and to extend European plantations over the greater part of the lands of the original inhabitants'. His emphasis was on people not on physical impediments. West African nations were not reduced to subjection because they 'are by no means so weak and defenceless as the miserable and

---

[1] C.O./267/5, quoted by Wyndham, op. cit., p. 59.
[2] Wyndham, op. cit., p. 61.   [3] Ibid.
[4] Bosman, *A New and Accurate Description of the Coasts of Guinea* (2nd edn., 1721), p. 20.
[5] K. E. Knorr, *British Colonial Theories, 1570–1850* (Toronto, 1944), (p. 175, footnote 1).

helpless Americans'; Africans 'were besides much more populous'. Density of population and the ability of the indigenous peoples to resist the European invaders were important factors; where these were lacking conquest and subjection was the rule. 'The Cape of Good Hope was inhabited by a race of people (the Hottentots) almost as barbarous and quite as incapable of defending themselves as the natives of America.' The area in comparison with the west coast was sparsely populated. Thus the success of the Dutch settlement at the Cape was due partly to the strategic commercial position it occupied and partly to the absence of opposition from the natives.[1] Adam Smith might have greatly underrated the resistance to the invaders offered by the American Indians and the Hottentots but he was not unaware of the situation in West Africa. Up to the beginning of the nineteenth century, therefore, the hostility of the well-armed coastal states was a factor in preventing European invasion of their territories and of their politics. This state of affairs lasted so long as Africans had the equipment, the means, and the numbers to maintain their independence. Physical barriers to penetration were indisputably present. The factor of climate and physical impediments have been more than adequately treated in existing works and we do not wish to underrate them. A nodding acquaintance with the sources of West African history reveals a high mortality rate among the merchant-adventurers. This high mortality was due, however, not to the climate but to unaccustomed diseases. Medical authorities attributed the cause of malaria to the unwholesome miasma that emanated from the coast swamps. No one suspected that the mischief-maker was the malaria-carrying anopheles. Quinine was unknown and some of the deaths were due more to intemperance[2] than to 'the effects of the climate'. As this study will show, in the nineteenth century the factors of climate and physical impediments did not prevent the appearance of European empires when Europeans had overcome African opposition.[3]

We have shown that from 1481 to 1807 trade with the foreigner did not alter the political contours of West Africa. During these

[1] Adam Smith, *The Wealth of Nations* (Everyman edn.), ii, 130 f.
[2] W. Winwood Reade, *Savage Africa* (London, 1864), and W. Simpson, *Niger Expedition* (London, 1843).
[3] We do not wish to imply that African opposition was the sole impediment to European penetration: we emphasize it here because some authors tend to write as if it did not exist. See Chap. IX.

centuries the flag did not, in the main, follow trade. The lands of Guinea remained under native governments and the European concerned himself almost exclusively with trade. There were, of course, local modifications to this generalization and the degree of abstention from African politics differed from one trading area to another. In the area of the forts, more particularly in the Gold Coast, European settlements situated near African territories were inevitably involved in local politics. The colonizing experiments in Freetown, the Senegambia, the kingdom of Kongo and Angola and others were exceptions to the general rule.[1] But the political subjection which accompanied nineteenth-century trade expansion was of recent origin and in many areas of West Africa less than a century old. With abolition the radical change in the economic sphere soon wrought corresponding changes in the social and political planes. The 400 years old political systems built on the slave trade gradually declined and by the 1880's collapsed.

These revolutionary changes were due to a complex variety of factors, political, economic, strategic, and humanitarian, all worldwide in their implications and, although occurring in the main in Europe and America, having decisive effects on the commerce of West Africa. The slave trade, its abolition, and the economic, military, and humanitarian forces which contributed to its extinction, are more or less well known.[2] The aspect of this many-sided movement most forcibly felt in contemporary West Africa was the economic. At the end of the eighteenth century a predominantly mercantile epoch was being succeeded by a predominantly industrial age. In Britain, where the industrial change was greatest, the slave trade, which had fitted perfectly into the scheme of mercantilist economics, was being rendered obsolete by the rapid technological advance in industrial production. Abolition of the slave trade was therefore only one manifestation of the major changes from the era of mercantilism to that of the industrial revolution and aggressive free trade.

The humanitarianism so widely advertised at the time was, in one sense, the reflection on the ideological plane of changes taking place in the economic sphere. This explains the 'curious affinity' between the two forces that has been noted by many writers. The two aspects were complementary and any attempt to explain the one without

[1] Martin, op. cit., and Wyndham, op. cit.
[2] See W. K. Hancock, *Survey of British Commonwealth Affairs* (London, 1942), ii, pt. 2, 154–72, Lloyd, op. cit., Eric Williams, op. cit., and Martin, op. cit.

reference to the other will lead to an over-simplification of a complex issue.

Consider one aspect of the economic change taking place in Britain at the time of the abolition. Towards the end of the eighteenth century Liverpool capital, reared on the slave trade, was being diverted to a new channel—the cotton trade with America. Inventions connected with the cotton industry followed each other in rapid succession. Industrialized Lancashire claimed the attention of the capitalists and of powerful slave interests. British shipping was to find employment in a new direction as the cotton trade began to render the British slave trade obsolete. The change-over was gradual, yet it was this mounting economic change which reduced slave interests to manageable proportions and enabled the abolitionists to attack it successfully. On the other hand, had it not been for the spirited and inspired attack of the Christian humanitarians such as Wilberforce and Clarkson, slavery and the slave trade might have lingered on—as indeed other decadent systems did linger on—long after they had outlived their usefulness.

It is necessary to emphasize again that these contemporary movements connected with the industrial change were a European not a West African phenomenon. This is particularly true of happenings on the ideological plane. The nineteenth-century West African middleman was not only ignorant of the ideological battle raging in Europe on the question of abolition, but his ideas of life, of society, and of man belonged to a world poles apart from that in which the Benthamites argued and the Clapham sect preached.

Along the coast of West Africa, particularly in those parts where the slave trade formed the basis of the economy of the communities concerned, opposition to abolition was the rule. In the Gold Coast, where European forts and settlements were situated close to the African states, local native resentment against the Act of 1807 led to serious riots. When Parliament rebuked the Committee of the Company of Merchants for failing to convince Africans that abolition was for the good of the natives, the committee retorted,

Can the wildest theorist expect that a mere act of the British legislature should in a moment inspire . . . natives of the vast continent of Africa and persuade them, nay more, make them practically believe and feel that it is for their interest to contribute to and even acquiesce in, the destruction of a trade . . . by which alone they have been hitherto accustomed to acquire wealth and purchase all the foreign luxuries and conveniences of life?[1]

[1] Martin, op. cit., p. 152.

On this point the attitude of the white slave-trader and the African middleman was identical, for the economic basis of both their lives was threatened. To contemporary Africans the European movement for abolition was extremely puzzling, especially as Englishmen who were foremost in the trade became overnight the most zealous in opposing it. Not only had the slave trade been the mainstay of their economics, but slave-trading kingdoms such as Lagos, Dahomey, Bonny, and many others owed their origin and greatness to the rise of the slave trade. The king of Bonny, Africa's greatest slave market, spoke for the rest when he declared to Captain Crow in 1807:

> We [i.e. the king and Council] think that this trade must go on. That also is the verdict of our Oracle and the priests. They say that your country, however great, can never stop a trade ordained by God himself.[1]

Yet in spite of the determined opposition of slave interests the old order began gradually to yield place to the new. Economists argued that Africa had other commodities more lucrative than slaves to offer to the growing industries of England, and urged that the West African labour force, instead of being denuded to exploit the West Indies and the Americas, should be turned to agricultural production in Africa itself.

The new industrial order demanded above all markets and raw materials for the rising output of British factories. The quest for markets is reflected in Captain Cook's voyages in search of the 'Terra Incognita Australis'—that mythical continent of the eastern Pacific that turned out to be another El Dorado. The same consideration turned Europe's attention to Africa, and in England the African Association, founded in 1788 and representing a galaxy of interests, sent expedition after expedition to scour the interior of the continent. These ventures, directly or indirectly, received government support. The student of West African history cannot fail to note that from the late eighteenth century to the end of the nineteenth there was a concerted movement, directed chiefly at first from Britain and later from France, Belgium, and Germany, to enter the West African interior, exploit its resources, and open new markets for European manufactures. The movement derived its impetus from a variety of patrons: scientists, humanitarians, industrialists, and government agents. These interests were represented by a constellation of illustrious

---

[1] H. Crow, *Memoirs* (London, 1830), p. 137. The quotation is a paraphrase of the king's pidgin English.

names: Sir Joseph Banks, F.R.S., botanist; Josiah Wedgwood, industrialist; Fox and Pitt, politicians; Wilberforce, Clarkson, and Buxton, humanitarians; James McQueen and Reichard, geographers; John Ledyard and Mungo Park, Clapperton, Richard and John Lander, explorers, to name but a few.

Diverse non-economic forces affected this movement for the penetration of the West African interior: love of adventure, ardour for scientific discovery, abhorrence of the slave trade, missionary zeal, and national rivalry, yet in a curious way writers have tended to harp unduly on these external manifestations of a movement that was at root economic. It was the economic change taking place in Europe at the time that canalized these discordant elements into one channel and provided a common ground for unity or alliance among such strange bedfellows. Take the London Society Instituted for Exploring the Interior of Africa, commonly known as the African Association. Its aims originally were more scientific than commercial, yet no sooner did Mungo Park reach Sego on the Niger in 1796 than the Association tried to stir up England to take advantage of the discovery. 'A gate is opened to every commercial nation to enter and trade from the West to the eastern extremity of Africa.' Park and Hornemann, who had been equally successful from the North,

have explored roads which shortly mercantile adventure will, and must enter. In this new race of commerce, shame indeed would it be to our national councils . . . that the default of patronage and support of Government, our commercial people may lose the start for a priority of factories and establishment of trade, and permit other nations to usurp the vantage ground which British enterprise shall have explored.

In 1799 the Association followed this up with a suggestion that a British Consul be appointed for Senegambia,

such an opening for the consumption of the Manufactures of Great Britain, where millions of Natives who are now supplied by a Land Carriage of near 2,000 miles across burning Sands, and who give Ivorys, Drugs and Gold in return for the goods they consume, may be furnished with British Articles by a Land Carriage of 500 Miles only, across a fertile and well-watered Country.

It did not take contemporary West Africans long to perceive the nature of this movement and to view it as a powerful challenge to the *status quo*. Captain James K. Tuckey, R.N., during his ascent of the River Congo in 1816, noted that 'the native merchants do not wish Europeans to penetrate into the country, lest they should inter-

fere with their business'.[1] Even before the death of Mungo Park
Africans had begun to notice the change in European trade requirements, the increasing pressure they were exerting to enter the hinterland rather than trade on the coast as formerly. 'White man now
come among us with new face, talk palaver we do not understand,
they bring new fashion, great guns, and soldiers in our country.'[2]

In the years 1822–4 Major Dixon Denham, F.R.S., and Captain
Hugh Clapperton visited Hausaland and sought to open trade relations with the Fulani empire and the kingdom of Bornu. In a letter to
George IV Sheikh Mohammed El Kanemy, Emir of Bornu, favoured
the proposal but warned against the influx of English merchants into
his dominions. 'Our country', he said, 'does not suit any heavy [rich]
traveller, who may possess great wealth. But if a few light persons
[small capitalists], as four or five only, with little merchandise,
would come, there will be no harm. This is the utmost (number of
people) that we can give permission for; more than this number must
not come.'[3] Even Bello, Sultan of Sokoto, who was favourably disposed towards the travellers in 1824, proved hostile in 1825 when
Clapperton returned to inaugurate a treaty of commerce and friendship.[4]

On the coast, as in the hinterland, challenge to African authority
was emerging with the opening years of the nineteenth century. The
rising industrialism manifested itself in various ways, not only in
the travels of the intrepid explorers and the consequent advancement
of African geography but in the increasing interest displayed by the
British Navy in the topography of the coast. In this connexion the
work of Captain W. F. W. Owen may be cited. Between the years
1822–6 he was ordered by the Admiralty to direct the survey of the
African coast line. It was during these years that the thousand-mile
stretch from Cape Mount on the termination of the Windward coast
to the bights of Benin and Biafra was first surveyed.[5]

[1] J. B. Williams, 'The Development of British Trade with West Africa, 1750–
1880', *Political Science Quarterly*, l (1935), 194–213.

[2] J. Corry, *Observations Upon the Windward Coast* (London, 1807), p. 127.

[3] Denham, Clapperton, and Oudney, *Narrative of Travels and Discoveries in
Northern and Central Africa* (London, 1828) ii, appendix I, 415–19.

[4] Ibid., appendix II; also Howard and Plumb, *West African Explorers* (London,
1951), pp. 15–17.

[5] Captain W. F. W. Owen was born in 1774 and served in the Royal Navy. He
explored the Maldive Islands in 1806, and surveyed the lakes of Canada in 1815.
Between 1821 and 1825 he carried out his famous survey of the coast of Africa. In
1826 he supported British troops in the Ashanti War and in 1827 was sent to found

In the course of this operation an incident occurred which illustrates that although eighteenth-century conditions survived into the nineteenth century, the coastal principalities had already begun to feel the impact of European power. In 1824 Owen's party arrived at Bonny (in the Niger Delta), then West Africa's leading slave-trading kingdom. The captain himself, a typical product of the industrial order, paid scant regard to native governments and was contemptuous of their institutions.

Accordingly when he led his squadron into the coastal waters of the Bonny country he did not bother to present his credentials to the king. Instead he dispatched a junior officer 'to state the purpose for which we had come', and without specific permission from the authorities or, according to his own account, 'without further consideration of King Peppel [i.e. Opubu][1] or his etiquette', Owen embarked on a survey of the coastline of Bonny and its rivers. This unauthorized activity on the part of the English commander provoked prompt action by the king. In retaliation he ordered that all trade with the British community should instantly cease.[2] 'He expressed the most violent indignation at our presumption' in entering his territorial waters 'without his permission'.[3]

Two significant points emerged from this incident. At the meeting with the English community in which the 'palaver' was amicably settled King Opubu made statements which illuminate the African attitude to the politics of the time. A paraphrase of his brief and broken sentences delivered in the current pidgin English reveals the workings of the king's mind: If the king of England (George IV), Opubu declared, a brother monarch, ordered his warship to embark

---

a British settlement in the Spanish island of Fernando Po. From 1827 to 1829 he was Superintendent of the settlement. It is by his accurate surveys of the coast of Africa, though, till then only explored, that Owen is best known. Charts of the west and east coasts of Africa, &c., drawn under his direction are very numerous and form the basis of those still in use.

[1] 'Peppel' is spelt variously in contemporary documents, viz., Pepperel, Pepple, and 'Pepper'. It is not the name of the reigning kings but of the Dynasty to which they belong. Thus Owen referred to 'King Peppel' when in fact the king at the time he wrote was 'Opubu' (of the House of Pepple). There is little doubt that Opubu was the 'Peppel' in Owen's narrative. In 1846 Hope Waddell saw at Bonny the following inscription on a bell: 'This bell was cast for Opoboo Foobra, King of Grand Bonny, by William Dobson, founder, Downham, Norfolk, England, 1824.' See H. M. Waddell, *Twenty-nine Years in the West Indies and Central Africa* (London, 1863), p. 314.

[2] W. F. W. Owen, *Narrative of a Voyage to Explore the Shores of Africa*, pp. 343–61.   [3] Ibid.

on a survey of the coast of Africa, I see nothing objectionable in that aim. If brother George commands his battleships to attack the slave ships of foreign nations that is no concern of mine. But he has no right whatever to send his men-of-war at will into my dominions. It was the plain duty of the English commander to have waited upon me and explained the import of his mission. I declare emphatically that I can never compromise my sovereign powers. On this issue I am adamant. Consider my kingdom, this land which I hold in trust for the Bonny country and the spirits of my ancestors. What would be my excuse if my father or grandfather were to rise from their graves and demand to know the reason for the presence of English warships in the territories they had entrusted to my charge. 'In which strain of oratory', Owen declared 'the old man continued, until from mere rage and exhaustion he could say no more.'[1]

Commenting on this incident after its settlement Owen declared that he could not understand why the British traders at Bonny during this crisis treated an African king with great 'deference and respect. They administer to his whims and caprice, as if the advantages derived from their traffic was not mutual; and when his anger is raised, instead of opposing his menaces they try to win him back to good humour by the most servile flattery and gifts. Had a stranger heard the earnest consultation held by these people when the trade was closed upon this occasion, he would have been more inclined to think himself in the purlieus of St. James's than in a Negro town on the West Coast of Africa.'

Yet the English traders who cringed to win King Opubu's favour knew the reality of his power. They knew that however magnificent 'the purlieus of St. James's' might have been, at Bonny the Pepples ruled: and like practical men of affairs they judged native governments not by their trappings but by their utility. This incident was also a portent of things to come. Incursions were to be made into the traditional abstentionist policy, as well as the territories, of African states. Increasing in range and intensity, as the century advanced, they represented a serious challenge to the *status quo*.

---

[1] Ibid. The following is the king's original pidgin: 'Brudder George . . . send warship look um what water bar ab got, dat good, me let um dat. Brudder send boat chopum slave, dat good. E no send warship, for cappen no peake me, no lookee me face. No, no, no; me tell you, No; Suppose you come all you mont full palaver, give e reason whye do it, me tell you, you peake lie, you peake lie, you peaked-n lie. Suppose my fader, or my fader fader come up from ground and peake me why English man do dat, I no sabby tell um why.'

The persistent search for 'a highway into the heart of Central Africa', commonly known as 'the quest for the course and termination of the River Niger', came at a time when the new industrialism was endowing Europe with the technical instruments of effective action in Africa. This quest Europe consciously and energetically pursued from 1788 to 1830. 1830 was the year of destiny. It was the year when the twin problems of geography and commerce were solved by the momentous discovery of the brothers Richard and John Lander that the Niger entered the Atlantic in the Bight of Biafra. Throughout Europe the event was hailed as one of cardinal importance.

Though the knowledge of interior Africa [said Dr. Martin Leaks, F.R.S., in a paper read in 1830 before the Royal Geographical Society] is the progressive acquisition of many enterprising men . . . it cannot be denied that the last great discovery has done more than any other to place the outline of African geography on an basis of certainty. When to this is added the consideration that it opens a maritime communication into the centre of the continent, it may be described as the greatest geographical discovery that has been made since that of New Holland.

This epoch-making event altered the emphasis, so far as the Niger basin and its Delta were concerned, from exploration to commerce. The river became to the trading Europeans an arm of the Atlantic Ocean, the main road to the gold and treasure, real and imaginary, of the vast interior. Significantly, this discovery coincided with the development of the steam-engine, for had the steamboat not begun to displace the sailing ship, river navigation on a commercially important scale would not have been possible. From the thirties to the end of the century the Niger and its Delta became the focus of attention and witnessed the long series of scientific and commercial expeditions organized by the new school of inland (as opposed to coast) traders, a movement that was to make Nigeria a British protectorate. This region provides the best illustration of the process by which the trading activities of 500 years led in the nineteenth century to the political subjection of West Africa to Europe. The history of the Niger Delta in the years 1830–85 is therefore the history of one of the highways of imperialism in West Africa; like the more famous Congo the Niger was considered a dazzling prize by the competing great powers—Britain, France, and Germany. In order to appreciate its importance as a means of transport and a highway of commerce it is necessary to look at the land and the people.

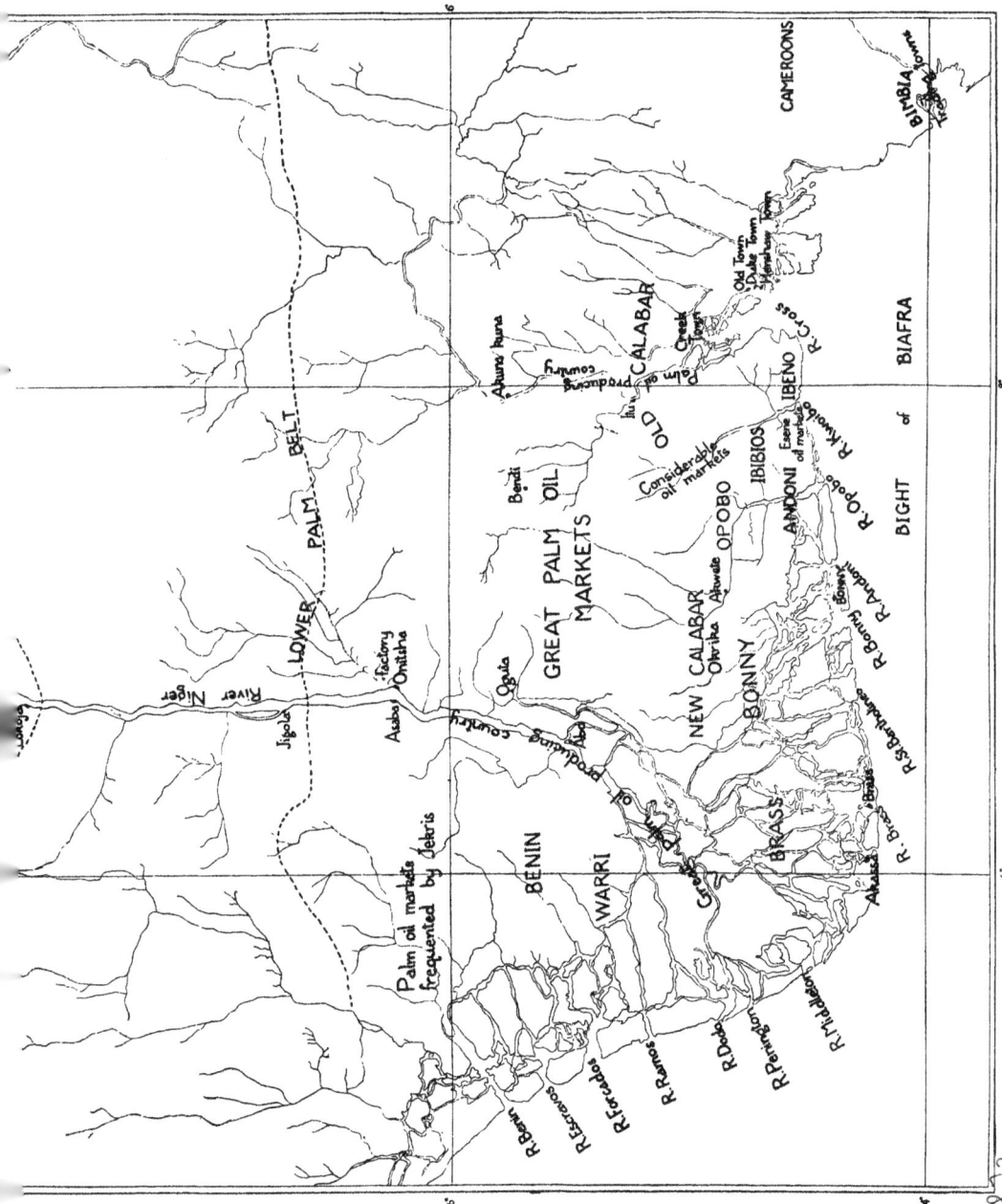

THE NIGER DELTA, 1830

LOWER PALM BELT

River Niger

Jigola

Asabo · factory Onitsha

Palm oil markets frequented by Jebris

BENIN

WARRI

Great ...

to Sumppond country

Aba

GREAT PALM OIL MARKETS

Ogula

Bendi

Considerable oil markets

Palm oil producing country

Akuna Kuna

OLD CALABAR

Old Town
Duke Town
Henshaw Town

Great Town

R. Cross

IBENO

Esene old markets

IBIBIOS

ANDONI

OPOBO

Abuate

Otriba

NEW CALABAR

BONNY

R.Opobo

R.Kwaiba

R.Andoni

R.Bonny

BRASS

R.Brass

Akassa

R.Middleton

R.Pennington

R.Dodo

R.Ramos

R.Forcados

R.Escravos

R.Benin

CAMEROONS

BIMBIA

Trading Towns

BIGHT of BIAFRA

CHAPTER II

The Delta and its People[1]

FROM Lagos to the Cameroons lies the low country of the Nigerian coastal plain. The Niger Delta occupies the greater part of this low-land belt and may be described as the region bounded by the Benin river on the west and the Cross river in the east, including the coastal area where the Cameroon mountains dip into the sea. It covers an area of some 270 miles along the Atlantic coast and is 120 miles in depth. The two mouths of the Niger are the Forcados and the Nun, but the rivers Benin, Brass, Bonny, Kwa-Ibo, the Cross, and other separate streams are linked to these by a labyrinth of creeks and lagoons. 'I believe', wrote Mary Kingsley, 'the great swamp region of the Bight of Biafra [Niger Delta] is the greatest in the world, and that in its immensity and gloom, it has a grandeur equal to that of the Himalayas.'[2] There remains, however, the intriguing paradox that this area, notorious among nineteenth-century travellers for its unhealthiness, with a soil too poor 'to produce a ton of oil' as Mac-gregor Laird put it in 1832, and practically uninhabited by the tribes of the Nigerian interior before the Portuguese adventure to the Guinea coasts began, had become by 1830 the greatest single trading area in West Africa.

It was as navigable waterways that the rivers of the Niger Delta became so important in the economic history of modern Nigeria. A canoe could be taken from Badagry on the west coast of Nigeria to Rio del Rey in the east without going into the open sea. This 'Venice of West Africa', as Winwood Reade described it in 1867, linked together not only places in the Delta but towns and villages along the 2,600 miles of the Niger valley. 'The Oil Rivers are chiefly remarkable among our West African possessions', wrote Sir Harry Johnston in 1888, 'for the exceptional facilities which they offer for penetrating the interior by means of large and navigable streams and by a wonderful system of natural canalization which connects all the branches of the lower Niger by means of deep creeks. There are hardly

[1] See Map at end.
[2] *Travels in West Africa* (1897). Cf. A. C. C. Hastings, *The Voyage of the Day Spring* (London, 1857), pp. 73–74.

any roads existing in the Delta; the most trivial distance that a native requires to go, he generally achieves in a canoe.' This water system links the Delta with 'the markets and sources of production far inland.'[1]

Geographically the Delta divides easily into two sections. The northern section is comparatively drier and higher than the area of swampland to the south. Even in the lowland belt the dank and humid surroundings are interspersed with vast stretches of dry land, a maze of islands intersected by creeks and rivers, and on these settlements have been built. Some of these southern colonies, being placed on points of control for internal and external commerce, quickly grew in importance and became the trading centres on the Atlantic seaboard. Just as the growing volume of Atlantic commerce drew Europe irresistibly to the lands of Guinea, so the natives of tribal areas, impelled by the urge 'to traffic and exchange', flocked to the coast to do trade. From now on the coastland became the frontier of opportunity. As in medieval West Africa trade with the Arabs by way of the Sahara caravans led to an outcrop of commercial cities on the Niger bend such as Jenne, Timbuktu, Gao, and others, so the rise of Lagos, Accra, Dahomey, and the Delta states must be attributed to the development of maritime commerce. The seaboard trading communities which emerged with this commerce transcended tribal boundaries; their history belongs both to Atlantic and to tribal history.

Every item of the export trade in the ports of Biafra was a product of the tribal interior, and the carrying-trade on which the prosperity and greatness of the Delta states rested linked their fortunes decisively with those of the producers in the tribal locations. The coastal communities united in their blood and institutions elements of the Atlantic and tribal societies which fashioned them. Each of the adventurous groups that pioneered these settlements was different in language and culture and in political and social organization. The Jekris of Warri (on the Benin river) could not understand the Ijaws on the Brass river. These migrants represented many Nigerian tribes in movement—Ibos, Binis, semi-Bantus from the Cameroons Highlands, Ijaws, Efiks, Ibibios, to name only a few and the most important. This fact must be noted. It helps to explain the haphazard way in which the Delta communities grew. Down to the nineteenth

---

[1] F.O.84/1882, Memorandum by Consul H. H. Johnston on the British Protectorate of the Oil Rivers, Part II.

century this movement of populations continued. Opobo, the main centre of trade and politics in the eighties, was founded in 1870.

Perhaps the Niger Delta was peopled by three distinct waves of migration from the tribal hinterland. The earliest, that of the Ijaws, appears to have preceded the Portuguese advent. A detailed analysis of their traditions of origin indicates that they believe Benin to have been their ancestral habitat. This claim, which may be true of some places, must be received with reservations in the case of others until more supporting evidence is forthcoming, especially as the temptation to claim Benin origins is very strong.[1]

Throughout medieval West Africa the kingdom of Benin was the dominant power in southern Nigeria and extended its conquests from Lagos in the west, to Bonny river in the east, and northwards to Idah. It was the one state with which the Portuguese, during their early visit to the Delta, maintained diplomatic relations.[2] The persistence and universality of the claims to Benin origin in Delta traditions is evidence, at the least, of the powerful influence which this kingdom exerted over the imagination of her neighbours, particularly in south-eastern Nigeria, where her military power was felt by Ibos and Ibo-speaking peoples east of the Niger.

According to tradition the kings of Benin had become absolute and oppressive at the time of the first migration. For example, Prince Ginuwa, son of Oba (King) Olua and heir to the throne, was popularly believed to be the power behind the Oba and the instigator of many acts of cruelty visited by his father on the people. Led by the Iyase (Prime Minister) Ogbue, the nobility joined forces with the common people and resolved that the wicked prince must be barred from the succession. So unanimous was the opposition that the king advised his son to flee. Followed by his admirers, mainly young hot-heads, and powerfully aided by his father with arms and men, Prince Ginuwa secretly left Benin by night and taking the direction of the

---

[1] Conclusions reached in this chapter, particularly on the question of migrations, are tentative. Until authoritative local histories of the Delta states are written, and the conflicting theories now in circulation carefully sifted and checked, one can only write in very broad terms. See Jacob Egharevba, *A Short History of Benin* and his *Famous Iyases of Benin*, published locally. Chief Egharevba's dating of epic events in Benin history is arbitrary, but his knowledge of local history is wide. Cf. J. W. Blake, *Europeans in West Africa* (London, 1942), i. 78–79.

[2] P. A. Talbot, *Peoples of Southern Nigeria* (London, 1926), i. 155–6. Cf. J. W. Blake, *European Beginnings in West Africa* (London, 1937), pp. 11–12, and E. Prestage, *The Portuguese Pioneers* (London, 1933), pp. 212–16.

sea, finally settled at Warri and founded the Itshekiri kingdom. Epics like this die hard in tribal memory. The founder of the Brass city-state is said to have been a Benin general ordered by the Oba to reduce to obedience a rebellious tribe on the outskirts of the empire. The campaign ended in total defeat for the Benin forces—a great 'loss of face' not only for the general but also for the king. Rather than face his master he led his men to found Nembe on the Nun river, one of the two mouths of the Niger.[1] This town is still referred to by Brassmen as their ancestral habitat. Although Benin provides, how-ever imperfectly, some clue to the history of the early migrations to the Delta, the user of oral tradition in the reconstruction of centuries-old migrations is constantly aware of the fragmentary and conjectural nature of his evidence.

The route which the migrants took suggests the second and perhaps the more important reason for their exodus: it led invariably towards the sea coast, and the inaccessible Niger Delta, where the exiles hoped not only to escape from the long arm of the Oba, but also to engage in fishing and salt-making, for fish and salt were commodities highly prized in the hinterland. These industries, according to tradi-tion, were the earliest occupations of the migrants. European records support this. About 1505, according to Pereira, people in the hinter-land 'exchanged yams, cows, goats and sheep and sell them for salt at this village'—an Ijaw village in the Delta.[2] Economic need was undoubtedly the main reason determining the direction they took. The salt-making industry persisted and increased up to the nineteenth century. Captain John Adams, writing between 1786 and 1800, recorded that at Warri 'neptunes or large brass pans are used during the dry season for purposes of evaporating sea-water to obtain its salt . . . and a great trade is carried on in this article with the interior country'.[3] Consul H. H. Johnston noted in 1888: 'A native salt industry of old standing continues. The salt is made extensively by Jakrymen from the leaves of a willow-like tree not unlike the man-grove; which are burnt; the ashes are soaked and washed, then evaporated; the residue represents native salt, which is even now preferred for many uses to introduced salt.'[4]

[1] Variations of these accounts are legion and the versions reproduced here serve merely to illustrate the nature of the material available.
[2] Talbot, op. cit., i. 184.
[3] J. Adams, *Sketches Taken During Ten Years Voyage to Africa between the Years 1786–1800* (London, undated), pp. 33–38, 1st edn.
[4] F.O.84/1882, Memorandum on the British Protectorate of the Oil Rivers.

Attempts have been made from time to time to trace the origin of the Delta peoples, and of these works the most important is that of Dr. P. A. Talbot. His researches have been widely used by subsequent writers and must be given consideration. He took the view that the Ijaws were driven to their present home by 'the coastward-moving Ibos', but frankly admitted that apart from this conjecture their origin is wrapped in mystery. 'The Niger Delta, therefore, is, with the exception of a few small tribes, occupied by these strange people (the Ijaw)—a survival from the dim past, beyond the dawn of history,—whose language and customs are distinct from those of their neighbours (the Ibos) and without trace of any tradition of a time before they were driven southward into those regions of sombre mangrove.'[1] Dr. Talbot, whose contributions to Delta studies are indisputably great, strangely overlooked the fact that the clue to the early Ijaw migrations might be sought for, not only among the Ibos—with whom they appear to have had little relation until about the middle of the sixteenth century—but also in the kingdom of Benin.

His neglect of Benin sources is all the more surprising since another scholar, Major A. G. Leonard, had explored the same subject in 1906 (Talbot's publications appeared in 1926 and 1932), and had collected many traditions from various city-states, all of which allude to the Benin origin of the Delta tribes. In this connexion Major Leonard's study is perhaps an advance on Talbot's position. Ijaw tradition, which Talbot disregarded, Leonard collected and used rather shyly, but it enabled him to trace the Benin origin of some of the Ijaw towns. Although the data he assembled were meagre and in some respects deficient, his approach to the subject seems correct.[2] The migrations from Benin were, however, pre-fifteenth century, and took place possibly centuries before the advent of the Portuguese. The settlements which sprang up as a result of those migrations were just fishing and salt-making villages, and were on a small scale when compared with that which followed the rise of the Atlantic trade.

[1] Talbot, *Tribes of the Niger Delta* (London, 1932), p. 5; cf. id., *Peoples of Southern Nigeria*, esp. vols. i and ii.

[2] A. G. Leonard, *The Lower Niger and Its Tribes* (London, 1906), pp. 17–47. It is surprising that Talbot, who recorded these traditions in his *Peoples of Southern Nigeria*, i, made no use of them in *Tribes of the Niger Delta*.

On the issue of the Benin origins of some of the Delta tribes, see also J. W. Hubbard, *The Sobo of the Niger Delta* (Zaria, 1953).

The most important movement of populations occurred between
1450 and 1800, and gradually converted the little Ijaw fishing villages
into the city-states. This second wave of migration followed the
development of the slave trade and involved all the tribes to the
Delta hinterland; it was a movement in which the Ibos, being numerically superior, were predominant. Points on the Delta coast, suitable
as harbours for the European sailing ships, were quickly occupied.
Such was the case with Bonny. According to tradition, a famous
chief and hunter, Alagbariye, on his regular hunting expeditions to
the coast, came upon the site on which Bonny now stands, and aware
of its potentialities for directing the new trade, brought his people
there to found the town. Variations of this account have been
recorded by European travellers from Barbot to Baikie and Leonard.[1]
The site so admirably chosen by the newcomers proved to be the
best port of the Niger Delta and remained so till the nineteenth century. 'By its safe and extensive anchorage', wrote Hope Waddell in
1846, 'its proximity to the sea, and connection with the great rivers
of Central Africa, Bonny is now the principal seat of the palm oil
trade as it was formerly of the slave trade' in West Africa. That it
was practically uninhabited before this migration is indicated by its
original name. According to tradition the first settlers on arrival
found the island full of birds, mostly curlews, and called it 'Okoloama' (*Okolo*, curlew; *Ama*, town; the town of curlews).[2] Similarly
the occupation of the site now known as Old Calabar by the Efik
tribe, who were formerly domiciled in Ibibio territory, shows that
everywhere vantage points for the Atlantic trade were quickly seized
upon. The port they occupied is, as a natural harbour, second only to
Bonny in importance. Various accounts of the Calabar migration
have been given by European travellers and traders since the seventeenth century, and in the nineteenth century a number of writers
have dealt with Efik tribal history.[3] By the end of the sixteenth century
the process of forming the city-states may be said to have been

[1] Talbot, *Peoples of Southern Nigeria*, i. 238. Cf. Leonard, op. cit., pp. 22-23.
[2] It is important to note that 'Bonny' is the corruption of the word 'Ibani'
(name of the Patriarch of the founders of Okoloama) by Europeans; Ubani by
the Ibos; Umani by the Ibibios; and Ebi-nya by the Andonis.
[3] Waddell, op. cit., H. Goldie, *Old Calabar and Its Mission* (Edinburgh, 1890),
p. 12, and M. D. W. Jeffreys, *Old Calabar* (Calabar, 1935), pp. 1-22. The Efiks
disagree with Jeffreys that they are Ibibio and with Goldie that they occupied
their present site in the seventeenth century. They believe they arrived at their
present site during the fifteenth century. Their traditions of origin indicate that
they came from the region of the Cameroons.

complete. From the seventeenth century onwards the Delta became the most important slave mart in West Africa.

Once the states were founded and the settlers' position as middlemen consolidated, fresh voluntary migrations from the hinterland to the coast were practically impossible. Yet large accessions of people continued to flow into and swell the Delta population, mainly by way of the slave trade. It was during the era of traffic in human beings that the Delta gained the bulk of her population. A study of contemporary literature will reveal that in the nineteenth century by far the greater number of the Delta population were 'in a state of serfdom' and not a few of the great chiefs were of slave descent. Particularly was this the case with Bonny. The influx of slaves seemed to have reduced the number of freemen to an absolute minimum. In 1848 Koehler noted that 'only a small proportion' of Bonny population is 'free-born'.[1] In 1863 Richard Burton recorded that apart from the Bonny royal family and one or two others, the rest were of slave origins and of the latter 'some few are "Bonny free" [born in Bonny] but none "proper free" '.[2] Hugh Goldie, whose knowledge of Old Calabar was unrivalled, stated in 1890 that the 'slaves greatly outnumber the freemen'.[3] It would appear that marriage between slave women and freemen led inevitably to the greater absorbing the less. Few men were free from the stigma of slavery, and consequently the surviving free classes wielded power out of all proportion to their numbers.[4]

With further migrations to the coast barred by the rise of the city-states, the lure of the great commercial highway of the Niger valley itself stimulated another migration within the hinterland, and the hardy and adventurous people from the Benin area once again established themselves at places on the river bank favourable to trade. The Ibo-speaking people living to the west of the Niger call themselves Ika, and the people of Arbo, Assay, and Onitsha on the west bank have a tradition that their ancestors came from Benin. This third migratory wave is generally accepted to have taken place about the middle of the seventeenth century, at a time when the Delta middlemen having fortified their privileged position on the Atlantic coast brooked no rivals. According to an Onitsha writer the date of

[1] Talbot, *Peoples of Southern Nigeria*, i. 256.
[2] Ibid., p. 269.
[3] Goldie, op. cit., p. 18.
[4] See Chapters VII and VIII.

their arrival at the present site was about 1630.[1] The tradition of these seventeenth-century migrants, which is closely related to that of Benin, shows that although they are Ibo-speaking, they were not originally Ibos. Moreover, whereas the Ibos east of the Niger have no kings—an Ibo proverb has it, 'Ndi Igbo Echi Eze', i.e. 'the Ibos make no kings'—yet these Ibo-speaking riverine towns to the west of the Niger have a society patterned after the semi-divine kingship of Benin. Even in the nineteenth century their Benin origin was perceptible to European observers. In 1832 Macgregor Laird said of Obi Ossai, king of Abo, 'From his fondness for coral ornaments, I should imagine him to be of Benin extraction.'[2]

But not all the migrants came from Benin. The principal Ibospeaking towns on the banks of the lower Niger between Brass and Onitsha claim, according to their traditions, to have originated from the following tribes:

Ibos	Igala	Benin	Mixed tribes[3]
Atani	Ossomari	Aboh	Utoku
Ogwu	Okoh	Onitsha	Adawai
Osuche	Odekpe	Assay	Akrai
Umunankwo	Umuolu	Uchi	Okpai
		Onya	Ndoni
			Asaba

The significance of this later movement of peoples lies in this: just as the Delta states captured commercial points on the Atlantic coast, so the migrants from Ado na Idu[4] and other areas controlled strategic and commercial points on the Niger valley through which flowed the hinterland products to the sea. Both gained a monopoly of trade in their respective spheres. A century ago the town of Abo exercised what amounted to a monopoly of trade up and down the Niger valley. It occupied a strong strategic position 147 miles from Forcados—the most important mouth of the Niger—and was about the same distance from Bonny, Brass, New Calabar, and Akassa on the sea. The entire trade of the Niger was held up at will by her war-canoes armed

[1] M. O. Ibeziako, *Some Aspects of Ancient Civilization* (1937), p. 13; also Talbot, op. cit., pp. 167–9 and 234–5.

[2] Laird and Oldfield, *Narrative of an Expedition into the Interior of Africa* (London, 1837), i. 101.

[3] The towns shown under the heading 'mixed tribes' are settlements in which the original inhabitants are known to have come from more than one tribe. I owe my information in this section to Mr. R. R. Olisa, of the Inland Revenue Department, Lagos. Mr. Olisa has carried out a detailed research on the population of the Niger valley.   [4] The Ibo term for the 'kingdom of Benin'.

with brass and iron cannon. This explains why Abo loomed so large in the narratives of the British Niger expeditions of the first half of the nineteenth century, and why the Abo chief, Obi Ossai, who had no power beyond the banks of the Niger, was wrongly styled by them the 'king of the Ibos'.[1] All of these expeditions bear testimony to the commercial importance of Abo.[2] Laird noted its strategic position in 1832 as being 'at the head of the three great outlets of the Niger,—the Benin, the Bonny and the Nun'.[3] And following Laird, Captain William Allen and Dr. T. R. H. Thomson, members of the Niger expedition of 1841, declared: 'Abòh is much the largest town in the [northern] Delta. . . . Obi Ossai, King of Ibu [Ibos], is therefore one of the most powerful and influential rulers on the banks of the river, which is aided much by the position of this town, Abòh, at the upper part of the Delta enabling him to control very much the trade towards the sea.'[4]

The eastward movement into Iboland from the Benin area, stimulated by trade in the Niger valley, was paralleled by a comparable movement from the north. The northern branch was a direct result of the slave trade. The indigenous home of the Ibos, which lies mainly to the east of the Niger valley, is within the forest belt where the cavalry used by the Fulani in their annual slave-raids could not operate. These raids were conducted mainly in the plains north of the forest region, and were organized from Kano, Sokoto, Bida, and Ilorin. They inevitably led to the movement of tribes, south of the Benue, to inaccessible areas and places of safety such as the Ibo forest area provided.

Here and there are still to be found people who have a vague tradition of their fathers having been driven from the Ilorin-region, and settled among a people of a strange tongue which they adopted. At Ukwu-Nzu are to be seen ancient ivory tusks in a shrine which it is said were deposited by an Oba or King of Benin, whose mother came from that town, which is one of the small group speaking both Ibo and a corrupt Yoruba called 'Onukwumi', who say they were driven by slave-raiders in the neighbourhood of Ilorin.[5]

The effects of these migrations on Iboland and its history may now be assessed.

[1] Richard and John Lander, *Journal of an Expedition* (London, 1832), iii. 176–84.
[2] Lander, op. cit., iii. 183.   [3] Laird and Oldfield, op. cit., i. 102–4.
[4] W. Allen and T. R. H. Thomson, *A Narrative of the Expedition . . . to the River Niger, 1841* (London, 1841), i. 239–40.
[5] S. R. Smith, 'The Ibo People' (unpublished manuscript, 1929), pp. 1–7.

The density of population which was and still is a main feature of the Ibo country was due in part at least to this accession of new blood from the west and north. The Ibos might be, as has often been asserted, a prolific race, but there can be little doubt that the new migrants from the seventeenth century onwards added not a little to the existing population and occupied lands the original tribe could ill afford to lose. Professor W. M. Macmillan has in various writings consistently maintained that Africa is underpopulated, and he attributes much of her backwardness to her lack of human resources necessary for taming what, according to him, is an inhospitable and poor continent.[1] This view cannot apply to Iboland.

Perhaps the most important factor conditioning Ibo history in the nineteenth century and in our own time is land hunger. Yorubaland, occupying a greater area of land, has a smaller population. Hence the Ibos pressing against limited land resources had, of necessity, to seek other avenues of livelihood outside the tribal boundaries. In the nineteenth century and earlier the growth of a large non-agricultural population in areas where the land was too small or too poor to sustain the people gave rise to some measure of specialization among sections of the tribe: the Aros became the middlemen of the hinterland trade; the Ada and the Abam constituted the mercenaries; Awka men were the smiths and doctors, while Nkwerre people, in addition to their work in iron, played the role of professional spies and diplomatists. If we may judge from nineteenth-century records, in spite of this specialization, over-population was the rule in all sections of the tribe. This reservoir of manpower accounts for the fact that Iboland supplied the greater part of the slaves shipped to the New World from the bights of Benin and Biafra. Professor M. J. Herskovits has shown that there were four principal slaving areas in West Africa: 'the Senegal and the Guinea Coast' are two of the areas mentioned in contemporary writings. 'The regions about the mouth of the Niger, named Bonny and Calabar in the documents, and the Congo are the other two.' He went on to show that 'large numbers of slaves were shipped from the Niger Delta region, as indicated by the manifests of ships loaded at Calabar and Bonny, the principal ports. These were mainly Ibo slaves representing a people which today inhabits a large portion of this region.'[2] Contemporary sources clearly indicate that the Delta formed the most important slave mart

[1] W. M. Macmillan, *Africa Emergent* (London, 1938).
[2] M. J. Herskovits, *The Myth of the Negro Past* (New York, 1941), p. 36.

in West Africa, equalling the trade of all West Africa put together. Delta ascendancy in this traffic dated from the closing years of the seventeenth century. Between 1786 and 1800 Captain John Adams carried out a scientific research into the West African trade and people. In 1822 he wrote:

This place [Bonny] is the wholesale market for slaves, as not fewer than 20,000 are annually sold here; 16,000 of whom are members of one nation, called Heebo [the Ibos], so that this single nation . . . during the last 20 years [exported no less] than 320,000; and those of the same nation sold at New Calabar [a Delta port], probably amounted, in the same period of time, to 50,000 more, making an aggregate amount of 370,000 Heebos. The remaining part of the above 20,000 is composed of the natives of the Brass country . . . and also of Ibbibbys [Ibibios] or Quaws.[1]

These figures have been borne out by other witnesses. Macgregor Laird put the Delta export slave trade between 1827–34 'at the lowest calculation' as 200,000 slaves.[2]

This over-population explains the great preponderance of the same tribe in the Delta itself, even in areas like Old Calabar and the Cameroons not dominated by the Ibo interior. In 1853, when Creek Town was the leading trading community of Old Calabar, Ibos formed more than half the population.[3] 'The King of New Calabar . . . and Pepple King of Bonny, were both of Ibo descent, of which also are the mass of the natives.'[4] This was confirmed by Dr. W. B. Baikie after an interview with King William Dappa Pepple at Fernando Po in 1854.[5]

Impressed by this Ibo ubiquity, Dr. J. A. B. Horton, a West African writing in 1868, declared that Iboland 'is separated from the sea only by petty tribes [the Delta communities], all of which trace their origin from the great race'.[6] The mistake of ascribing Ibo origins to all the Delta peoples was common among nineteenth-century writers. It can only be accounted for by the great influx of Ibo migrants which blurred the lines of the earlier migrations. The statement fails to take note of the fact that in the peopling of the Delta no one Nigerian tribe had a monopoly. Benis, Ijaws, Sobos, Jekris,

[1] Adams, op. cit., p. 38.
[2] Parl. Pap. 1842, XI, Pt. I, Appendix and Index, No. 7.
[3] *Church Missionary Intelligencer* (London, 1853), xiv. 255; cf. H. Goldie, *Efik Dictionary* (Edinburgh, 1874), p. 355.   [4] H. Crow, op. cit., p. 197.
[5] W. B. Baikie, *An Exploring Voyage into the Rivers Quorra and Tchadda* (London, 1854), p. 355.
[6] J. A. B. Horton, *West African Countries and Peoples* (London, 1868), p. 171.

Ekoi, Ibibios, Efik, and even the northern Nigerian tribes were represented. The following contemporary statement on the composition of Old Calabar's population was true of almost any Delta state: 'We have amongst us [in Old Calabar] captives of the slave-raids of the Tibari, as the Fulatos or Fellani [Fulani] are called here. Thus about 13 different tribes are represented in our population.'[1]

To sum up, it is broadly true to say that owing to their numerical superiority[2] and consequent land hunger the Ibo migrants (enforced or voluntary) formed the bulk of the Delta population during the nineteenth century. They bequeathed their language to most of the city-states—to Bonny, Okrika, Opobo, and to a certain extent influenced the language and institutions of Old and New Calabar. But the population which evolved out of this mingling of peoples was neither Benin nor Efik, Ibo nor Ibibio. They were a people apart, the product of the clashing cultures of the tribal hinterland and of the Atlantic community to both of which they belonged. The tribal Ibos called them Ndi Mili Nnu (People of the Salt Water), and so long as the frontier of trade was confined to the Atlantic seaboard so long did they remain the economic masters of these territories.[3]

In the peopling of the Delta the points occupied by the migrants were widely separated from each other. Usually they were islands. like Bonny dominating the mouth of a river which linked the hinterland to the sea. In time each community developed the independence and individualism so typical of island dwellers. Every river mouth, every centre of trade, and, in some areas, every town had its overlord. Each city-state had all the apparatus of rule which enabled it to maintain law and order, administer justice, make war and peace, organize and prosecute peaceful commerce for four centuries. The

---

[1] H. Goldie, *Calabar and Its Mission* (Edinburgh, 1890), p. 18.

[2] Horton, ibid., pp. 174–5, estimates Ibo population in the middle of the nineteenth century 'at from 10,000,000 to 12,000,000' people. This seems an exaggeration, but confirms the common nineteenth-century belief that the population density was high.

[3] The term 'Ijaw', still used to describe the Delta inhabitants, although convenient for purposes of classification, takes no account of the co-mingling of peoples we have just discussed. For Ibo influence on Old Calabar language, &c., see Jeffreys, op. cit., pp. 44–45. For European influence, e.g. in language, ibid., pp. 55–59:

amik	hammock	*ankisi*	handkerchief	*bhibe*	bible
abranken	blanket	*bensin*	pencil	*etombit*	tumbler
tasen	thousand	*nwaba*	guava	*suap*	soap

term 'city-state' as applied to the Delta communities embraces not only the settlements on the coast but also their extensions (by way of trading posts) in the interior. This is in line with the Greek idea of city which means a community of people rather than an area of territory; for although the Delta trading colonies were all outside her political boundaries, they were indissolubly bound by strong economic ties. Moreover 'city-state' is a more appropriate designation than 'tribal-state', since the period of migrations disorganized the tribal entities and the slave trade further accentuated the mingling of peoples. In the nineteenth century, therefore, the Delta states were grouped not by considerations of kinship but by contiguity, and in the period under survey citizenship came increasingly to depend not on descent but on residence.

The city-states divide broadly into two political groupings—the monarchies and the republics. The former include Bonny (Ibani), New Calabar (Kalabari), and Warri, not to mention petty monarchies such as those of Bell Town and Aqua Town in the Cameroons. The republics were in reality single trading units with divided political authority as in Old Calabar, Brass, and the Cameroons. Bonny and Old Calabar best illustrate these two types of political systems.

Bonny was the economic and political centre of the Niger Delta during the greater part of the nineteenth century, and even its successor from the 1870's, Opobo, was an offshoot of the older kingdom. The former has always been a monarchy as far as can be ascertained; a list of her kings from the foundation of the monarchy to the end of the nineteenth century was recorded by A. G. Leonard in 1906.[1]

[1] Leonard, op. cit., p. 47.

Kings of Bonny

1. Alagbariye.	6. Edimini.
2. Opkraindole.	7. Kamalu.
3. Opuamakubu.	8. Dappa (Great or Opu).
4. Okpara-Ashimini.	9. Amakiri.
5. Ashimini.	10. Appinya.

11. Warri.

King Holliday Owsa⎱
  (Igbani ⎰ Short quartumvirate—
  (Bupor. ⎰ all princes of the blood.
  (Ipor. ⎰

12. Perekule, afterwards King Pepple.
13. Foubra (Agbaa).
14. Foubra ⎱ Sons of
15. Opobo ⎰ Perekule.
16. Bereibibo.
17. Dappa (William).
18. George.

A more detailed list and a fuller account of their reigns, corroborating Leonard, is preserved by the descendants of the Pepples at Bonny.[1] If, as is generally supposed, the monarchy was founded around the mid-fifteenth century, in 1830 that institution was almost 400 years old.

The reigning king in that year was Opubu (of the House of Pepple). The first king of this House was Pelekule or Perekule (anglicized Pepple) and although Opubu was the third of the Pepples he was the fourteenth king (Ama-nya-na-bo) in an unbroken line of succession. The monarchy was therefore a deep-rooted institution at Bonny. Moreover, the Royal House of Pepple which reigned from the eighteenth to the nineteenth centuries had a knack of producing remarkable men. In the Pepples Bonny found, New Calabar excepted, a focal point for unity and strength unknown to the other Delta communities.

Impressed by the might of the Pepple monarchs European observers have tended to credit them with autocratic powers; indeed, Adams's statement in 1790 that the power of the king of Bonny 'is absolute' and that 'the surrounding country, for a considerable distance, is subject to his dominion' represents the general contemporary opinion.[2] Nor was this view altogether unfounded. The Pepples sought by alliance and conquest to gain ascendancy over the entire Delta and the markets of the interior. In this they well nigh succeeded but for the stubborn opposition of the kingdom of the Kalabaris (New Calabar) which refused to accept subjection. The recurrent wars between the two kingdoms not infrequently ended in the defeat of New Calabar, yet that state's powers of recuperation were demonstrated time and again.

In 1790 it was reported that the king of Bonny had 'destroyed the town of New Calabar twice', had compelled its 'inhabitants . . . to take their merchandise to Bonny for sale', and had not permitted them 'to have any communication whatsoever with the shipping'.[3] In 1826 Captain Owen noted that one of the titles of the reigning Pepple was 'Conqueror of the Callabar', a title 'he derived from his grandfather, who subdued that country, but which has long since been independent, although the present king threatens again to reduce

---

[1] In 1949 I was permitted to study several well-preserved documents and other relics relating to the Bonny monarchy in the possession of the present Head of the Royal House.

[2] Talbot, *Peoples of Southern Nigeria*, i. 250–1.

[3] Ibid., p. 250.

it to his dominion'.[1] Notwithstanding this threat New Calabar was a thriving independent state in 1830.

Even in home affairs the powers of a Bonny king were limited by the country's constitution. This did not altogether escape the attention of contemporary European observers and one of them made this significant comment: 'The Kings of Bonny, although in many respects they appear to exercise absolute power unrestrained by any fixed principles, may be properly termed heads of an aristocratic government. This is evinced by having a grand palaver house, in which they themselves presided, but the members of which composed of the great chiefs or great men, were convened and consulted on all matters of state urgency.'[2] The king was nothing if not king in council, and as the analysis of the social organization will reveal the king's powers were everywhere limited by the peculiar political system of the city-states.

In contrast to the hereditary monarchies of the Pepples at Bonny and of the Amakiris at New Calabar there was the divided authority of the Efik community on the mouth of the Cross river. At Old Calabar, from the eighteenth century onwards, there were four trading towns—Creek Town, Henshaw Town, Duke Town, and Obutong, each—except on questions of common interest—under separate and independent rulers. As an eyewitness put it in 1847, 'The towns of Calabar, are, in fact, a number of small republics, each with its own chief and council, united only by the Egbo confraternity.'[3] The Egbo Society was a sort of freemasonry, a secret cult, uniting the ruling classes in all four towns; membership was open to freemen only. This 'confraternity' came into being because the nobility felt the need for 'a bond of union', a 'supreme authority' for 'enforcing peace and order among equals and rivals', and for safeguarding the interests and privileges of the nobility. 'It seemed especially designed to keep' women, slaves, and the masses of the population in subjection.[4]

For all practical purposes the Egbo Order was the supreme political power in Old Calabar; it exercised not only executive and legislative functions but was the highest court of appeal in the land. Its President became the first citizen of the community. Hutchinson reported that at Duke Town (the seat of Egbo power) there was in 1856 a 'Palaver-House, a species of senatorial forum, where all

[1] Owen, op. cit., p. 345.
[2] H. Crow, op. cit., pp. 215–16.
[3] Waddell, op. cit., p. 314.
[4] Ibid., pp. 313–15.

matters public or private, are discussed and settled by the Egbos'.[1] Similar organizations existed in communities of divided authority, such as the Cameroons, primarily to protect the privileges of the nobility against the insurrection of the lower orders.

The pivot of Delta social organization was the 'House System' or 'House Rule'. This peculiar constitution is common to all the trading states and was the direct result of the trade with the Europeans. As used in the Delta it is a European term and a descriptive one at that. The mixture of peoples often meant that African law and custom vanished and a new law and order was evolved based partly on African precedent and experience and partly on the lessons of the contact with Europe. In its full development the House became at once a co-operative trading unit and a local government institution. As a rule every trader of any importance owned so many slaves bought from various tribes. These, along with the trader's family, formed the nucleus of a 'House.' Even in the hey-day of the slave traffic the Delta middlemen retained the best slaves in their personal service, some of whom manned the fleet of canoes indispensable for the trade with the interior or engaged on agricultural work on the farms. The smaller Houses numbered anything from 300–1,000 members; others, such as the royal Houses, numbered many thousands. In 1847 King Eyo of Creek Town, Old Calabar, 'had in his House many thousand slaves, and four hundred canoes with a captain and crew for every one. Besides his extensive trade, which amounted to several puncheons annually, he employed his people reclaiming waste land, founding towns, and planting farms in well-selected positions which gave him command of the rivers and channels of trade.'[2] Along with the king's House there would be scores of smaller Houses, each presided over by a wealthy merchant.

The House system, which grew out of the needs of Delta society, followed, in a measure, the pattern of social organization of the interior tribes. Among the Ibos and Ibibios each town or village is composed of a group or of several groups, at the head of which is the eldest member of the group. Such a group among the Ibos is called 'Umunna' and among the Ibibios 'Ekpuk', i.e. an extended family. In each group all the members are related by blood. It is significant that with the emergence of the 'House' the words 'Umunna' and

[1] T. J. Hutchinson, *Impressions of Western Africa* (London, 1853), p. 119.
[2] Waddell, op. cit., p. 320.

'Ekpuk' disappeared from the vocabulary of the extribal Ibibio and Ibo-speaking peoples in the Delta; in their place we have 'Ulo' and 'Ufok'—House, expressing the new coast relationship based not on kinship but on common interests and economic necessities. Master and servant, the bond and the free, all became members of one House, a veritable hierarchy, with numerous gradations, each rank with its duties and responsibilities, its privileges and rewards.

But, unlike the 'Umunna' and the 'Ekpuk' the House system did not make for 'excess of democracy'; the House Head, unlike the Elder of the interior, was not just a mere figurehead, registering the people's will. He was in theory absolute, with powers of life and death over his subordinates. How far this power was exercised is another matter. It cannot be denied, however, that the element of autocracy in House rule was very strong: it had to be, particularly if the discordant and often rebellious elements composing a House in the semi-military society of the Delta were to be welded into a coherent whole.

Estimates of the House system vary considerably. There are some, like Dr. Jeffreys, who would declare that 'the authority of the Head of a House' was based on the principle that 'might is right'. He spoke of the 'iniquitous reign of the Houses' and from his account one would derive the impression that the system was all darkness and no light.[1] It cannot be denied that an element of cruelty and even brutality was ever present. A cruel master could, on occasion, take the life of his slave for very trifling offences. de Cardi enumerated punishments that could be inflicted on the domestic slaves:

ear cutting in its various stages, from clipping to total dismemberment; crucifixion round a large cask; extraction of teeth; suspension by the thumbs; Chilli peppers pounded and stuffed up the nostrils, and forced into the eyes and ears; fastening the victim to a post driven into the beach at low water and leaving him there to be drowned with the rising tide, or to be eaten by the sharks or crocodiles piecemeal; heavily ironed and chained to a post in their master's compound . . . and reduced to living skeletons; impaling on stakes; forcing a long steel ramrod through the body until it appeared through the top of the skull.[2]

These speak plainly of the dark side of the system.

Yet, as he himself emphasized, these extremities were resorted to only in exceptional circumstances, and he admitted that the chances of a slave 'improving his condition are manifold'. While allowing,

[1] Jeffreys, op. cit., pp. 55–62.
[2] M. H. Kingsley, *West African Studies* (London, 1899), p. 535.

therefore, that the life of a slave before he 'gets his foot on the first rung of the ladder of advancement' could be terrible, once he had graduated beyond the domestic hierarchy progress was usually rapid. In the nineteenth century, European observers, who were by no means uncritical of some aspects of House rule, did not overlook its merits. This peculiar system defies definition and does not lend itself to generalization. It cannot be assessed apart from the context of the society which produced it. Delta society in the nineteenth century rested on a foundation of slavery; terror and despotism were normal features of a system that had to keep the masses in subjection. Yet if house rule may be judged from its practical results, on the whole it met the needs of the day. 'Absolute authority on the one part, and entire subjection on the other, is the theory; but in practice both the · authority and subjection are checked and limited in many ways . . . the harsh terms master and mistress are not in the Calabar language. The sweet and precious names, father and mother, alone are used to express the relation. The children of both classes (slave and free) grow up together as playmates, and equally regard the Head of the House as their father. In our schools they sat side by side, read in the same classes, and were treated as they deserved, without reference to their relation.'[1] Another observer declared that 'it is remarkable how clannish the slaves belonging to the same house become. Each one considers that he partakes of the honour of the house, and is zealous in maintaining it. Any slight upon his master or father [the one word "ete" signifying both] is resented as a personal offence.'[2]

The British Consul to the Bight of Biafra, T. J. Hutchinson, declared in 1861 that 'in many of the palm oil trading rivers slavery is purely mythical. In Bonny, the men who rule the roost in political debate, as well as on the palm oil change, are of the slave class.'[3] 'The best thing in it' [the House system], said another, 'is that it gives to the poorest boy who paddles an oil canoe a chance of becoming a king.'[4] That many slave boys rose to the rank of the nobility in the city-states is writ large in Delta history of the nineteenth century. Forceful and energetic Ibo slaves such as JaJa and OkoJumbo took advantage of the peculiar constitution of the House system and became the Heads of the Houses to which they were attached.

It was in the interest of every House Head to foster and increase

[1] Waddell, op. cit., p. 315.   [2] Goldie, op. cit., pp. 19–20.
[3] *Ten Years Wandering Among the Ethiopians* (London, 1861), pp. 2–6.
[4] M. H. Kingsley, op. cit., p. 427.

the trade of his people: as trade cannot flourish under conditions of terror, the Heads must have used their absolute power with great discretion and restraint. Discipline might have been severe and brutal in certain cases,[1] but as a general rule, loyalty from the slaves and confidence from the master (father) was the prevalent mood. For the difference between the plantation slavery of the New World and the domestic slavery as practised in the Niger Delta lies in this: whereas in the former the slaves performed, on the whole, an indirect and impersonal service and were regarded as some form of capital goods, in the latter the wealth produced by a slave eventually set him free, for the master knew his slave intimately and the value of his work and rewarded him accordingly. It was this incentive, ever present in the House system, that made it in the nineteenth century an institution full of vitality, flexible, and in a large measure beneficial to all.

The 'House' was primarily the unit of local government in the Delta, and as each occupied a separate quarter in the community the Head of the House was responsible for law and order in his section. It followed then that in a place like Bonny the king, who was as a rule the leading merchant in the state, had no direct power over the Houses of his chiefs. He could intervene to resolve a conflict between one house and another, to confirm the election of new House Heads and to determine the rank a chief might occupy in the state. But although he was in direct control of foreign relations, war and peace, and was the initiator of commercial policies, he always acted within his authority as king in council.

The trading organization of the hinterland was closely linked with the Delta states. No tribe in eastern Nigeria achieved a highly centralized political organization in the nineteenth century; and the clans, local government units, recognized few authorities higher than themselves. Although this 'excess of democracy' was the characteristic feature of the political organization, it must not be imagined that there were no threads of unity in the commercial and cultural spheres nor that the fragmentation of authority necessarily impeded the flow of trade.

Two types of trading organization operated in the hinterland. The first, centred upon the Aros, obtained mainly in the period of the slave trade. Their influence was based on the Aro Chuku Oracle which was universally respected and feared throughout Iboland, and in

[1] M. H. Kingsley, op. cit., pp. 533-8.

fact by every tribe in eastern Nigeria. This Oracle was supposed to reside in the territory of the Aros, a section of the Ibo tribe. In 1854 Baikie wrote of the 'noted City of Aro where there is the celebrated shrine of Tshuku [God], to which pilgrimages are made, not only from all parts of Igbo proper, but from Old Calabar, and from the tribes along the coast, and from Oru and Nembe. The town is always mentioned with great respect, almost, at times, with a degree of veneration, and the people say "Tshuku ab yama", or "God lives there".'[1] Aro people (whom the Ibos call "Umu-Chukwu"—the Children of God) exploited this belief in their Oracle in many ways, principally in order to dominate the life of the region economically, and they made themselves the sole middlemen of the hinterland trade. This they did by establishing Aro colonies along the trade routes of the interior[2]—like the Greeks, the course of whose coloniz-ing expeditions was largely directed by the priests of the Delphic Oracle. In its wake they organized a trading system which had its ramifications throughout practically the whole of the country between the Niger and the eastern side of the Cross river. Every quarter of Aro Town had its 'sphere of influence' in matters of trade. 'For instance, the country between AroChuku and Awka belonged to the quarters of Utari, Amove and Ndizioggu.'[3] Acting as mediators between God and the clans and assuming themselves to be the spokesmen of the Almighty, they held a privileged position through-out the land, erecting what amounted to a theocratic state over eastern Nigeria. Aro colonies became the divinely ordained trade centres in the interior; Aro middlemen the economic dictators of the hinterland. During the time of the slave trade and in the period of legitimate commerce they acquired immense wealth through a monopoly all believed to be divinely appointed, and with wealth came great political influence.[4]

The numerous political units represented by the clans, admirable as organs of local government, proved inadequate for handling matters of common interest such as commerce and justice. A central

[1] Baikie, op. cit., pp. 310–11.

[2] See K. Umo, *The Aro Settlements* (Lagos, 1945). The author traced more than twenty-five of these settlements.

[3] Talbot, *Peoples of Southern Nigeria*, i. 182–3.

[4] The predominant position held by the Aros during the slave-trade period is acknowledged by all sections of Ibo country. Today sites of Aro colonies exist, and although no longer trade routes, are still inhabited by descendants of the Aros. The great Oracle, known to Europeans as 'Long Ju Ju', was destroyed by the British in 1900.

organization was needed to facilitate inter-tribal trade, and provide a 'pax' without which commerce could not flourish.[1] It was this vacuum existing at the centre of the tribal organization that the Aros, working through the medium of their Oracle, filled. The trading settlements they established at the crossing of rivers and at the intersection of the main routes became the 'free cities' to which all who wished to 'traffic and exchange' safely repaired, international courts where individuals and clans in conflict sought justice from the undisputed authority of the Oracle.[2] 'From most parts of the Niger Delta and the Cross River litigants proceed to invoke the aid of the oracle in the settlement of their claims and disputes', wrote Sir Harry Johnston in 1888. That the astute Aros abused the use of this Oracle and diverted it to their own ends must not obscure the need which called it into being.

The position of power the Aros occupied was of course dependent on the universal belief in their Oracle as the supreme deity. This belief they sought by every means at their disposal to sustain. They hired the services of the famous professional warriors of Iboland— 'the Abam, Abiriba, Awhawfia, and Edda' (or Ada)—whenever there was fighting to be done, arming these mercenaries with 'the guns obtained from the white traders' and 'conquered all the people who resisted their influence or killed their agents'.[3] Thus to the super-natural powers of the Oracle was added the military might of its adherents. This explains the contemporary fear and dread of the Aro name. Even in the Niger Delta the fear for this hinterland deity was great. 'The terror inspired by the threat that if a slave gave trouble to his master he would be sent to Chukwu [the Oracle] was sufficient to enable the numerically inferior people of the Delta to hold thousands of slaves in subjection, and herein probably lies one of the reasons for the establishment and maintenance of the Oracle at Aro-Chukwu.'[4]

---

[1] In *The Ibo People* S. R. Smith describes the conditions requisite for the establishment and development of oracles. These are (1) A quiet place remote from main routes. (2) Some natural features which inspire the sense of dread, such as rocks, caves, steep valleys with water, groves, or dense bush. (3) A system by which travelling agents get to know local disputes and encourage reference for settlement to their own oracles. (4) An easy and secret method for the disposal of the victims of the oracles. As an example a victim sold in slavery would be announced as having been 'eaten' by the Oracle.

[2] F.O.84/1882, Memorandum of Sir Harry Johnston on Oil Rivers.

[3] Talbot, *Peoples of Southern Nigeria*, i. 184. Cf. Smith, op. cit., pp. 135–45.

[4] Smith, op. cit., p. 136, where he also states that the Aro Oracle 'was some 80

The intimate link between the interior trade organization and that of the Delta led many writers to suggest that the Aros might have emigrated originally from the Delta itself and founded the towns of Aro-Chukwu 'primarily for the supply and forwarding of slaves to the coast', and that the Oracle was a device in the name of religion for attracting people from the surrounding country, and so kept up a steady flow of human beings whose lot was represented as being 'eaten by Chukwu'.[1] The theories of Aro origin are legion. Their close economic ties with the Delta have never been disputed. There is no doubt that 'they sold most of the slaves at Bonny'[2] and that the Obi-Nkita quarter (the leading Aro town) monopolized the trade with that city-state. Thus it was that Bonny became a leading slave market in West Africa.

The system of obtaining slaves by use of oracular devices was fairly widespread in the Ibo country and, apart from the Chukwu at Aro-Chukwu, there were other oracles such as the Agballa at Awka, the Igwe at Umunora in the Owerri district, the Onyili-ora near Nri, and Ogba, a cave in the Nkisi stream at Ogbunike in the Onitsha district,[3] all of which merely supplemented the work of the all-powerful Aro Oracle, undoubtedly the dominating power in the country.

The belief that the bulk of the slaves handled in the Atlantic trade were captives from tribal wars or that kidnapping and raids were the normal methods of obtaining the human victims is now seen to be but a half truth when applied to the tribes east of the Niger. The Oracle, directed by the Aros, was the medium through which the slaves exported from Delta ports were largely recruited. As the highest court of appeal, this deity was supposed to levy fines on convicted individuals and groups. These fines had to be paid in slaves who were believed to be 'eaten' by Chukwu (the Oracle), although in fact they were sold to the coast middlemen. This recruiting campaign, carefully staged under conditions of awe and reverence, was rarely attended by violence. Only when the injunctions of the Oracle were defied did the Aros, in his name, turn their fierce mercenaries on the offending

miles from Bonny, 60 miles from Kalabar [New Calabar], and 70 from the mainstream of the Niger above Abo, it was sufficiently remote for its purpose, while at the same time it was in close touch with the dense populations of the Ibo people, and the neighbouring tribes, the Ibibio, Ijo, Isokos, Jekiri, Usobos, and the Benis of the Niger Delta'.   [1] Ibid., p. 136.
[2] Talbot, op. cit., pp. 184–5.
[3] Smith, op. cit., p. 135.

party. Then the process of terrorizing the victims began and with their superior arms and immense wealth they invariably emerged victorious. But the dominant power of the Oracle was widely understood and rarely opposed, so that the slaves obtained by violence and kidnapping could not have greatly exceeded, and may even have been fewer than, those who surrendered to the dictates of the Oracle. Nevertheless, both methods of recruitment—whether by violence or the invocation of superstitious fears—led to unsettlement and terror, and exposed the interior tribes to exploitation by the middlemen.[1]

The second, and for the nineteenth century the most important, trading organization was connected with the trade in palm oil. Early in the century the oil trade was developing and in 1830 had become more vital to the economy of the city-states than the trade in men. The determined attack on the slave trade by the British Naval Squadron had greatly undermined it, and the Delta middlemen, eager to maintain their position, turned to the new trade.

The area from which the bulk of the oil was derived lay immediately within the Delta hinterland. The famous 'oil markets' which loomed so large in the consular reports of the last century were situated in the palm belt, at the heads of the creeks and rivers linking the interior to the coast. Each city-state had its own exclusive markets in which it maintained trading posts and in which hundreds of its subjects lived for the greater part of each year. Over half the oil handled in the Delta trade was sold at Bonny, all of which came from the exclusive markets of Essene, Obunku, Imo, Akwete, Urata, Azumiri, Ohambele, Ngwa (landing port, Aba), and Ndele. In theory these tribal states which came under the Bonny sphere of interest were politically independent but in practice they were virtually the protectorates of the latter.[2]

In the period under survey Bonny was undoubtedly the first among the 'great powers' of the Niger Delta. Her commercial supremacy was based on her military organization and the unit of her fighting force was the war-canoe. This craft functioned as the warship of the creeks and rivers, and the Bonny command of these waterways was

[1] In *Tribes of the Niger Delta*, p. 289, Talbot confirmed the statements already quoted and declared that the greatest source of Aro wealth was the slave trade.

[2] I am indebted to Mr. Adadonye Fombo, of Customs House, Port Harcourt, for information with regard to the Bonny oil markets of the nineteenth century. Mr. Fombo is a well-known local historian of Bonny.

due to the overwhelming preponderance of her war-canoes. The continual demand for weapons of war by her kings and chiefs, so evident in nineteenth-century records, is a clear indication that a large proportion of her national income was expended on armaments.

The war-canoes were of various sizes, all equipped with brass and iron cannons. Some 'are capable of carrying 140 persons each, and have often a gun of large calibre mounted on the bow'.[1] Others, such as those Owen reported at the Bonny magazine and depot for war-canoes in 1826, were smaller in size and did not 'exceed 70 feet in length, mounted with guns of small calibre, and carrying when on a war expedition upwards of 80 men the greater number armed with muskets'.[2] The number of war-canoes must have been considerable since they were common to all the Delta states. It was customary at Bonny that the confirmation of a chief's election by the king was dependent on the former having equipped and manned a war-canoe and demonstrated that he had adequate resources to maintain it in peace and war. Since most Bonny Houses had as many as ten or more 'war-canoe chiefs', the amount of war vessels at the disposal of that city-state must have been formidable.

As was to be expected the Delta states were, in comparison with the tribal communities, far better armed; moreover, being the capitalists of the Atlantic trade they were greatly sought after as financiers by the hinterland traders. The result was that the interior producers of the oil were firmly bound to the coastal middlemen. To strengthen their friendship with the latter they married their daughters to the great chiefs and sent their children to Bonny to be trained in the business methods of the West. On their part the Delta states protected their tribal customers and allies in time of war, appointed reliable family heads as produce buyers on commission, and advanced them barter goods on credit for business ventures further inland.

Market laws were enacted to regulate the relations between the two communities and these were administered by equal numbers of the Bonnymen and the owners of the territory concerned. 'The severity of market laws shows the importance in which these institutions were held. Quarrel or fight entailed a heavy fine, while, should a man chance to be killed as the result of a dispute, the slayer was hanged in the middle of the market place, usually from the branches of a tree set aside for this purpose. Should a trader refuse to accept

[1] Talbot, op. cit., pp. 250–1.
[2] Owen, op. cit., ii. 345–6.

a particular kind of manilla[1] agreed upon as local currency, he was sacrificed to the market ju-ju, unless able to provide a substitute.'[2] It was on the ruthless enforcement of the market laws that the tranquillity of the trading areas depended; the Delta states learnt from hard experience that commerce could not flourish in lawlessness and disorder. Anything, therefore, which disturbed the peace was quickly stamped out. It was not uncommon in a time of crisis for a Bonny king to go to the tribal interior specifically to restore order in the markets. Indeed, one of the regular taxes levied on the white merchants by the city-states was 'for fostering of trade in the hinterlands of their district, for which good offices they were paid a duty called "comey" which amounted to about two shillings and sixpence per ton on palm oil exported'.[3]

The social organization of the tribes south-east of the Niger—the Ibos, Ibibios, Ekoi, Ijaws, and Efiks has often been described as lacking in cohesion and as being low in the scale of political organization, especially when compared to the highly centralized monarchies and states of the Western pattern. There is really no scientific basis for such comparison, as modern ethnographers have repeatedly emphasized. No universal criteria for comparisons of this sort exist, and as Professor M. J. Herskovits has said 'scholars drawing comparisons of this nature have merely re-acted to their own conditioning which has given them a predisposition to favour their own customs and to place differing cultures on levels which are deemed less advanced'.[4] In the emphatic words of Piddington, 'No human community is any lower, earlier, or more ancient than any other. All represent highly specialized human adaptations, the product of millennia of traditionalized cultural life'.[5]

Viewed in this light the Delta and the eastern Nigerian political organization served well the needs of their day.[6] The notion, still

---

[1] The 'Manilla' is a Delta coin shaped like a horse-shoe; it has, however, many variations some of which are in popular demand. They all look alike to the uninitiated, but to the practised eye of the middlemen the subtle differences between them are easily discernible. To avoid interruption to trade market laws would declare all manillas acceptable.

[2] Talbot, *Tribes of the Niger Delta*, p. 281.

[3] M. Le Comte C. N. de Cardi, quoted by Kingsley, *West African Studies*, p. 443. [4] Herskovits, op. cit.

[5] Quoted from *Man* by V. Gordon Childe in *Social Evolution* (London, 1951).

[6] K. O. Diké, 'History and Self-Government', *West Africa* (London, Feb.–Mar., 1953).

widely prevalent, that the multiplicity of independent political units was indicative of the non-existence of some form of authority at the centre is, to say the least, a superficial view. Beneath the apparent fragmentation of authority lay deep fundamental unities not only in the religious and cultural spheres, but also, as has been indicated, in matters of politics and economics.

Throughout the nineteenth century the great majority of the Ibos claimed Nri town in Awka district as their ancestral home, and it has been suggested that around Nri town is to be found 'the heart of the Ibo nationality'. The priests of this town enjoy the privilege 'of walking untouched or unharmed through any portion'[1] of the Ibo country, 'their semi-sacred character indicated by a short staff . . . affording a passport and protection everywhere'.[2] The theocratic sway of Eze (king of) Nri was almost universally accepted and the itinerant priests ministered to the religious needs of the whole community.[3] Inter-marriages, attendance at inter-clan festivals, blood-covenants between neighbouring political units, and the many communal-market groups in the tribal interior, were effective instruments of cultural unity. The alliances which existed between Bonny and other trading towns were, properly speaking, 'covenants', solemn leagues, which in the illiterate society of the Delta played the part of treaties. But they were more than treaties in that, being ratified or cemented with human blood, individual members of the contracting parties regarded one another as 'blood brothers'. The bond thus created was not limited by time or space. Wherever Bonny and Brass-men met they looked on one another as brothers, bound perpetually by the blood covenant linking their two countries.[4] The hidden strength of this ill-defined and apparently loose political organization was demonstrated towards the end of the century when it succeeded in holding at bay the organized and well-armed European attempts to

---

[1] Leonard, op. cit., pp. 34–35.   [2] Smith, op. cit., p. 146.
[3] Talbot, *Peoples of Southern Nigeria*, i. 234. A few other clans performed religious functions similar to that of the Nri people in some sections of the Ibo and Ibibio tribes.
[4] 'There is one point on which Bonny people seem to be fairly well agreed, and that is the relationship existing between themselves and the Brassmen. According to tradition they have always been on the very closest terms . . . and have never made war on each other, and this they attribute to the fact that their gods are in some remote ancestral or spiritual way derived from the same stock—Ogidiga, the Brass, and Ekiba, the Bonny God, having been somehow related in spirit-land.' Leonard, op. cit., pp. 23–24. I found no evidence of any war between the two peoples throughout the period under survey.

break through to the markets of the hinterland. It was not till Britain by conquest and diplomacy weakened the allegiance of the tribal areas to their Delta masters that she won the battle for the control of the eastern Nigerian interior.

In the sphere of politics and economics these underlying unities have already been demonstrated. No less an authority than Dr. P. A. Talbot asserted that throughout the period of the slave trade 'the administration of the whole region was so organized that an Aro compound, or quarter, was established in most Ibo towns of any size. These settlers acted as agents and were kept in constant touch with the central authority [at Aro-Chukwu]. The whole country was covered with a network of routes along which the unfortunate captives were passed from depot to depot, until finally sold on the coast.'[1] In this region a change in the commodity of trade was always accompanied by a change in the institutions through which it was carried on. The powers of the Aro Oracle waned with the declining trade in men which called it into being, and in its place arose the 'market governments' presided over by the powerful Delta states although the membership of the governing councils included equal numbers of the coast middlemen and the oil producers.

It is true that throughout the nineteenth century and before it 'tariff walls' existed between one trading area and another, both in the hinterland and on the coast, but, as has been shown, numerous devices were found to overcome this, and the Bonny alliances enabled her to tap the resources of every unit while not competing with them in the smaller markets under their control. An age-long covenant which forbade the Okrika trader to settle on the coast also made it illegal for a Bonny trader to enter the Okrika 'sphere of interest' in the interior. Benin, Old Calabar, and the Cameroons were, strictly speaking, not in the Delta system and therefore outside the orbit of Bonny ambitions. But these city-states dominated in similar fashion the areas to their hinterland. That the alliances between the coastal states and the tribal areas worked smoothly is an indication that all fared well from the arrangement.

Perhaps the overriding genius of the Ibos, Ibibios, Ijaws, Ekoi, and Efiks and their political institutions lay in their extraordinary powers of adaptability—powers which they displayed time and again in the nineteenth century and throughout the period of the Atlantic trade in face of the constantly changing economic needs of Europe. No less

[1] Talbot, *Tribes of the Niger Delta*, p. 289.

was their genius for trade. 'They are a people of great interest and intelligence', declared Dr. Talbot, 'hard-headed, keen-witted, and born traders. Indeed, one of the principal agents here, a [European] of world-wide experience, stated that, in his opinion, the Kalabari [a Delta people] could compete on equal terms with Jew or Chinaman.'[1]

[1] Talbot, op. cit., p. 9.

CHAPTER III

Trade in the Thirties

IN 1830 the task which confronted West African traders was one of adjustment to the new economy and changing society engendered by the abolition of the slave trade. Because for two centuries Britain had controlled the lion's share of this traffic,[1] her dramatic withdrawal in 1807 precipitated an economic crisis among the African traders. Both the British merchant and the slave trader had sunk much capital in the African trade. None could retire without prospects of financial ruin, for investment in the slave trade did not merely consist in the acquisition and equipment of a slaver; expensive shore establishments were maintained and an immense quantity of goods distributed on credit to reliable African middlemen to secure their interest. This was true of every Delta port and conditions there typified the position in West Africa generally. Dr. Talbot in his researches on this subject showed that although the 'European traders usually lived on their ships, which stayed several months in the river, they had also, on the lands of friendly chiefs, stores and yards called Barrikos [barracoons] where the slaves brought down to the coast were kept'.[2] The Portuguese and Spaniards not only built barracoons but substantial houses where their chief factors resided permanently. In 1863 Sir Richard Burton discovered the ruins of such houses 'in the old Portuguese town of Akassa' in the Niger Delta. 'A tomb was lately found there, bearing the date A.D. 1635 ... the Portuguese must have known the Upper Niger centuries before we did.'[3] It was therefore not an easy proposition for traders so entrenched to abandon expensive equipment designed for a very profitable coast trade.

To the Africans themselves, whose whole prosperity had for centuries depended on this trade, abolition was a drastic change.

---

[1] Bryan Edwards, *History of the British West Indies* (London, 1819), ii. 65–67. 'Around 1798, slaves exported annually by Britain from the West Coast were 38,000, by the French 20,000, by the Dutch 4,000 and by the Portuguese 10,000, totalling 72,000.' The official British Foreign Office annual total for the same period was 100,000.   [2] *Peoples of Southern Nigeria.*
[3] *Wanderings in Western Africa from Liverpool to Fernando Po* (London, 1863), p. 261.

Besides, as they were ignorant of European movements and world economic changes, the very idea was puzzling. Whilst Portuguese and French merchants told them that slavery was right and ordained by God and encouraged them to hunt for more, British merchants who not long ago had partaken liberally of the same business now said that it was all wrong and savage and that palm oil, 'elephant's tooth', and timber were the things to look for. The African believed neither party but met the demands of each group according to his ability. Captain Vidal, who was in Bonny in 1826, said that 'there were 12 sail of slavers there, and 12 British merchant vessels at the same time' taking palm oil.[1] Obi Ossai, king of Abo, impatient of the contradictory nature of European professions and practice, put the African case bluntly to the members of the Niger expedition of 1841. 'Hitherto we thought it was God's wish that Black people should be slaves to White people. White people first told us we should sell slaves to them, and we sold them; and White people are now telling us not to sell slaves. If White people give up buying, Black people will give up selling.'[2]

Caught up in this medley of economic cross-currents the Delta middleman was bewildered and suspicious. According to Lieutenant Levinge of the West African Naval Squadron, Africans in the Delta often asked him if England were at war with the slave-trading nations of Europe. 'They cannot understand why we take them [the slavers]. We carried on the slave trade so shortly before ourselves, that I do not think they clearly understand why we should be so anxious to suppress it now.'[3] So deep-seated was this suspicion that in August 1841, when Britain concluded a treaty with Bonny to abolish the foreign slave trade, the king of that city-state insisted that the following clause be inserted: 'That if at any future time Great Britain shall permit the slave trade to be carried on, King Pepple and the Chiefs of Bonny shall be at liberty to do the same.'[5] Plainly Africans were more concerned with the business of finding a means of livelihood than with moral judgements on the commodity—men or oil—which they bartered for European manufactures.

Traders in the thirties were soon divided into two camps: those

[1] Parl. Pap. 1842, XI (551), Pt. I, Q. 356.

[2] *Journals of the Rev. J. F. Schön and Mr. Samuel Crowther on the Expedition up the Niger in 1841* (London, 1842), p. 70.

[3] Parl. Pap. 1842, XI (551), Pt. I, Q. 4034–5.

[4] F.O.84/385, vol. iii, Bonny River, No. 49, Tucker to O'Ferral, Adm. 22 Aug. 1841 and its enclosures.

who vigorously prosecuted the old trade in defiance of British naval blockade and those who struggled to establish a trade in the products of the West African forest. The latter were often referred to in contemporary British literature as 'legitimate traders' and the others were sometimes designated 'man-stealers in Africa'. It must be confessed that the lot of the British merchant was the harder. At first the search for a new commodity yielded little fruit. The articles on which hopes for an alternative commerce were based were ivory, gold dust, timber of various kinds, pepper, rice, and gum copal. Of these ivory was generally considered to be the most valuable. Captain Deane, who traded in this product, said 'it was the great object of the voyage' to the coast. Timber, including camwood, barwood, redwood, and bleeding wood, was next in value to ivory. Of these camwood was the most lucrative at £28 to £30 a ton according to Syndenham Teaste, a Bristol merchant.[1] But in summing up the prospects of legitimate trade Teaste said the outlook was not very promising and that the ivory supply was nearly exhausted.[2]

Palm oil, the commodity that was to save the situation, was little known at the beginning of the century. Mr. Poplett, a trader, spoke of the 'palmetto tree' from the roots of which 'they draw the oil'.[3] In spite of this ignorance it was not long before palm oil began to come into its own. Whereas in 1801 the largest shipment was 96 casks, in 1813 781 casks were consigned by one ship to the Liverpool brokers, Henderson, Sellar & Co., and 750 casks by another ship to the firm of James Penny & Co., also of Liverpool.[4] It is interesting to note that the pioneers of the oil trade came mainly from Liverpool and that some of the leading slave traders were at the top of the list. They include Captain E. Deane, owner of the former slaver *Cumberland*; James, John, and William Aspinall, owners of several slave ships; Jonas Bold, James Penny, John Tobin, and many others.[5] Above all the times favoured the enterprising merchants of Liverpool because the demand for palm oil was great.

With the increasing population at the time of the industrial revolution in Britain came changes in social customs and industrial requirements. As British people began to take washing seriously, the demand for soap rose considerably, and palm oil was the chief

[1] N. H. Stilliard, 'The Rise and Development of legitimate Trade in Palm Oil with West Africa' (unpublished thesis, University of Birmingham, 1938), p. 7.
[2] Ibid., pp. 7–8.   [3] Ibid., pp. 10–11.
[4] Ibid., p. 14.   [5] W. E. Williams, op. cit. pp. 17–22.

constituent in its manufacture. The substitution of metal for wooden machinery and the development of railways caused a steep rise in the use of oil as a lubricant. The existing sources of animal fats were not only inadequate but sometimes unsuitable. West African palm oil was found to satisfy these needs. In 1830 the Delta was known to be the chief source of this commodity. Henceforth to the British merchant prohibited by the law to deal in men, the slave coasts gained a new prominence as the oil rivers.

The palm-oil figures for 1828 were as follows: 4,461 cwt. from regions around Sierra Leone and the Gambia, 7,350 cwt. from the Gold Coast, and 114,335 cwt. 'southward from the River Volta, including Fernando Po. This actually covers the bights of Benin and Biafra.[1] But at that date the export from the Bight of Benin was almost nil,[2] so that the 114,335 cwt. can be assigned almost entirely to Delta ports. From the start the trade in the Bight of Biafra was in the hands of private merchants and the first Delta port to deal in that commodity on a commercial scale was Old Calabar,[3] where the pioneers, J. O. Bold and James Penny of Liverpool, had a monopoly for three or four years.[4]

In the Bonny river, which about the middle of the century produced more palm oil than all the West African ports put together, the pioneer was Mr. Tobin, a former Liverpool slave trader, who in partnership with Charles Horsfell, also of Liverpool, started a firm that was foremost in the trade for many years.[5] The slow but steady growth of that commodity was borne out by Mr. Tobin, who stated that in 1814 'not more than 450 tons a year from all parts [of Africa]',[6] yet in 1832 'our House alone imports 4,000 tons of palm oil per annum, the import duty on which amounts to £10,000'.[7] The average price per ton was then £28 in England. The local price per ton averaged £14, although it could be as low as £5 in the less frequented rivers, where competition was not very keen.[8] The Governor of Fernando Po stated the price per ton at £26–£28 in 1830.

In 1841 and 1842 three reports by well-known figures in the West African scene appeared. Robert Jamieson, a Glasgow merchant,

[1] Parl. Pap. 1830, X (661), Imports into U.K. from W.C.A.
[2] Owen, op. cit., pp. 357–9.   [3] Adams, op. cit., pp. 42–43.
[4] Stilliard, op. cit., pp. 23–24.   [5] Ibid.
[6] Parl. Pap. 1848, 3rd Report, XXII (536), QQ. 5676–8.
[7] C.O.82/5, 1464, F.P., Tobin to Goderich, Liverpool, 14 Apr. 1832.
[8] See C.O.82/3, 2009, F.P., No. 1 of Nicolls's Report; cf. Owen, op. cit., pp. 343–5; also Adams, op. cit., pp. 109–12.

attacked in a pamphlet the Niger expedition of 1841,[1] but in the process surveyed the trade of West Africa, concentrating on the Niger Delta which all considered the centre of that trade. In two papers submitted to parliamentary select committees, Macgregor Laird and Dr. Madden dealt with the same subject. According to Laird, who had made a study of the situation, 'the trade from the Delta increased from 4,700 tons of palm oil in 1827 to 13,945 tons in 1834, besides exporting, at the lowest calculation, during the same period, 200,000 slaves'.[2] In the thirties the price of palm oil per ton, duty paid, varied from £33 to £34,[3] and in 1834 the trade was worth £450,185—little short of half a million pounds sterling. Meanwhile the slave trade flourished alongside the trade in oil. In spite of the work of the Preventive Squadron slave-traders were active in the Bight of Biafra and, as in the case of the oil trade, the demand for slaves was stimulated by industrial and agricultural developments in the Old World and the New.

The industrialization of Britain had a direct effect on the slave trade to the Americas. Liverpool capital, reared on the slave trade, had been directed to a new channel—the cotton trade with America. Industrialized Lancashire, whose phenomenal growth is closely linked with the fortunes of Liverpool, needed the slave-grown cotton of the Americas. Tentative experiments on the rich, broad fields of the southern United States proved a great success and the whole of the south began to extend its cotton culture and more and more to throw its energy into this one staple. 'The enhanced price of slaves throughout the American slave market brought about by the new industrial development and the laws against the slave trade, was the irresistible temptation that drew American capital and enterprise into the traffic. In the U.S.A., in spite of large interstate traffic, the average price of slaves rose from about 350 dollars in 1840, to 360 dollars in 1850, and to 500 dollars in 1860. At the same time the consumption of raw cotton in England rose from 572,000 bales in 1820, to 871,000 in 1830, to 3,366,000 in 1860.'[4] In Brazil and Cuba, as the sugar industry expanded, thousands of Africans were landed to work in the plantations. Dubois has estimated that between 1800 and 1850 probably two million Negroes were poured into Brazil.[5] This might

[1] *An Appeal against the proposed Niger Expedition* (London, 1841).
[2] Parl. Pap. 1842, XI, Pt. I, Appendix and Index, No. 7.
[3] Parl. Pap. 1842, XII, Pt. II, Appendix and Index, pp. 33–36.
[4] Dubois, *The Suppression of the African Slave Trade to U.S.A. 1638–1870.*
[5] Id., *Black Folk: Then and Now.*

be an exaggeration, but the enforced migration from West Africa to the Latin American states in the nineteenth century involved many thousands of men, the bulk of whom came from the shores of the bights of Benin and Biafra.

On the mainland, every Delta port was frequented by the slave dealers, particularly Bonny. When the naval blockade became effective in this vicinity, the Portuguese and Latin American slave trade centred on Brass river. This place had been, commercially speaking, a Portuguese stronghold for upwards of two centuries and was not open to English legitimate trade until about 1850. Hidden in the deep recesses of the Niger valley and approached by creeks with no outlet in the Atlantic, Brass became the centre of a gigantic smuggling trade. The organization of this underground traffic was a closely guarded secret never fully probed by the British Navy and merchants; they were, however, aware of its existence, to judge by contemporary records. A legitimate trader at Bonny stated that 'the principal slave trade is carried on in the Brass River by a Spanish resident at Brass Town, and others of Spanish and Portuguese birth'. They did not trade on their own account but acted as agents for the commercial houses of Brazil and Havana.[1] The man in charge of the network that linked the mainland trade with the slavers at sea, and who was himself resident at Brass, was Don Pablo Frexas. With the king of Bonny and the chiefs of Brass, he was the leading architect of this smuggling ring and worked, no doubt, in close alliance with Pereira at Prince's Island. He died at Bonny in 1842,[2] but Africans to the end of the century remembered him under the name of 'Pa Pablo' and recalled his exploits. It is noteworthy that at Bonny and Brass the old people still remember the methods and subterfuges used to evade the British naval blockade at this time. These accounts were handed down by the fathers and grandfathers of the older men.

During the thirties the ineffectiveness of the naval blockade was common knowledge among Africans. Captain William Allen and Dr. T. R. H. Thomson in 1841 reported an interview with Obi Ossai, king of Abo in the northern Delta. This chief was told by his European visitors: 'You cannot sell your slaves if you wish, for our Queen has many warships at the mouth of the river, and Spaniards are afraid to come and buy there.' The king 'seemed to be highly amused on our describing the difficulties the slave-dealers have to encounter'. They

[1] Parl. Pap. 1842, XII, Pt. II, Appendix A, No. 34 (pp. 67–68).
[2] Parl. Pap. 1842, XI (551), Pt. I, QQ. 6079–87. Evidence of Captain Blount.

suspected 'that much of his amusement arose from his knowing that slaves were shipped off at parts of the coast little thought of by us. The abundance of Brazilian rum in Abòh, shewed that they often traded with nations who have avowedly no other object'.[1] Independent of the Latin American group were the pirates and French slavers who braved the British blockade and traded openly and directly with Delta ports. In 1833 the 'notorious slave-dealer called Gaspard, a Frenchman . . . aided by Parriera the slaver, who resides constantly at Princes', appeared in Old Calabar on one of his periodic visits carrying away hundreds of slaves, 'to the great detriment of commerce'. Their vessels were 'well armed and numerously manned'.[2]

The central aim of the British party in the Delta trade was to eliminate the slave trader and to create conditions favourable to the growing trade in palm oil. It is quite clear that interest, as well as philanthropy, lay behind the British movement for the suppression of the slave trade. The converted African Company as far back as 1812 declared that 'British trade cannot exist where the slave trade exists. Those in the latter will monopolise the former.'[3] In 1821 Commodore Sir George R. Collier reported that owing to the slave trade 'the trade in palm oil which a few years ago was encouraged by the Chiefs of Bonny is again lost'.[4] In 1833 the Government learnt from the report of the Governor of Fernando Po that there were thirty-six slavers in the Delta at one time.[5] At Old Calabar, in the same year, the notorious Gaspard arrived and immediately 'all legitimate commerce ceased, and a general scramble of robbery and plunder commenced to supply him with slaves'. British palm-oil vessels at the port were 'obliged to remain there in expensive and sickly indolence, until the slavers and pirates are supplied with their unhappy victims'.[6] In Bonny a legitimate trader, on 25 November 1835, wrote to his employer in England: 'We are doing but little business, as the slave trade is carrying on with the utmost vigour. We have in the River ten Spanish vessels' taking slaves.'[7]

Between 1830 and 1837 disorders caused by the slave trade showed

[1] Allen & Thomson, op. cit., i. 220–2.
[2] C.O.82/6, Fernando Po, 67, Nicolls to Hay, 28 Oct. 1833.
[3] Quoted by Hancock, op. cit., ii, pt. 2, 161 from Parl. Pap. 1816, VII (506) and Parl. Pap. 1817, VI.
[4] Admiralty 1/1675, Report to Admiralty, 1821.
[5] C.O.82/6, Fernando Po, Nicolls to Hay, 28 Oct. 1833.
[6] C.O.82/6, F. P. Nicolls to Hay, 28 Oct. 1833.
[7] Parl. Pap. 1842, XI, Q. 3957.

no signs of subsiding, and since one fight is very much like another, we will cite only a few instances by way of illustration. In 1830 John Beecroft, an English trader at Fernando Po, complained that at Old Calabar British merchants were hopelessly outnumbered by nine French slave-trading vessels newly arrived in that river, and that they laughed at his remonstrances, knowing that he 'was not in a condition to enforce them, the French being nine to one against me, the smallest vessel having double the number of men that I had'.[1] A merchant in the same river, Richard Cummins, appealed to the Navy for protection because a hostile French slaver fired a bullet through the belly of one of his officers and killed him.[2] According to a naval officer it was not very safe for legitimate traders to move about freely. 'Wherever there are so many Spaniards and Portuguese about, they are likely to stick you with a knife.'[3] The British, of course, fought back. On the shores of the Bight of Biafra were to be met from time to time white crews of captured slavers—victims of this collision of economic interests—who had been dumped at Delta ports without shelter or food. Most of them soon died of malaria or starvation. In February 1841 fifty of these were landed 'in the neighbourhood of Bonny'. By the end of May 'not ten remained alive'.[4]

An eyewitness graphically described the situation which this undeclared war between slavery and legitimate commerce created in the Niger Delta.

'A slave-trader arrives in the river: the trade with the British vessels is instantly stopped . . . and until these slaves are procured, no legitimate trade is pursued. I submit that this involves the loss of British capital in the following way: there are about 15,000 tons of British shipping employed in the palm oil trade, which are sailed at the expense of about £10 per ton, per annum.

The loss of time, depreciation of vessel and extra insurance @ £3 per ton = £45,000. The extra insurance on their cargoes valued at £500,000 @ 2% = £10,000—Total £55,000. This applies to the existing trade, south of the Rio Volta, (Niger Delta) the port most frequented by slave-vessels'.[5]

As was to be expected, those in the oil trade were dissatisfied with this state of affairs. The humanitarian squadron had failed in its task of

---

[1] C.O.82/4, No. 3, Fernando Po, Beecroft to Nicolls, 17 Nov. 1830.
[2] V.O.82/1, Old Calabar, Cummins to Lieutenant Bagley, 26 July 1828.
[3] Parl. Pap. 1842, XI (551), p. 230, QQ. 4062-3.
[4] Parl. Pap. 1842, XI, Pt. I (551), Q. 1729.
[5] Laird and Oldfield, op. cit., pp. 355 f.

suppression; organized slave trading, such as the Delta traffic was, proved too strong for its slender resources.

As far back as 1826 Captain W. F. W. Owen had suggested that a base for suppressing the trade should be established on the mountainous island of Fernando Po which occupied a position dominating the Delta coast line. This island although belonging to Spain was last occupied by her in 1777. Owen suggested that two steamers stationed in the centre of the worst slaving area would shortly put an end to the trade: his own sailing ship based there captured five slavers in twelve months.[1] Owing largely to the importunity of Owen and his friends a British base was finally established on this island in 1827, permission having been obtained from the Government of Spain. Owen himself was the superintendent of the new settlement.

Much of 1828 and 1829 was occupied by the erection of prefabricated bungalows brought out from England for the new colony and the construction of a hospital, quarters for a military officer and European artificers, a bakehouse, and shops. The island was fast becoming a British fort in the Niger Delta. Owen wanted many more men for 'the works of external defence' and reported: 'I have mounted on Adelaide Islet Twenty Guns ready to be applied whenever they may seem necessary.'[2] In 1828 the settlement consisted of a superintendent, a director of works, an overseer of workmen, a master house carpenter, a storekeeper, 14 European and 36 African mechanics, and 110 labourers and Kroomen, making a total of 165.[3] This hive of activity entailed immense expenditure and Owen suggested that the use of slave labour would cut expenses.

In April 1828 he reported the capture of two slavers and instead of ordering these to Freetown, where the Court of Mixed Commission was still located, he illegally detained them on the plea that many slaves lost their lives on the long sea voyage to Sierra Leone. Of the 350 slaves involved Owen said: 'The men are a valuable acquisition to us as Labourers and the great disproportion of our Males to the Females in our community renders the women no less valuable.' In the same month he reported that 'the number of our Establishment at present is more than seven hundred individuals; nearly one half of which are no present charge to His Majesty'.[4] Through the illegal

---

[1] Lloyd, op. cit., p. 22.
[2] C.O.82/1, Fernando Po, Owen to Hay, 11 Feb. 1828.
[3] Ibid., 25 Feb. 1828.
[4] C.O.82/1, No. 6, Owen to Hay, 28 Apr. 1828.

landing of slaves Owen was speedily increasing the population of the settlement, and naturally the authorities at Sierra Leone, the head-quarters of British administration in West Africa at the time, viewed this with disfavour. Fernando Po was in fact aspiring to rival long-established Freetown.

Meanwhile the situation on the coast was engaging the attention of Parliament. The Select Committee of 1830 examined the subject and its sixth resolution declared 'that by far the greater number of the slaves are shipped from the ports on the Coast of Africa in and near the Bights of Benin and Biafra and are mostly captured near to these places, and within two or three days sail of the Island of Fernando Po'. The committee therefore recommended that Fernando Po should replace Freetown, Sierra Leone, as the place for the sitting of the Court of Mixed Commission.[1] The opposition of Sierra Leone and other factors connected with British tenure of the island prevented the implementation of this resolution.

It is necessary to emphasize that the importance of Fernando Po was not limited to its strategic position in the suppression movement. Legitimate traders desired it because they needed a British base affording them protection in the vicinity of West Africa's leading oil ports and, as will be shown, the island was important to the prosecution of the oil trade itself. Early in 1828 Owen was reporting that palm-oil ships from the ports of the Delta 'requested me to receive money from them for its security against plunders . . . by this means our treasury is overflowing of these transactions'.[2]

In 1832 Mr. Tobin stated that some of the ships used in the oil trade 'are of large tonnage, and on account of the shallow water in the mouth of the River Bonny are unable to load there'. The mer-chants were 'accustomed to have smaller vessels' to convey the oil to Fernando Po, where the larger vessels could be loaded. He said that this practice had been going on long 'before the British Govern-ment had any footing' in the island.[3] Soon after the establishment of the settlement British palm-oil traders were applying to Owen for permission to erect mercantile posts there. The vessels of Britain, America, and other nations made use of the facilities of Port Clarence,[4] where the swift servicing of damaged vessels led Owen to

---

[1] Parl. Pap. 1830, I (661), Resolution 6 f.
[2] C.O.82/1, Owen to Hay, 11 Feb. 1828.
[3] C.O.82/5, 1464, Liverpool, Tobin to Goderich, 14 Apr. 1832.
[4] C.O.82/1, F.P., No. 6, Owen to Hay, 28 Apr. 1828.

claim: 'There is not another point on all the coast of Africa from the Red Sea to the Mediterranean where the same thing could have been done, so quickly and with so much ease.'[1]

There was no doubt at all in the minds of contemporaries that Fernando Po was an almost indispensable base for the growing trade with the Niger Delta. Owen's successor, Colonel Edward Nicolls, emphasized in numerous dispatches its importance for the future development of the Delta and the Niger valley. In fact, in 1832, when the news that Spain was willing to cede the island to England for the sum of £100,000 reached Nicolls, he instantly advised the Government to pay that sum and acquire it. He showed that although Fernando Po was valueless to Spain—who had no economic interests there, except of course the slave trade—its acquisition must be to Britain 'a certain source of riches and prosperity'.[2]

The consternation created among the palm-oil merchants can therefore be imagined when the Government, for reasons to be explained later, decided to abandon the island. One of them, Richard Dillon, protested to Lord Goderich that the occupation or purchase of the island from Spain would be the sole means of affording 'protection for British Commerce—and confidence to British Capitalists in pushing a trade with the interior of Africa'.[3] Twenty-four merchant houses with interests in the Delta trade petitioned Goderich in 1833, saying that the Government's decision meant, in effect, the evacuation of a point which made the palm-oil trade possible, and that as soon as the British establishment was removed the island would become 'a slaving piratical nest under the name of Spanish independency. It is a matter of fact as appears from our Customs House reports, that the importation of palm oil has at least been trebled since a British establishment has been located at Fernando Po.' They quoted the following figures from Marshall's Trade Report to substantiate their argument. Palm oil imported into the United Kingdom:

1827	1828	1829	1830[4]
94,246 (cwt.)	126,553	179,946	213,477

The growth of British commerce, as seen in the rise of the palm-oil trade and commodities such as timber, ivory, and bees-wax, drew her irresistibly to the Delta coasts and the Niger valley. The tendency

[1] C.O.82/1, No. 14, Owen to C.O., 8 Sep. 1828.
[2] C.O.82/5, 2004, F.P., Nicolls to C.O., 30 Jan. 1832.
[3] C.O.82/4, London, Dillon to Goderich, 25 July 1831.
[4] C.O.82/6, 307, F.P., Merchants to C.O., London, 8 Jan. 1833.

was not movement away from strategic points like Fernando Po or from trading posts on the mainland, but quite the reverse. This was clear enough to Nicolls, Laird, and the better class of merchant. Responsibility for the shortsighted policy of withdrawing from Fernando Po was due in part to the unenlightened financial policy of the Government and in part to the conflict between the West India interest and the abolitionists, centred upon the African Institution. To understand the background to these events it must be remembered that Fernando Po had been suggested as a better locality than Freetown for the suppression of the slave trade. Friends of Sierra Leone not unnaturally feared that the success of the Fernando Po experiment might mean the death of Freetown.

This colony was supported by the Government, aided by bodies of which the principal was the African Institution. The influence of the latter on all matters of policy relating to slavery was sufficiently great to leave the impression that it, and not the Government, was the spearhead of the anti-slavery movement. An anti-slavery society was necessarily a danger to the West India interest. Therefore if the African Institution and the abolitionists could be discredited through their association with Sierra Leone, so much the better for the West Indies.[1] But Sierra Leone had not the trade of the Niger Delta and was not looked upon as a successful experiment. In 1830, for instance, Joseph Hume (a voice of the West India interest) tabled a motion on 15 June asking for the withdrawal of the Sierra Leone settlement. At Mr. Buxton's suggestion it was altered into a motion for a select committee to inquire into the state of the colony. It was this committee which recommended the transfer of the Mixed Commission Court from Freetown to Fernando Po.[2] It is noteworthy that the West India interest had already recommended the acquisition of Fernando Po in a memorial to Liverpool, Bathurst, and Huskisson.[3]

The important point in all this was that the enemies of Sierra Leone and of the African Institution became the friends of Fernando Po. The island which needed no one to advertise its merits was unfortunately dragged into the broils of opposing economic and ideological groupings. Led by the African Institution the humanitarians in sheer self-defence began to spread unfavourable reports of

[1] G. R. Mellor, 'British Policy in relation to Sierra Leone' (unpublished thesis, University of London), ff. 58–59.
[2] W. H. Scotter, 'International Rivalry in the Bights of Benin and Biafra' (unpublished thesis, University of London), ff. 32–33.
[3] Mellor, ibid., p. 141.

Fernando Po and to oppose its acquisition from Spain. As early as 1828 Owen was complaining that the officials of the Sierra Leone Government, who were responsible for supplying the island with provisions and equipment, sadly neglected the infant settlement. They were driven to depend on Duke Ephraim, the African chief of Old Calabar, for their food supplies.[1] Nicolls repeatedly complained of Sierra Leone opposition. In fact, when he was ordered to evacuate the settlement he believed that Sierra Leone opposition was a factor in Britain's decision to abandon the island.[2]

There is no attempt to suggest that Sierra Leone opposition was the only obstacle. Suggestions for its acquisition, made from time to time and approved by the Foreign Office and the Colonial Office, were held up at the Treasury. But the task of acquiring the island would have been infinitely easier if there had been unanimity on the British side—particularly as Spain was favourable during the early stages of the negotiations towards the sale or exchange of the territory for another British possession. In 1841 Palmerston, as Foreign Secretary, renewed the attempt to effect a purchase, but the Spanish Government could not swallow his reasons for desiring it. He had claimed that although the Cabinet did not feel it necessary to acquire the island, the abolitionists clamoured for it and he needed their support in Parliament. In Spain itself the atmosphere had changed. When the proposal was made public there was a national display of 'indignant patriotism' against the insult to the honour and dignity of the Motherland in the alienation of this 'Key of the Niger' and 'hence of the commerce of the interior'. Other nations were awakening to the possibilities of the Niger trade.[3]

In France the proposals of Palmerston were attacked and cited as 'a further step in Britain's course of universal encroachment, which France had a direct interest in preventing'. The methods by which she attempted to obtain this valuable island were spoken of as part of 'the hypocritical and torturous course so peculiar to her diplomacy'.[4] The failure of the negotiations was hailed as a triumph for French diplomacy.[5] This was the last British attempt to acquire Fernando Po. The loss of that island meant that the only possible base for the establishment of a British administrative post to guard

[1] C.O.82/1, F.P., No. 18, Owen to Hay, 26 Nov. 1828.
[2] C.O.82/6, F.P., Nicolls to Hay, 9 Sept. 1833.
[3] Scotter, ff. 48–52.
[4] *The Times*, 22nd July, 30th Aug. 1841, quoted by Scotter, p. 53, as originating in *Le Nationale* and *La Presse*.   [5] Ibid.

the growing trade of the oil rivers disappeared. In 1832, when the Government decided to abandon the settlement, British trade with the Delta was worth half a million pounds. Laird had foreseen in the thirties that a trade of that magnitude, and one which showed signs of rapid growth, would require a 'pax' to bestow law and order on the lawless piratical society of the coast. Such a government would provide 'an impartial tribunal' to which African and European traders could appeal for justice and fair play 'in case of dispute or aggression from either side'.[1] The absence of a permanent base from which to control the activities of British traders in the Delta gave free rein to the elements of violence, disorder, and instability in the first fifty years of 'equitable traffic'.

The white coast traders—whether in slaves or in palm oil—really belonged to one fraternity with the Delta as their operational base. They had become too much a part of the four-centuries-old trade practice on the coast to wish to alter it. The revolution which occurred in the trade therefore was to come from a new group of men for the most part unacquainted with the old order. In breeding and outlook they were a race apart from the coast fraternity, for whatever the virtues of the latter they made no pretentions to humanity, Christianity, or civilization. This is not to suggest that individual exceptions to the general rule did not exist. But as an American accomplice said, with little exaggeration, the slave trade 'ruins the health or takes the lives of ninetenths who are concerned in it, and poisons the morals of most survivors'.[2] Most of the coast traders were among the abandoned desperadoes of their race and aptly nicknamed 'palm-oil ruffians'. They 'were rude, uneducated men, who prided themselves upon coming in at the "hawse-hole, and going out at the cabin windows". Acts of wanton cruelty to white men, as well as to Negroes, have been handed down by generations of this fraternity.'[3]

In 1830 the Landers' discovery introduced a new element in the trade. A school arose which advocated the shifting of the traders' frontier from the seaboard to the Nigerian hinterland. It was natural that the old Liverpool traders, for whom inland penetration would mean heavy losses in capital equipment, should ally them-

[1] Laird and Oldfield, op. cit., pp. 391–3.
[2] J. W. Russell, *The Romance of Old-Time Ship Master* (ed. R. D. Paine, New York, 1907).
[3] J. Whitford, *Trading Life in Western and Central Africa* (Liverpool, 1877), p. 288.

selves with the African middlemen, as we shall see, and attack the intruders. Success in inland trading would cut off their supplies and the ensuing decline and eventual disappearance of coastal business was a prospect they fought bitterly to prevent.

The activities of the newcomers were canalized into the well-known Niger expeditions of the nineteenth century, organized by the humanitarian and industrial forces that decisively influenced the passing of the Abolition Act in 1807. Their views are well preserved in the voluminous literature of the time, in such works as James McQueen, *A Geographical and Commercial View of Northern Central Africa*, 1822; Laird and Oldfield, *Narrative of an Expedition into the Interior of Africa*, 1837; and Thomas Fowell Buxton, *The African Slave Trade and its Remedy*, 1839. All pleaded that the 'civilization of Africa' could come only through the 'cultivation of the habits of industry' which must be accompanied by the preaching of Christ and the substitution of honourable trade for the slave trade. 'Left to themselves', said McQueen in 1822, 'the Negroes will never effectually accomplish this. It must be done by a mighty power, who will take them under its protection till Africa is shown that it is in the labour and industry of her population, and in the cultivation of her soil, that true wealth consists. Were we once firmly established, in a commanding attitude on the Niger . . . the progress of Improvement will be rapid, and the advantages great.'[1]

The Niger expedition of 1832 was purely commercial and symbolized the end of one epoch and the beginning of another. Macgregor Laird,[2] a world pioneer in steam navigation, led the vanguard

[1] T. F. Buxton, *The African Slave Trade and its Remedy* (London, 1839), pp. 415–17.

[2] Macgregor Laird: b. Greenock, Scotland, 1808; son of William Laird, founder of the famous Birkenhead firm of shipbuilders. Educated at Edinburgh and afterwards entered into partnership with his father, a position he relinquished in order to promote a company 'for the commercial development' of Lander's discoveries. He accompanied the 1832 commercial expedition, arrived in the Delta and ascended the Niger beyond Lokoja in the first iron steamer to make a sea voyage. He returned to Liverpool in 1834 and in 1837 became Secreatry of the British and North American Steam Navigation Co. formed to run steamers from England to New York. In 1844 he removed to Birkenhead and was concerned with the construction and development of steamships till 1850. According to his family records he was offered but rejected the post of first Governor of South Australia. The last twelve years of his life were devoted exclusively to the development of the resources of the Niger basin. In 1849 he founded the African Steamship Company. In 1854 he sponsored the first successful commercial expedition to the Niger, and contracted with the Government for regular steamship service between

of men anxious to exploit Lander's discovery and open 'a direct commercial intercourse with the inhabitants of Central Africa' by way of the Niger. Conscious of the industrialists' need for oil and the value (£1,000,000) of Delta exports produced with 'imperfect means of transit' (the canoes), he argued that with better transport and direct contact between consumers and producers (on whose industry the Delta middlemen waxed rich) the trade would greatly increase and its profits multiply.

To this end the 1832 commercial expedition was fitted out and its two steamships, the *Quorra* and the *Alburkah*, were the first ocean-going iron steamers ever built. 'It was generally allowed', Laird declared, 'that better-found vessels had never left the port of Liver-pool.'[1] Great hopes were lavished on the outcome of this venture but it proved a total failure and of the forty-eight men who accompanied Laird and Lander only nine survived. The 1841 expedition fared little better, the deaths being fifty-three out of a total complement of 303. When the hopes of great commercial gains were not realized—especially after so much had been lost in men and money—many people in Britain began to lose their early enthusiasm for the hinter-land trade. The humanitarians, the 'devils of Exeter Hall', who by their optimistic propaganda had raised high hopes of a valuable and extensive trade in these regions, were subjected to heavy attacks by literary critics and commercial publicists.

As always in history during times of failure and reaction there are men who see beyond the happenings of the present to the possibilities of the future. In the 1840's their champion was Macgregor Laird. It is refreshing to turn from the didactic and pious language that flooded the journals of the humanitarians to the realistic, terse, and direct statements of Laird. His belief in the hinterland trade and African regeneration is all the more surprising since he had himself expected much from the expeditions and lost most by them. Un-deterred by the loss of his entire fortune in the 1832 venture, he remained the guiding spirit in all the commercial expeditions until his death in 1861.[2]

England and Africa. He laid the foundations of British supremacy in the Niger valley before his death on 9 Jan. 1861.

[1] Laird and Oldfield, op. cit., i. 9.

[2] The Niger expeditions of the years between 1832 and 1857 have been ade-quately described in existing works. See A. F. Mockler-Ferryman, *British West Africa* (London, 1900), pp. 120–93; A. Norton Cook, *British Enterprise in Nigeria* (Philadelphia, 1943), pp. 38–45. The contemporary literature on the expeditions is listed by Cook, op. cit., pp. 300–5; W. N. M. Geary, *Nigeria Under British Rule*

His faith in the Niger enterprise was almost inspired. Nature has given us the River Niger. 'By the Niger the whole of Western Africa would be embraced. . . . British influence and enterprise would thereby penetrate into the remotest recesses of the country, one hundred million people would be brought into direct contact with the civilized world; new and boundless markets would be opened to our manufacture; a continent teeming with inexhaustible fertility would yield her riches to our traders.'[1] Yet what distinguishes Laird from the crowd of journeymen was not his pronouncements, notable as they were, but his tenacity of purpose, his unfailing vision even in the darkest hour, his healthy realism, and freedom from prejudice. All these are reflected in his reaction to the 1832 disaster. It had been Laird's plan, in view of Lander's tales of the vast resources of the interior, to by-pass the Delta and concentrate on the trade of the hinterland. His experience in 1832 taught him that long years of hard work must pass before Delta ascendancy could be successfully challenged. He determined to reverse 'the plan which we pursued; that is by making the palm oil trade [on the coast instead of ivory, &c., in the interior] the first, and the trade with the interior the secondary object'.

His constant theme was that the foundations of inland trade must be laid by men of the right type, Europeans and Africans who had little in common with the 'degraded' fraternity of the coast. His ships had been attacked in 1832 and Lander killed at Angiama by the coastal middlemen who had begun their opposition to inland trade. Laird had no illusions on this issue. Until Delta 'monopoly is broken down, and the natives of the interior are allowed to visit the coast, or Europeans ascend beyond their influence, not much good will be done'. Yet his hostility to the coast merchants did not blind him to their achievements. Among prejudiced observers the sloth of Africans in the Delta was proverbial. One might have expected Laird to sing the usual song. Yet characteristically he disposes of this view with reference to the facts of the situation:

In 1808, the import of palm oil did not exceed one or two hundred tons per annum: it is now (1837) 14,000 tons, having been trebled in the last eight years. Twenty years ago, African timber was unknown in the European market: there are now from 13 to 15 thousand loads annually

(London, 1927), pp. 153–76; and C. W. J. Orr, *The Making of Northern Nigeria* (London, 1911), pp. 5–16.
[1] Laird and Oldfield, op. cit., ii. 388–9.

exported. I fearlessly assert, that there are no people on the face of the globe more desirous and capable of trading than the present race of Africans, with all their disadvantages.[1]

The methods Laird advocated were those of partnership with hinterland Africans, gradual elimination of the Delta middlemen, substitution of African for white labour, and the opening of local trading and collecting centres in the interior. But the conditions of trade, the stubbornness of the African middleman, and the rivalry of Europeans were such that forty years were to elapse before his objective was realized.

[1] Laird and Oldfield, op. cit., ii. 402.

CHAPTER IV

The City-states and the Treaty System

COLONEL (later GENERAL SIR) EDWARD NICOLLS,[1] the enthusiastic and industrious Governor of Fernando Po, 1829–34, had taken
a distinct liking to the Niger Delta, and during his tenure of office
indulged in activities few of which the Colonial Office sanctioned.
Foremost among these was his passion for treaty-making. In dispatch
after dispatch he claimed that the most effective means of exter-
minating the Delta slave trade was not the suppression movement
led by the Navy, but the negotiation of alliances with the Delta states
who through treaty obligations would side with Britain against the
slave-dealer. Such city-states as did support the British Navy against
the dealers in men signed the treaties because it paid them to do so.
Principalities like Bonny, on the other hand, where the slave trade
was vital to her economy, resisted the abolition movement. The Delta
states were as divided among themselves as were the nations of
Europe.

Nicolls advocated the treaty system in the hope that the British
Government would share his sense of urgency in the matter. His
enthusiasm led him to unauthorized treaty-making and acquisition
of bases on the coasts of Biafra. In 1833 he obtained a voluntary
cession of all the lands from Bimbia Island to the Rio Del Rey
(Cameroons) from King William of Bimbia, who asked for 'nothing
but to be considered as the King's subject. The land ceded is high,
dry, fertile, well wooded and watered. And the three islands in the
Bay of Ambosey may be made perfect Gibraltars with little expense.'[2]
At the back of the Governor's mind, no doubt, there lurked the

---

[1] Nicknamed 'Fighting Nicolls' through having engaged in 107 battles and
skirmishes on land and sea, he was born in 1779 and served in the Royal Navy
and Marines. From 1823 to 1828 he commanded Ascension garrison and greatly
improved the island's amenities. When appointed Governor of Fernando Po
in 1829 he strove to improve conditions there and devoted himself to the suppression of the slave trade. After the disastrous Niger expedition in 1832 he
nursed Magregor Laird to health, who afterwards became his son-in-law. He was
promoted to the rank of Major-General and later retired on account of ill health.
In 1850 he received a knighthood.
[2] C.O.82/6, 1143, F.P., Nicolls to Hay, 10 Dec. 1833.

thought that the Government who refused to pay £100,000[1] for the purchase of Fernando Po would not object to a free grant of land on the Delta Coast. Undaunted, Nicolls continued his thankless task. In 1834 he entered into a 'Treaty Offensive and Defensive' with a chief of the Brass country, and before he was recalled convinced the king and chiefs of Old Calabar that the slave trade was against their best interests. They promised to 'meet the Chiefs of Bimbia, Cameroons, Malimba and Bonny whom I propose to assemble here [Fernando Po] . . . to form a defensive league against the slavers and pirates'.[2]

However good the intention behind Nicolls's treaties, it is questionable whether he served any useful purpose by contracting agreements which were no sooner signed than they were repudiated by the British Government. Neither was he very discriminating in his choice of African allies. King Boy (real name, Ammaï-kunno),[3] a well-known slave-trading chief of the Brass river with whom he concluded the treaty of 1834, was not to be expected to honour an agreement that would put an end to his means of livelihood. Moreover, behind every treaty was the unmistakable hand of the Governor himself, even in passages where Africans were quoted as signing away their rights voluntarily and asking for 'protection'. No sooner did the king of Bimbia sign the treaty of 'protection' in 1833 than Nicolls 'ordered him' as 'subject of His Majesty to cause all the money secreted from the pirates and found at Bimbia, to be sent to me, this money amounting to 1,100 dollars, I shall take it into the public chest'.[4] The coercive element embodied in these treaties was made manifest even to the Africans who, at this date, had little notion of treaty obligations.

Nicolls had been ordered to evacuate Fernando Po in February 1833, but much to the exasperation of the officials he did not return to England until April 1835. He had dreamt of making British interest predominant in the Bight of Biafra and that Fernando Po would under him 'become a glory and advantage both to British Commerce and the cause of Humanity'.[5] There was little evidence when he left that any of these aims would come to fruition. Yet the Governor was not hopelessly ahead of his time. Exactly four years after his departure, on 31 March 1839, the first slave-trade treaty between Britain and Bonny was signed.

[1] C.O.82/5, 2004, F.P., Nicolls to Hay, 30 Jan. 1832.
[2] C.O.82/6, F.P., Nicolls to Hay, 14 Sept. 1833.
[3] Allen and Thomson, op. cit., i. 237.
[4] C.O.82/6, F.P., Nicolls to Hay, 24 Aug. 1833.
[5] C.O.82/3, 2009, F.P., No. 1 of Nicolls's Report, 1830.

The view still widely held that 'the coastal tribes of West Africa were their allies [the slave-dealers] in the fight against legitimate commerce'[1] is not accurate. What really determined the side the African took in the struggle was the importance or otherwise of the trade to the economy of the community concerned. From 1830 and earlier Old Calabar had been the friend of the legitimate British trader because the slave trade had ceased, or was ceasing, to be vital to her economy. Writing at the end of the eighteenth century Captain John Adams stated that the people of Old Calabar had directed their attention 'to the manufacture of palm oil, in large quantities, in conquence of Bonny becoming the great slave market, and monopolising the trade in slaves, which Old Calabar carried on to a considerable extent before it; but which the chiefs of Old Calabar lost by exacting from the vessels trading there, exorbitant duties or customs'.[2] When the Bonny palm-oil trade was still in its early stages, Old Calabar was exporting 2,000 tons.[3] This figure is also borne out by Captain W. F. W. Owen's report in 1828.[4]

Moreover, during British occupation of Fernando Po, 1827–34, the two governors, Owen and Nicolls, commented on the friendship and co-operation of the kings of that city-state with the British party and their eagerness to promote legitimate commerce. In 1828 Owen reported the repeated demands made to him by the chiefs of Old Calabar 'to be instructed in the methods of making sugar, and to obtain the necessary machinery for which they say they have repeatedly applied to their friends in Liverpool without success. For these advantages they are ready to pay handsomely. It would appear that the West India Interest has always operated too successfully against these legitimate desires.'[5] As late as 1842 the Calabar chiefs were still eager to employ their slave population in agricultural pursuits, and sought British help in securing the machinery needed for sugar manufacture and cotton culture.[6]

Nicolls was much impressed with the character of Duke Ephraim, the leading chief in 1832, describing him as 'a man of great knowledge and humanity' whom he thought would abolish the slave trade in his territory were he to enter into an agreement with the British.[7]

[1] Hancock, op. cit., ii, pt. 2, 161.
[2] Adams, op. cit., p. 42.   [3] Ibid., pp. 113–15.
[4] C.O.82/1, Sierra Leone, Owen to C.O., 2 Feb. 1828.
[5] C.O.82/1, No. 6, 2144, Sierra Leone, Owen to C.O., 28 Apr. 1829.
[6] F.O.84/495, No. 171, H.M.S. *Madagascar* at Sea, Foote to Herbert, 12 Dec. 1842.   [7] C.O.82/5, 2004, F.P., Nicolls to Hay, 30 Jan. 1832.

In the forties, therefore, when Britain initiated the slave-trade treaties with the Delta states, she had no difficulty in getting Old Calabar to abolish the foreign slave trade. On several occasions the Calabar community played the part of informers to the British Navy on the movement of slavers. In December 1842 they sent a canoe to warn Commodore Raymond at Fernando Po of the presence of French slavers and warships on the river.[1] The senior naval officer, William Tucker, reporting on Old Calabar to the Admiralty, said that 'the slave trade there is of no importance'.[2]

The chief of Bimbia 'kept humbugging' with a slaver for three weeks and meanwhile 'sent to tell Beecroft [a British merchant] of the slaver's presence'. This gentleman 'despatched a vessel of war, H.M. Brig *Rapid* and took the slaver after an exchange of volleys of musketry'.[3] Instances such as these can be multiplied. In time the slavers came to regard the Old Calabar and Cameroon natives as the allies of the British, and treated them as enemies. Raymond reported in 1843 that the French man-of-war *La Vigie* threatened 'to blow their town [Old Calabar] about their ears if they did not supply the French Schooner, *Luiz D'Aubuquerque*, with slaves'. The chiefs refused to comply and, after a protracted palaver, the French ship 'took palm oil in lieu of the traffic'.[4] Taken as a whole the slave trade of this city-state was not important to her economy in the nineteenth century. Legitimate commerce was therefore as much the need of the Efiks at Old Calabar as of the merchants from Britain.

The opposition to the British movement for suppression in the Bight of Biafra was concentrated at Bonny. Her politics in the thirties were complicated owing partly to the disintegration within the kingdom following the death of Opubu and partly to the international complications consequent on the working out of the Equipment Treaty of 1835 concluded between England and Portugal. The state of domestic politics may be briefly summarized. The famous king of Bonny, Opubu the Great, died in 1830.[5] His reign which began in 1792[6] saw great changes in the economic sphere, but he proved himself equal to the situation. Early in the century, perceiving that

---

[1] Proceedings of the Anti-Slavery Convention, op. cit., pp. 261–2.
[2] F.O.84/384, vol. ii, No. 56, Tucker to O'Farrell, 30 July 1841.
[3] F.O.84/549, Encl. 2 in Nicolls to Barrow, 39 Shooter Hill, 5 June.1844.
[4] F.O.84/495, Encl. 2 in No. 12, Raymond to Foote, 10 Jan. 1843.
[5] A. Fombo, the Bonny historian, supplied this date. Cf. E. M. T. Eppele, 'Ja Ja of Opobo' (unpublished manuscripts), f. 2, gives 1829 as the date of Opubu's death.   [6] Talbot, op. cit., i. 251.

the British attack on the slave trade was a determined one, he took the initiative in opening the palm-oil markets in the Ibo country while still vigorously prosecuting the slave trade in alliance with the Portuguese.

Opubu was essentially an innovator and his audacious acts set the tone of politics throughout the century. The Bonny constitution required that a king must relinquish the headship of his private House on ascending the throne. Succession to the royal House was a plum much sought after by the aristocracy. Opubu raised an Ibo ex-slave Chief Madu (Maduka) to this elevated position. From all accounts Madu was a man of rare ability, religiously dedicated to the service of the monarchy. Yet his appointment remained to the end unpopular with the free classes and but for the king's strong personality and Madu's strength of character there would have been an open split over the unprecedented latitude Opubu allowed the ex-slave classes in the affairs of state.

At the time of King Opubu's death his son and successor, William Dappa Pepple who was born on 23 August 1817, was a minor. Chief Madu therefore became regent from 1830 to 1833. During his headship of Opubu House he had by his industry and efficient administration made it the wealthiest in the land. He was in turn succeeded as Head of the House by his eldest son, Alali, who also became regent.[1] Beneath this appearance of order old animosities rankled and soon after King Opubu's death in 1830 the opposition, first against Madu the regent and later against Alali his son and successor, crystallized around the crown prince. This young man, unlike his father, was in character and bearing openly contemptuous of the new class of ex-slaves rising with the developing trade in oil, who formed the majority of the population and were naturally the supporters of King Opubu's innovations from which they stood to benefit.

The regent was quick to sense the tactics of Prince Dappa and upon Opubu's death planted himself firmly in the saddle; as the balance of domestic politics was in his favour, he in turn treated the crown prince with contempt and ruled despotically. In 1835, when Prince Dappa Pepple ascended the throne, he discovered that the regent Alali clung to the powers of the monarchy leaving him king only in name. So strong was the position of Alali within the kingdom that there was little chance of a successful insurrection.

But the usurpation of the regent must never be interpreted to mean

[1] Epelle, ff. 3–4.

that he aimed at occupying the throne. Bonny theories of kingship, unwritten though they might have been, completely barred an ex-slave from such an office, and if Alali had been an aspirant to that high position he would have lost his mass following in a day. A naturalized foreigner or an ex-slave could rise to the status of a leading chief but the rank of king was exclusively reserved for princes of the blood—*Ama-nya-na-bo*. As a matter of history the regent's popularity derived largely from his defence of the monarchy and his uncompromising stand for Bonny independence. The crisis in the thirties was therefore not constitutional but factional: the regent fought the crown prince because his hopes that the former would support him as did his father before him did not materialize. In fighting his enemies the regent found himself in the embarrassing position of fighting his king who had chosen to ally himself with the former.

We have shown that the late king's commercial policy gave equal encouragement to the trade in men and in palm oil. This policy was pursued until 1835 when Britain concluded the so-called 'Equipment Treaty' with Spain, which put an end to the ridiculous provision in former agreements whereby Spanish ships fully designed and equipped for the traffic could not be taken by the Navy unless they carried slaves on board. In January 1836, armed with this agreement and without any warning to the government of the city-state, Lieutenant Tryon, commander of H.M.S. *Trinculo*, entered the port of Bonny and seized four Spanish ships waiting to embark slaves for the New World. This unparalleled interference in Bonny affairs was the first challenge to her 'open-door' policy.

The news of the naval action caused great indignation in the city-state and the regent summoned the National Assembly to discuss the matter and decide on the appropriate steps to be taken. The British community immediately dispatched a representative to explain to the regent the legality of the naval officer's action and to make it quite clear that the capture of the slavers was in conformity with the Anglo-Spanish Treaty of 1835. The British envoy, Mr. Jackson, a respected supercargo, found the regent 'in his palaver or Assembly House, surrounded by his Chiefs, furiously excited at what they termed the violation of their rights, professing to be the protectors of every flag that waved in their territory'.[1]

Mr. Jackson succeeded in pacifying them with the promise that

[1] F.O.2/1, No. 1 (Encl. after Encl. 8), Bonny, Jackson to Craigie, 13 Mar. 1837.

the captured vessels would remain in the river until the treaty between Spain and England had been explained to the Bonny Government. The British traders were apprehensive of the outcome of the incident and feared that if a satisfactory settlement were not reached before the man-of-war departed, the Bonny chiefs 'might revenge themselves on us' aided by the 360 Spaniards whom Tryon had landed. But from 'the pacified appearance of Anna Pepple' (Alali) 'we dreaded no insult either to ourselves or Lieutenant Tryon'. In the Foreign Office records the regent is referred to as 'Anna Pepple', the name of the House of which he was the Head. 'Anna', Bonny and Opobo sources affirm, is a corruption of 'Hanno', the name bestowed on Opubu the Great by the Portuguese slave traders.

A meeting of all the parties was held next day, 23 January 1836, 'for the purpose of explaining to them [the regent and his councillors] the treaty with Spain, a copy of which, after a friendly reception, was read to them' by Capsios, leader of the Spanish traders. This gentleman deliberately misrepresented the document to the Bonny chiefs. He went further. In order to arouse the suspicions of the regent he insinuated that the document might be a forgery in spite of British protestations that it was a correct copy of the treaty in question. When the British in desperation pressed him to declare emphatically his views on its authenticity or otherwise 'he returned an equivocal answer as to its validity'.[1]

It is clear that the Spanish slave-trading party had the ear of the regent and his chiefs and that the economic policy which England pursued ran counter to that of the city-state. The outcome of this meeting was therefore never in doubt. Spanish and Portuguese influence and intrigue won the day while British protestations that their action was legal and justified went 'unregarded, and after some violent language among themselves, Anna Pepple, foaming with rage struck the table'. He ordered the English delegates to be arrested. Thereupon his men seized 'Lieutenant Tryon by his collar' while the regent declared, 'You lie, you be my prisoners and on this we were dragged off various ways and ushered into a dark place of confinement . . . chained by the neck and legs.'[2]

The imprisonment of the British naval officers and palm-oil merchants was followed by a concentration of the West African Naval Squadron at Bonny. The show of force had the desired effect and

[1] F.O.2/1, No. 1. Encl. 8, 9, 10, Bonny, Jackson to Craigie, 15 Mar. 1837.
[2] Ibid.

Alali was forced to release the prisoners and sign a treaty guaranteeing that such an outrage would not be repeated. This 1836 agreement was not a slave-trade treaty. The sole object was to protect British lives and property in Bonny river, as witness some of its principal clauses. The mood of the regent and of the people generally was such that any mention of the abolition of the slave trade would have met with uncompromising opposition.

Three of the clauses forbade the imprisonment, detention, or 'any form of maltreatment' of a British subject by the Bonny authorities. Further, the treaty provided that disputes between the two parties should in future be settled by a committee of English traders 'with the King and Gentlemen of Bonny', who would be held responsible for any loss or damage to British property or persons on the river. Finally, the Government of the city-state was warned that an infringement of any article of the treaty 'will bring them . . . under the displeasure of the King of England, and be declared Enemies of Great Britain', and that 'men-of-war, on any complaint, will immediately come up to Bonny to protect the English vessels'.[1]

This treaty was signed almost under duress. The regent, although he released the English captives, was not convinced of the legality or the justification for the British seizure of Spanish slavers in Bonny river.[2] The treaty itself was in some respects openly one-sided and left the African community sullen and dissatisfied. To take just one example: Article III stipulated that if any 'English seaman shall illtreat a Bonnyman [as often happened] he shall be punished by the Captain of the vessel to which he may belong'.[3] In other words the Bonny Government had no control whatever over the misdeeds of culprits in her dominions. The question then arose: if the captain, the sole judge of the seaman, refused to convict the criminal and set him free, or was himself the offender as was not unusual, what means was there by which the Bonny victim could obtain redress?

The part played by the Navy in Delta politics must be assessed. The treaty of 1836 signalized naval power as the new and disintegrating factor in Delta society. Prior to the inauguration of the West African Squadron in 1810 there was no British standing force in the Bights. European and African traders looked to the Delta principali-

---

[1] F.O.2/1, Encl. 1 in No. 1, H.M.S. *Thalia* at Sea, Campbell to Craigie, 11 Mar. 1837.

[2] F.O.2/1, Encl. in No. 1 after Encl. 8, Hindostan, Rio Bonny, Jackson to Craigie, 13 Apr. 1837.

[3] F.O.2/1, Encl. 1, H.M.S. *Thalia* at Sea, Campbell to Craigie, 11 Mar. 1837.

ties to provide the protection so vital to commerce. For close on 300 years the Delta states served well the trade interests of both parties. It was these age-long institutions that the newly arrived naval power had begun to challenge and was later to undermine and destroy.

The planting of naval power on the coasts of Guinea followed hard on the abolition of the slave trade. In 1810 Captain Irby was instructed to proceed to West Africa and give effect to the Act of 1807 along some 3,000 miles of coastline. To carry out this duty he had at his disposal the *Amelia* (38 guns), *Ganymede* (24), *Kangaroo* (18), and *Trinculo* (18). In 1832 the number of ships was slightly increased and the new commander of the squadron, Sir George Collier, was given six ships—*Tartar* (36 guns), *Phesant* (22), *Morgiana* (18), *Myrmidon* (20), *Snapper* (12), and *Thistle* (12). Although the force was clearly inadequate for the tasks in hand yet the mere fact that their menacing guns could at any moment be turned against an offending native state—all of them situated near the sea—made them objects of dread and of detestation by the coast potentates.[1]

Naval operations on the coast had broadly two aspects. First and foremost it concentrated on the suppression of the slave trade and this at times involved the warships in actual combat at sea, in occasional blockade of the slave ports, and confiscation of foreign slavers which, ignoring solemn treaties made by their countries with Great Britain, pursued the contraband traffic in men. The commanders of the squadron were also instructed to protect British legitimate traders and, translated in practical terms, this meant that the Navy was required to terminate forcibly the slave trade of the African states and thereby promote 'equitable commerce'. As was to be expected British traders soon learnt that with the Navy on their side they had little to fear from the native powers. From the thirties, therefore, the white community sought to displace the authority of the coastal principalities and substitute for it the gunboat politics of the Navy.

It will be seen that although the Navy contrived the destruction of the old régime it proved disastrously incapable of administering law and order in the vacuum thus created. Ships of the West African Squadron were so few, the demand for their services so numerous and varied, that no warship was known to remain in a Delta port for more than a week. This incessant mobility rendered naval authority intermittent and uncertain, resulting ultimately in the breakdown of

[1] Lloyd, op. cit., pp. 62–68.

an orderly community to which anarchy succeeded until the last decades of the century.

The elimination of the old order was a gradual process effected in the face of determined opposition. At Bonny in the thirties the conflict was bitter and prolonged. No one who had studied the situation could have expected the 1836 treaty to last. Within a month an infraction of the first article had already occurred. Mr. Ralph Dawson, Master of the British palm-oil ship *Havannah Packet*, had been roughly handled and detained by the regent for his insolent behaviour during a trade dispute. Soon after two infractions of Article V were reported. The treaty had in fact become a dead letter as soon as it was signed.[1]

The regent's uncompromising support of the slave traders had rendered him *persona non grata* with the British community. In Bonny the weaker party led by the powerless king sought to exploit this hostility to its own advantage by intriguing with the English community against the regent. In March 1837 when Rear-Admiral Sir Patrick Campbell (in charge of the squadron) ordered his Senior officer, Commander Craigie, to proceed to Bonny, a plan had been hatched to overthrow the regent. Three reasons for this mission to Bonny were stated in Craigie's instructions. But there was more to it than these seemingly innocent phrases would convey:

'(i) The trade of Bonny, being of considerable importance and extent, I have to desire that you will cause all proper countenance and protection to be given to His Majesty's subjects engaged therein, sending . . . one cruiser into the river occasionally for that purpose.

(ii) To congratulate the new King on his accession to the sovereignty of the Bonny (Country) and

(iii) To obtain the ratification of the new King to these regulations respecting the trade in Bonny' [i.e. the trade regulations embodied in the 1836 Treaty].[2]

'The new King' who figured so prominently in these instructions was, of course, William Dappa Pepple, and the belated congratulatory messages on his accession (which took place in 1835) seemed designed to appear as adequate excuse for assembling the warships in Bonny river. There are indications in the dispatches connected with this period in the Foreign Office papers that the young king, in

[1] F.O.2/1, No. 1, Encl. 3, H.M. brig. *Lynx* off Rio Bonny, Huntley to Craigie, 23 Mar. 1837.
[2] F.O.2/1, No. 1, H.M.S. *Thalia* at Sea, Campbell to Craigie, 11 Mar. 1837.

order to fight a strong and formidable enemy at home, sought British alliance. Both the British and Dappa Pepple had a common interest in the downfall of the regent Alali, although for very different reasons. To the former he represented the old class of autocratic African slave-dealers in staunch alliance with the slave-trading nations of Europe and America. He had shown, by word and deed, that he was not willing to make concessions to the principles and interests for which the British stood. Such an uncompromising attitude was bound to meet with opposition from those engaged in the palm-oil trade. This explains the sustained tirade against the regent by the legitimate traders at Bonny in letters to the Foreign Office and the Admiralty in 1836 and 1837. They styled him the 'Usurper of Bonny', described his rule as 'savage and tyrannical', his treatment of British merchants 'brutal', and his mind as 'ferocious, malignant, and vindictive'.[1] Every attempt was made to present the regent in as unfavourable a light as possible to the home authorities. The young king whose power the regent usurped had good reasons for allying himself with the British against a common enemy.

In the meantime Craigie, while on a brief visit to Fernando Po, had dispatched one of his officers, Lieutenant H. V. Huntley, 'to proceed up the Bonny and inform the King of my intention, shortly, to appear there in order to wait upon him'. Huntley was 'to make himself generally acquainted with the state of the parties amongst the Chiefs of the Bonny',[2] and his report showed that at this time the king was 'nearly without authority' while the regent was still firmly in the saddle.[3] It would seem that the regent had sensed what was going on. Otherwise it would be difficult to explain his contemptuous treatment of the English delegation on their arrival without according them even the courtesy of a hearing. He evidently accepted the rumour circulated throughout Bonny that the British were in league with King Pepple for the purpose of dominating the city-state and eliminating the slave trade.

On 5 April Craigie arrived off Bonny and sent to inform the king that he intended 'to appear, attended by a retinue of officers, the Masters of the British ships, and a guard from my own ship'. This impressive British entourage landed in Bonny, expecting to be received

[1] F.O.2/1, No. 1, Encl. 7, Masters to Craigie, 4 April, 1837. Also F.O. 2/1, No. 1.
Encl. unnumbered after Encl. 8, Hindostan, Rio Bonny, Jackson to Craigie.
[2] F.O.2/1, No. 1, Encl. 2, Craigie to Campbell, 13 Apr. 1837.
[3] F.O.2/1, No. 1, Encl. 3, Huntley to Craigie, Bonny River, 27 Mar. 1837.

by the king and chiefs at the House of Assembly. Instead they were met by the lonely Pepple who explained that the regent's boycott of the meeting made it impossible for his chiefs to attend for fear of reprisals. This was proof, if proof were needed, that the regent's power at Bonny was absolute. Craigie then sent a personal message to the regent through Lieutenant Acland, accompanied by three ship's masters, who tried to convince him that he should meet the commander and the British party. When they arrived at the regent's house the latter sent them away 'in a grossly insulting manner, obstinately refused to attend, exclaiming that "one word from him to his men, would murder all the white men, in spite of their guard", and "that if he was wanted, the Captain of the Man-of-War could come to him"'.

Convinced that nothing could be accomplished Craigie rose to go. 'But the young King urgently pressed me, to go with him, to his own house: upon my declining he said "that if I did not go, he was sacrificed". Upon which I consented to accompany him.' King Pepple meant, of course, that if Craigie's mission failed his future and his existence in Bonny would be greatly imperilled: the regent would pillory him before the nation as the traitor that wanted to sell his country to the foreigner.[1] Bonny sources are at one in maintaining that the young king was a shrewd politician, avoiding in the long tussle with his adversary anything which would lead to an armed conflict. He knew full well that he would be hopelessly defeated in an open encounter. Instead he exploited the people's sentiment for the Royal House of Pepple, a sentiment which was still very strong among all classes of the population. He concentrated his tactics in exposing the illegality of the regent's position and attracted much sympathy to himself by the dignified and calm statement of his case in contrast to his enemy's haughty manners.

At the king's house Craigie met, in secret no doubt, the party of the king including some powerful chiefs and 'several Head Traders'. These had refrained from meeting the British openly lest their action be interpreted by the regent as an open defiance of his power. What transpired in this conference was not fully reported, but 'after a most amicable interview, it was arranged', said Craigie, 'that the King, and all the Chiefs of the Bonny, should meet me next day'.[2] On his return to the ship he held another conference with the British community and discovered that the masters of palm-oil

[1] F.O.2/1, No. 1, Encl. 2, Craigie to Campbell, 13 Apr. 1837.   [2] Ibid.

ships, who knew Bonny politics from within, were averse to risking another meeting on land unless they were certain of naval protection.[1]

Accordingly, Craigie assembled British warships in the Bonny river, 'the town being distant three cables length'. When all necessary military precautions had been taken, Craigie sent to the king and said that he 'was now ready again to meet himself and several chiefs on shore . . . and that I insisted on the presence of Anna Pepple' (the regent). By noon of 9 April 1837 all these conditions were complied with. The naval show of force had the desired effect. As soon as all the parties met Craigie 'called forward Anna Pepple, and distinctly stated, that, in consequence of the gross insults he had offered to British officers; also for the oppression and unjust manner in which he usurped the power in the Bonny country, and conducted the affairs of trade with the British merchants engaged here; that I had determined to remove him from all control over, or interference with, the British, excepting as a trader'. The regent, who 'at first assumed a haughty and menacing carriage, now seemed to fall, before just accusations', and 'signed a document accepting the terms of his deposition'.[2]

Without doubt the fall of the regent heralded the end of Bonny independence. The new king was a British creation, and whether it was clear to contemporaries or not, the power that put him on the throne had come to stay. For the usurper, in spite of the illegality of his position, breathed the spirit of the old order that was passing and to which, in reality, he belonged.

As a result of the regent's deposition, Bonny people were sharply divided into two camps. Alali was a fanatic: with him, as with Opubu, the defence of Bonny independence was a passion, almost an article of religious faith. He favoured and aided the Portuguese and Spanish slave-traders only because he stood for free trade, but he would have opposed the intrusion of the slave-trading nations as strongly as he opposed the British if they had interfered in Bonny politics. This point is important. The conflict between the ex-regent and his party and that of King Pepple ran through the whole period. Alali made the issue of Bonny independence a matter of life and death. It was the one question on which he admitted of no compromise. This principle gave an ideological basis to the group he led.

The young king was essentially a politician. He read the times correctly and saw that a new force had emerged with 'legitimate

[1] F.O.2/1, No. 1, Encl. 2, Craigie to Campbell, 13 Apr. 1837.   [2] Ibid.

commerce'. He recognized this force and tried, very intelligently, to co-operate with it. By nature he was a diplomat, and rarely lost his head in a situation however critical or intricate. These very qualities made him suspect in the eyes of Alali who regarded him from now on with great aversion.

The fall of the regent was followed by a revision of the treaty of 1836. The treaty of 1837,[1] like its predecessor, was designed to protect British commercial interests in the river, and was worked out by the Navy in the closest consultation with the legitimate traders at Bonny.[2] The signing of the treaty was a signal triumph for the British community. In a letter of gratitude to Craigie the legitimate traders declared that recent events had placed 'the British Trade and Character' in an 'elevated position', and acclaimed 'the total overthrow of the tyrannical chief and usurper, Anna Pepple. Neither the Foreign merchant, or Native trader, being no longer under the fear, of this ferocious and vindictive mind, we conceive the produce of the inland country will, when his fall is generally known, arise in great abundance.'

Moreover, 'we conceive, by the elevation of the rightful heir, Dappa Pepple, to the rule of the Bonny country, that the ascendancy of the British Flag is undoubtedly, and hence forward established in the River, namely, to the exclusion of the others'. And finally that, 'by the present treaty, the whole feature of the Trade, is greatly and advantageously changed for the British interest'.[3] This letter was signed by seventeen masters of palm-oil ships, sixteen of whom were British and one French. Craigie was under strong pressure from the masters to send the treaty to England for ratification 'with all despatch'.[4] Accordingly he ordered Huntley 'to proceed forthwith to England, in the ship *William Miles*, as requested in the representation'.[5]

Both the Foreign Office and the Board of Trade held the view that as the treaty was the work of the men on the spot and contained nothing objectionable, it should be ratified. The only scruples which the Foreign Office observed were to find out from the Legal Depart-

---

[1] Reproduced with modifications in L. Hertslet, *Commercial Treaties* (London, 1905), vii. 1.

[2] F.O.2/1, No. 1. Encl. 3, H.M.S. *Lynx*, Bonny River, Huntly to Craigie, 27 Mar. 1837.

[3] F.O.2/1, No. 1, Encl. 7, H.M.S. *Brutus*, River Bonny, Masters to Craigie, 11 Apr. 1837.   [4] F.O.2/1, No. 1, Encl. 7, Masters to Craigie.

[5] F.O.2/1, No. 1, Encl. 2, Craigie to Campbell.

ment whether there had been 'any precedent of such an agreement with savages, (called a treaty), and of the manner in which it was dealt with'.[1] The legal experts discovering nothing very irregular in the proceedings, Admiral Sir George Elliot, the new Commander-in-Chief of the African Station, was dispatched to Bonny to ratify the treaty. His letter of instructions 'was accompanied by a case containing three handsome long shawls of British manufacture, and three pieces of Broad Cloth, each of size sufficient for a large cloak; which articles Lord Palmerston conceives will be suitable to present to the King of Bonny, on the Occasion of ratifying the Treaty'.[2]

With the ratification of the treaty of 1837 a new stage was reached in Bonny-British relations. The young king proceeded to set his House in order. In foreign relations he discerned, quite rightly, that the fruitful source of British dissensions with Bonny was the 'trust' or credit system. This system, which will be treated in detail in another chapter,[3] was full of irregularities and abuses, and the large amount of unhonoured debts owing by the natives to the white traders was due to it. The frequent fights between the two communities were results of the attempts of the Europeans to recover debts owing to them by the African middlemen. The king therefore decided that if trusts were abolished and direct trade instituted, African traders would be compelled to pay directly in produce for the manufactured goods. This would stop the endless fights and disputes.

In 1838, therefore, the king entered into a treaty with Commander Castle of H.M.S. *Rylades* on the part of His Majesty's Government. This treaty forbade absolutely the giving of 'trusts' in any form, slightly increased the import duties, and enacted that the king could not be held responsible for debts or trusts incurred by his subjects with British merchants without his knowledge or consent.[4] To this treaty Elliot objected on the grounds 'that the import duties on British goods will be increased', and further that if the treaty were ratified, the king could not be held responsible for detained or lost British goods. Finally, that 'the difficulties of exacting the penalty on Masters for placing any part of their cargo in Trust, would be beyond the power of the King, and if attempted would lead to violence'.[5]

[1] Minutes on Bonny Paper, F.O.2/1 and its Encls. F.O., J.B., 30 Nov. 1837.
[2] F.O.2/1, F.O., 28/37, Admiralty, Palmerston to Wood.
[3] Chapter VI.
[4] F.O.84/340, King's House, Grand Bonny, Pepple to Elliot, 25 Apr. 1840.
[5] F.O.84/340, No. 53, H.M.S. *Wolverene* at Sea, Elliot to Admiralty, 3 July 1840.

This amounted to saying that although Pepple was right in tracking down the sore point of Afro-British relations to trust and its attendant evils, yet any attempt by the king to enforce a legally contracted agreement in his own dominions would call forth violence from the white traders. It was tantamount to a denial of Pepple's sovereignty and a confession that the British traders were a law unto themselves. King Pepple perceived the principles involved. Writing to Elliot on the subject he regretted 'sincerely . . . that the Articles of Convention entered into between myself and Commander Castle of H.M.S. *Rylades* on November 19th, 1838, has been cancelled in as much as the said Articles prohibited any trust whatsoever to be given out under a heavy penalty'. As the realities of the situation revealed themselves to him, Pepple became more vigilant and cautious in the defence of his position. Tactfully he reminded the Admiral that Britain recognized him 'as King of Bonny' in 1837, and that 'whilst he keeps the Treaties of Amity and Commerce inviolate, you will graciously be pleased to protect him from any undue or illegal interference in the exercise of his just prerogative as King of Bonny'.[1]

The truth was that the situation created at Bonny by the growth of the palm-oil trade had inevitably involved Britain in the politics of that country. The Bonny trade was worth nearly £500,000 in 1834. The struggles and disorders of the thirties and forties reflect the collision of two polities, that of Britain and Bonny, for the political and economic control of the city-state. Trade and politics are inextricably mixed. A nation with large economic interests in another's territory sooner or later, directly or indirectly, is implicated in its politics. Because of her property in Bonny river Britain had begun to challenge 'the exercise of [King Pepple's] just prerogative'. In issues involving great economic interests, legalistic arguments and questions of right do not often avail in international relations.

[1] F.O.84/340, Admiralty, vol. iii. Petition of Pepple to Elliot, Bonny, 25 Apr. 1840.

CHAPTER V

The Slave-trade Treaties

THE slave-trade treaties, which are more or less well known, were
initiated by Britain in 1810 and invariably embodied coercive clauses
designed to bring other nations into line with her policy of suppression. An essential feature of these treaties was the right of search
conceded to the naval squadron. They were first concluded with
Portugal and were later 'multiplied with every power in Europe
having a maritime flag; with every power in the Americas, except the
United States and one or two others'.[1] Nor were the treaties confined
to European nations. Britain had applied them with some success to
the suppression of the East African slave trade. In 1817 Radama, king
of eastern Madagascar, concluded a slave-trade treaty with Britain
and in return for his undertaking to put an end to the traffic the
British Government promised to pay him a subsidy of 10,000 dollars
a year for three years. Similar treaties were signed with the Imam of
Muscat and in 1822 with Seyyid Said, Sultan of Zanzibar.[2] In the late
thirties the British Government decided in face of opposition from
some quarters to extend the slave-trade treaties to the West African
states. Laird, a bitter opponent of these agreements, contended that
experience had shown them to be grossly ineffective. Subsidies paid
to European nations, such as Portugal and Spain, which amounted
to several million pounds, were largely wasted bribes, for in spite of
them the trade continued with 'unabated vigour'.[3] He ridiculed the
decision to enter into these treaties with African chiefs, declaring:
'The attempt to make Christian Powers adhere to them having failed,
seemed to be taken as the strongest proof that Pagan ones would
strictly comply with the most stringent conditions of a Slave-Trade
treaty.'[4]

There was much justification for the scepticism of the critics. In the
eighteenth century, when the trade was legal for all nations, the export
was between 70,000 and 80,000 a year. In the nineteenth century,

[1] Johnson, op. cit., pp. 238–53.
[2] Lloyd, op. cit., pp. 187–216. Cf. Coupland, *East Africa and Its Invaders*
(London, 1938).
[3] Johnson, op. cit.   [4] Ibid.

when nearly all the great powers (including Britain and America) had condemned the traffic, the annual export had risen to 135,000.[1] These figures may represent little more than official estimates, but the increase in the nineteenth century was an undoubted fact. In the thirties and forties Cuba and Brazil were the biggest markets; even after the United States had abolished the trade, slavery continued in the southern states and the demand for Negroes increased with the rise of cotton cultivation. It has been estimated that between 1808 and 1860 300,000 slaves were imported into the U.S.A.[2] In spite of the complicated bi-lateral treaties negotiated between Britain and foreign nations, treaties which filled some 1,529 volumes, little check was put on the traffic. Laird marshalled an impressive array of figures to support his case. He showed that in 1815 Great Britain paid £300,000 for the right to seize Portuguese vessels engaged in the trade, and in the same year 'gave up to Portugal her £600,000 for another treaty' designed to end the Portuguese slave trade. In 1817 a third treaty established the Mixed Commission Courts and the Preventive Squadron. 'In 1823 another treaty was brought forth' and by 1839 Britain had concluded five slave-trade treaties with Portugal. In spite of these solemn agreements, Laird argued, the slave trade of Portugal increased from 25,000 in 1807 to 56,000 in 1822:

and in 1839, 48 vessels, under the Portuguese flag [out of a total of 61 slave vessels] were condemned at Sierra Leone. With Spain we commence [treaty-making] in 1808; but did nothing until 1814, when we offered the Spanish Government a bribe of £800,000 to abolish the trade. . . . Having more honesty than the Portuguese, the Spaniards refused, and . . . the money was saved. . . . In 1815, we got her to sign, with other powers at the Congress of Vienna, a declaration 'that the slave-trade is repugnant to the principles of humanity and universal morality.' In 1817, another treaty was got on our paying £400,000 for it; and in 1822 a third; yet 'the sea swarmed with slave-ships, carrying on the slave-trade under the flag of Spain'.[3]

Viewed in retrospect the situation which faced statesmen was more complex than the critics would allow. So far as Britain was concerned the West African states were foreign territories. She had no other means of bringing them into line with her policy of suppression. The treaties concluded with the African chiefs therefore embodied clauses

[1] Lloyd, op. cit., pp. 24–27.
[2] Ibid., pp. 168 ff. Also W. L. Mathieson, *Great Britain and the Slave Trade 1839–65* (London, 1929).   [3] Johnson, op. cit., pp. 238–43.

stipulating that non-observance of the terms justified Britain in taking reprisals against the offending states. These served more as a cover for the employment of force which suppression tactics necessitated than as a guarantee that the treaties would be observed in their entirety by either Britain or the Delta states. We have shown that Nicolls's earlier attempts at treaty-making along these lines failed because he lacked government support. It was not till 1838 that the authorities were converted to his viewpoint and 'were moved to instruct the Naval Officers on the Coast of Africa to endeavour to dispose the Native Chiefs to enter into treaties' for the abolition of the slave trade.

The first of these agreements was concluded with Bonny on 11 March 1839. 'After a long palaver', Bonny agreed to abolish the trade 'provided they should obtain from the British Government, for five years, an annual present of the value of 2,000 dollars', which they stated was not more than half the revenue which they derived from the export slave trade.[1] This treaty was negotiated and concluded by Craigie on behalf of the British Government. Admiral Elliot wrote to Wood, Secretary of the Admiralty, saying that 'in the hope that the goods alluded to [i.e. the first year's subsidy] may be sent out, I have directed the Senior Officer in the West Coast of Africa to take an early opportunity of acquainting the King and Chiefs of Bonny with the intention of H.M. Government'.[2] No payment, however, was made throughout the first twelve months of the treaty and King Pepple the following year openly carried on the slave trade.

At this point Elliot was succeeded by Commander Tucker, who visited Bonny in September 1840 and reported that a 'constant supply of slaves are sent by canoe through the creeks to the rivers Nun and Brass for shipment. Three hundred and sixty having been taken by a Spaniard previous to my arrival in the River.' He quoted King Pepple as saying that it was impossible 'for him to put a stop to his subjects trading in slaves', and cited as evidence that the old trade was actively prosecuted the fact that 'dollars and doubloons are plentiful in Bonny which is always the case after the arrival of a slaver in the Nun or Brass River, as most of the slaves shipped off from there are purchased at Bonny'.[3] Pepple admitted that between

[1] F.O.84/383, Admiralty, vol. l, Memorandum on Negotiations with the Chiefs of Bonny, 7 Apr. 1841, Admiralty to F.O.
[2] F.O.84/340, No. 142, Simons Bay, Elliot to Wood, 5 Nov. 1839.
[3] F.O.84/383, No. 72, H.M.S *Viper* at Sea, Burslem to Tucker, 10 Sept. 1840.

1839 and 1840 he exported 2,000 slaves and would continue to do so through the Brass creek,[1] where in 1841 he sold 'a great number' to Don Pablo.[2]

To Tucker's constant accusation that Bonny still carried on the slave trade, Pepple could argue that she was free to do so until Britain ratified the treaty of 1839 and paid the subsidies as arranged. This was also the view of the Foreign Secretary, Lord Palmerston, whose protest on naval vacillation on this subject of honouring the 1839 treaty with Bonny called forth the long, but in parts inaccurate, 'Memorandum on Negotiations with the Chiefs of Bonny, April 7th, 1841'. It was his pressure and insistence that led the Admiralty to enter into a new treaty with Bonny the same year.

Lord Palmerston, unlike the Treasury and the Admiralty, held the view that since Britain had authorized these treaties to be negotiated, she was in duty bound to honour her part of the contract. On 31 March 1841 'Palmerston was of the opinion that the presents' to the Delta chiefs 'ought to be sent according to stipulation and should be discontinued in future, if the African chiefs do not keep their engagements'. That was precisely the point. It was no use complaining that the African chiefs still carried on the slave trade when Britain refused to ratify treaties for its abolition and withheld subsidies which alone could make those treaties effective. The truth was that on the British side, Palmerston excepted, few people believed that the treaties could ever be effectively enforced. The Treasury thought it 'inexpedient that any stipulation for the presents should be inserted in the treaty' and were averse to giving subsidies where the slave trade had not been 'actually prohibited'.[3]

In Old Calabar and the Cameroons, where the slave trade was no longer important, Britain, as we shall see, made treaties and honoured them. But however difficult the position at Bonny she had no justification for concluding agreements which were no sooner signed than they were repudiated. The confusion at Bonny serves to illustrate the lack of co-ordination between the government departments. Tucker, who was ordered to negotiate the 1841 treaty, was himself convinced that it would not work as the trade was too profitable to be given up easily by the Bonny people. He was certain that they would

[1] F.O.84/383, No. 96, at Sea, Tucker to Wood, 5 Nov. 1840.
[2] F.O.84/384, vol. ii, Encl. 1 in No. 164, Tucker to O'Farrel, 25 May 1841.
[3] F.O.84/383, Admiralty, vol. i, Memorandum on Negotiations with the Chiefs of Bonny.

use the annual subsidy, if paid, for prosecuting the trade with more vigour rather than for its suppression, and pointed out that means of evading the agreement by Bonny were numerous. He recalled the debt of gratitude which the king owed to Britain: 'Craigie in 1837 firmly established King Pepple on his throne' and the king had since received nearly £4,000 a year by way of tonnage duty levied on British ships. He therefore saw little reason why more subsidies should be paid to the king.[1] In point of fact King Pepple and his chiefs were in no mood for more treaties. Between 1836 and 1839 they had been called upon to sign four treaties—the one of 1837 excepted—and none of these had been ratified or honoured. Even the 1837 agreement had not been observed by the white traders in the river.[2] The king had come to view the business of treaty-making with disgust and angrily observed to an English merchant: 'One white man come, and make book [treaty] and another white man come tomorrow and break it; white man be fool, best treaty is in my head.'[3]

When, therefore, Commander Tucker arrived at Bonny for another treaty in 1841, his reception was cold. But 'after a great deal of trouble' he obtained the signature of the king and chiefs to an agreement for the abolition of the foreign slave trade. The difference between this treaty and that of 1839 was that whereas in the latter the subsidy was 2,000 dollars a year for five years, in the new treaty Bonny demanded and got 10,000 dollars a year for five years. 'I beg to inform your Lordship', wrote Tucker, 'that the King considered the treaty ratified, and expected the first payment will be sent to him immediately on receipt of this.'[4] Pepple would not have signed another treaty had not Tucker assured him that the treaty was ratified as soon as it was signed.

But in spite of these precautions the 1841 treaty went the way of its predecessors. Palmerston, who showed great interest and sympathy for the suppression movement, had been replaced by the earl of Aberdeen, who complained that the new treaty 'differed widely from those proposed in Lord Palmerston's letter of April 8th, and are not such as should meet with the concurrence of H.M. Government'. He protested against the greatly increased subsidy and the

[1] F.O.84/384, vol. ii, No. 164 (back of Des.), Encl. 1, Tucker to O'Farrel, 28 May 1841. See also F.O.84/383, No. 72, H.M.S. *Viper* at Sea, Burslem to Tucker, 10 Sept. 1840. In 1841 the duty was 'considerably above £3,800'.
[2] F.O.84/340, No. 53, at Sea, Tucker to O'Farrel, 3 July 1840.
[3] Parl. Pap. 1842, XI (551), Pt. I, QQ. 4240–3.
[4] F.O.84/385, Admiralty, vol. iii, No. 49, Tucker to O'Farrel, 22 Aug. 1841.

suggestion that payment be made, not as originally stipulated, in goods, but in money, 'and indeed a bill has already been drawn upon Her Majesty's Treasury, [by King Pepple] for the 10,000 dollars in question'. He urged the Navy to lose no time in informing the Bonny chiefs of H.M. Government's sentiments, and inducing them to accept the old treaty of 1839.[1]

The period of treaty-making at Bonny revealed a complete lack of policy behind British activities towards the Delta states. Naval officers did their best, but they were birds of passage, dependent for their advice on Liverpool supercargoes trading to these parts. Even the traders were dissatisfied with intermittent and confused interference that did no one any good. Captain Midgley, a Liverpool merchant at Bonny, told a parliamentary select committee in 1842 that these treaties were of great importance to trade provided they were honoured. Unless the British were ready to 'act up to' them 'with more energy than they have done they had better keep out of the River [Bonny] altogether. First comes a Captain and makes a treaty, and then another comes and says, "This treaty shall be null and void", and he tears it up. I allude particularly to Bonny. I piloted one vessel up and was party to a treaty, and in the course of a month or two afterwards, another comes and says, "I have orders from the Admiralty that this treaty shall be null and void".'[2]

Britain's difficulties in pursuing a consistent and well-conceived colonial policy at this time were enormous, nor were they confined to the West African states. In the working out of a policy many government departments were involved besides the Foreign Office. A parallel can be cited in the difficulties experienced by Sir James Stephen and the Colonial Office in having to deal with the Treasury and the War Office on colonial questions. Hence the situation in the Delta was part of the same problem—the out-dated, clumsy machinery of government in Britain which made swift consistent action so difficult.[3] Again throughout the nineteenth century the misunderstanding of the terms of treaties was a common feature of Afro-European relations. This is particularly true of the partition period in the eighties and nineties. Not only were the differing conceptions of 'sovereignty', 'suzerainty', and 'protection' frequent sources of conflict between the two peoples, but such a purely European term as 'ratification'

[1] F.O.84/385, Canning to Admiralty, F.O. 31 Dec. 1841.
[2] Parl. Pap. 1842, XI (551), Pt. I, QQ. 4240–4.
[3] P. Knaplund, *Journal of Modern History*, vol. i, 1929, pp. 40–66.

was alien to the traditional diplomatic practice of West Africans. King Pepple could never understand why a treaty must first be ratified before it could become binding on the contracting parties.

Meanwhile treaty-making after the pattern of that in Bonny had spread to the smaller states of the Delta. On the 18 and 19 September 1840 Lieutenant Pollard of H.M.S. *Buzzard* concluded a commercial agreement with the chiefs of the Cameroons. Later a slave-trade treaty was signed when chiefs Aqua and Bell of that place promised that if Britain granted them annual subsidies 'they will not allow their people, nor will they themselves trade for slaves'.[1] In January 1842 this treaty was ratified and the first annual subsidy paid. Here, as in Bonny, the treaties entered into were of two kinds.

The first was designed to protect British property in the rivers and to promote the growth of legitimate commerce. The other was specifically entered into with the object of abolishing the slave trade. Thus at Old Calabar in 1841, although the leading chief, Eyamba, signed a 'Treaty of Amity and Commerce' with the British, he would not conclude any agreement for the suppressions of the export slave trade, for, 'although the slave trade there is of no importance', it still paid them to indulge in what little there might be of it.[2] In 1842, however, both chiefs Eyamba and Eyo—rulers of the two leading trading towns of Old Calabar, Duke Town and Creek Town—signed a treaty abolishing the slave trade in return for 2,000 dollars subsidy for five years. Both the senior officer Captain Foote and Lieutenant Raymond who concluded the treaty spoke highly of their friendship, co-operation, and desire for legitimate trade. In every way Old Calabar was a striking contrast to Bonny. The people and their chiefs were, according to Foote, 'more disposed to be civilised here than at any other place I have yet been to'.[3]

The treaty was ratified and the subsidy paid in December 1843.[4] A similar agreement was reached with Bimbia (Cameroons), the only difference being that the subsidy was reduced to 1,200 dollars.[5] City-states like New Calabar and Brass, which were situated away from the sea and so inaccessible to warships, were unaffected until the establishment of the Consulate in the fifties.

So far as the king and people of Bonny were concerned, Aberdeen's

[1] F.O.84/436, Canning to Admiralty, F.O., 15 Jan. 1842.
[2] F.O.84/384, vol. ii, No. 56, at Sea, Tucker to O'Farrel, 30 July, 1841.
[3] F.O.84/493, No. 171 and its enclosures, Foote to Herbert, 12 Dec. 1842.
[4] F.O.84/493, Addington to Admiralty, F.O., 9 Dec. 1843.
[5] F.O.84/493, Canning to Admiralty, F.O., 3 Oct. 1843.

refusal to ratify the 1841 treaty amounted almost to a declaration of war. In 1843 his Lordship wrote to the Admiralty warning them that he had heard from Lord Sandon that King Pepple 'is said to have threatened to seize the British ship, *Lady Paget* . . . in order to compensate himself for the non-payment of the Bill for 10,000 dollars drawn by him on H.M. Government in virtue of the second article of the Treaty' of 1841: he therefore requested the Admiralty to instruct the Navy to be ready to take reprisals and to defend British interests in case of an attack.[1]

In February 1844 Beecroft reported that war had broken out between Bonny and the British merchants, 'the town and shipping firing into each other'. Not only had the 'Captains [British super-cargoes] had the worst of it', but King Pepple managed to get them ashore, threw them into prison, and threatened to roast them alive if they refused 'to land their guns'.[2] He surrounded the prison with armed men and demanded that their guns be placed under his care as security for their good behaviour.[3] This was done. The *Lady Paget*, for which Aberdeen feared, was seriously damaged.[4]

Anti-British feeling reached fever pitch. Awanta, the High Priest of Bonny, a person regarded as sacred by the native people and imbued with intense religious fanaticism, organized an underground terrorist group. From his residence at Juju Town, three miles away from Bonny Town, he controlled the activities of his followers, mainly young hot-heads, who patrolled the numerous creeks and killed and destroyed all the British men and property they could lay hands on. A Liverpool supercargo, Mr. Hartley, was murdered while on his way to claim a debt from the people of New Calabar.[5] Soon after two British sailors were killed in the river.[6] On one occasion, '16 masked men boarded a British boat carrying merchandise', and plundered her, wounding many men.[7] Incidents of this nature were very common. British merchants declared that so long as Awanta remained at Bonny their lives and property were unsafe. According to their own account he armed many men and set them loose to murder white men.[8]

[1] F.O.84/493, Canning to Admiralty, 8 July 1843.
[2] F.O.84/549, Encl. 2 in Admiralty letter of 12 June 1844, Beecroft to Nicolls, 20 Feb. 1844.   [3] Cf. Waddell, op. cit., p. 270.
[4] F.O.84/549, Encl. 2 in Admiralty letter of 12 June 1844, Beecroft to Nicolls, 20 Feb. 1844.
[5] F.O.2/3, No. 125, Misc. 69, River Bonny, Price to Clarendon, 15 Mar. 1847.
[6] F.O.2/3, No. 125, Misc. 80, Ward to Stanley, Admiralty, 9 July 1847.
[7] F.O.2/3, 5 Misc. Encls. 2, 4, 9, and 11.
[8] F.O.2/3, 5 Misc. Encl. 1, Hotham to Ward, 4 Nov. 1847.

The attitude of the Navy during this period of anti-British activities must now be explained. From 1836 to 1841 the view generally held by naval officers operating in the Delta was that British commercial interests must be protected against native encroachment, and although men such as Tucker were opposed to the slave-trade treaties, the majority favoured the treaty-system and not a few were at first zealous in upholding them. But during the forties experience was showing that the infraction of these treaties and trade regulations was not an African monopoly: commercial clauses, drawn up by the English traders themselves, were more often transgressed by their authors than by the native merchants. In 1840 Tucker pointed out that the masters and supercargoes of English vessels trading at Bonny 'and many even of those who signed the Treaty of 1837 are in the constant practice of evading the fifth article of that treaty by inducing natives to supply them with palm oil which had been previously agreed and paid for by other masters and supercargoes, thereby setting the natives a bad example and causing them to have a bad opinion of the honesty and justice of British Traders'.[1]

In other words the gentlemen of the Navy came to realize that it was not easy to legislate for the consciences of men schooled in the hard life of Delta trade. The ingrained instincts of piracy—a carry-over from the slave trade—which characterized a majority of the palm-oil merchants defied the laws of an orderly community. This fact is important. The commodity of the trade changed; palm oil was replacing men, but the traders did not alter.

It followed then that treaties, trade regulations, codes of conduct, all excellent in themselves, were rendered unworkable by the very nature of the men for whom they were devised. This was true of Europeans and Africans alike, for essentially both were the products of the same force. During the Bonny disturbances in the forties, therefore, the West African Squadron was inclined to leave the two parties to their own devices. When complaints from the traders reached the Foreign Office regarding the debts, persecutions, murders, and destruction of British property on the river—among other things the merchants complained that the cruisers on whose protection they depended had not been seen for a long time—Palmerston approached the Admiralty for more information on the matter.[2] Surprisingly the

---

[1] F.O.84/340, No. 53, H.M.S. *Wolverene* at Sea, Tudor to Admiralty, 3 July 1840.
[2] F.O.2/3, No. 125, Misc. 69 and 56, Bonny River, Price to Clarendon, 15 Mar. 1847.

latter showed little interest in the events at Bonny, observing that interference in commercial matters in that quarter was to be discouraged, but they promised to investigate.[1]

The change from enthusiastic defence of British interests to one of indifference by the Navy was defended in a dispatch to the Admiralty by the Commodore in charge of the African Station, Sir Charles Hotham, in 1847. His statement of policy was emphatic in its opposition to naval interference in the Delta. Sir Charles must have been unaware of the old policy of active intervention, judging from his statement that the 'policy of my predecessors has always been never to interfere in commercial matters'. Nevertheless, his reasons for wanting to abstain were sound. Like King Pepple he tracked down the sore point of Anglo-African relations to the 'trust' or credit system. By a clever manipulation of this system the British merchants derived fabulous profits, yet the disorder and dishonesty which accompanied it made for an unsettled and corrupt community. That was why the king demanded its abolition in 1838 and the white traders, aided by the Navy, opposed it to a man.

'The trade of Africa', declared Sir Charles, 'is formed on credit', and until the basis of that trade was altered it was little use trying to mediate between Africans and Europeans. Even in the imperfect state of trade 'the ignorant black adheres to all the stipulations, and performs his part creditably and well: there may be exceptions, but, on the whole, their behaviour will stand a favourable comparison with that of more civilized nations'. He put the blame for the disorders squarely on the shoulders of the white traders and condemned any attempt to use the warships in defence of those who were in the wrong. 'To lead the [British] merchants to believe that their speculations would be backed by military power' was a measure he would not support.[2]

To a petition from Bonny merchants asking for protection, Hotham replied that he was prepared to protect British lives and property where right and necessary, but if by protection they meant 'influence, either moral or physical, to recover your debts, I am bound to tell you that it will be denied. To adopt such a course might benefit the owners of ships at present in Bonny, but would for ever affect the interests of those who will succeed you, and sap the foundations of

[1] F.O.2/3, No. 125, Misc. 77, Admiralty, Ward to Addington, 5 July 1847.
[2] F.O.2/3, No. 125, H.M.S. *Penelope*, Ascension, Hotham to Ward, 3 May 1847.

legitimate trade.'[1] He might have painted a too favourable picture of the Delta middleman, and although a good deal of the upheavals could be traced to quarrels over the credit system yet there was also much discontent over Britain's unwillingness to honour the treaties.

Palmerston, now back in office, could not be expected to share Hotham's view considering the volume of letters and petitions which reached him from British merchants and owners of ships at Bonny, from the African Association of Liverpool, and others with interests in the Delta trade. Eleven supercargoes had petitioned early in 1847 stating that they were 'under a thorough conviction of the extreme insecurity of both life and property' in the river. They asked that their rights and privileges 'as subjects of Her Britannic Majesty may be enforced by the only power we consider ourselves entitled to call upon, namely, "Her Britannic Majesty's Vessels of War", cruising upon this part of the coast'.[2] In face of the wide publicity which the Bonny events received in Britain, Lord Palmerston decided to intervene.

A Board of Trade inquiry satisfied him that the amount of property at stake was considerable.[3] Palmerston therefore informed the Admiralty 'that Sir Charles Hotham ought to be instructed to compel King Pepple and the Chiefs of Bonny, by force, if necessary, to respect the lives and property of Her Majesty's subjects, and that the Commodore will be justified in enforcing the payment of debts due to British Subjects'.[4] On receipt of this instruction Hotham did not fail to point out that if it was made known to the merchants at Bonny, indiscriminate giving of 'trust' would be the result, making the task of recovering debts doubly difficult.[5] Palmerston concurred and left much to the discretion of the commodore.[6] Sir Charles entrusted the mission to one of his subordinates, Commander Birch, an officer who shared Palmerston's enthusiasm for action. One of his first acts was to put an end to the terrorism inspired by Awanta against British persons and property, a movement which had led to the loss of many lives in the river. King Pepple was powerless to intervene, as according to the laws of the country the High Priest

[1] F.O.2/3, No. 125, Encl. 2, Ascension, Hotham to Bonny Masters and others.
[2] F.O.2/3, No. 125, Misc. Encl. 14.
[3] F.O.2/3, Misc. 93, F.O., 16 Dec. 1847, Palmerston to Board of Trade, and F.O.2/3, No. 128, Board of Trade to F.O., 24 Dec. 1847.
[4] F.O.2/3, F.O., Palmerston to Ward, Admiralty, 6 Jan. 1848.
[5] F.O.2/3, No. 126, H.M.S. *Penelope*, Cabenda, Hotham to Ward.
[6] F.O.2/3, F.O., Palmerston to Ward, 3 June 1848.

was a sacred person and therefore above the law. Pepple explained that if he touched the person of Awanta, his action would bring disaster to the kingdom: such was the current belief. He indicated that the British would be given permission to capture and take him away if they so desired.[1] Birch, who knew that Awanta's capture was necessary for the safety of the British traders, did not scruple to use force to secure his arrest, and although his act was not openly condemned. by Hotham the commodore nevertheless warned against imprudent acts which might antagonize the natives and injure future relations.[2]

With Awanta imprisoned on board a man-of-war, the Foreign Office soon discovered that all sorts of legal tangles would be involved in his trial as he was not a British subject. Palmerston decided to avoid these difficulties by sending him 'to Norfolk Island, both as a punishment for his crimes and as a security against repeating the offence'.[3] But Lord Grey of the Colonial Office had a different idea. He was 'inclined to direct the Commodore to set this murdering High Priest on shore somewhere on the Coast of Africa as far as possible from the Bonny . . . leaving him to take his chance'.[4] With the execution of this order Awanta disappeared from Bonny and nothing further was heard of him.

There is little doubt that the Awanta terrorists were religious fanatics who fought to rid the country of the foreigners. The king secretly exploited this emotion to direct one wing of his anti-British measures and to lead his attack on New Calabar, the only city-state that defied Bonny supremacy in the eastern Delta. It had always been the policy of the Pepples to conquer and annex New Calabar. Thus the terrorist activities were concentrated on the sixteen-mile stretch of river linking New Calabar with Bonny, depriving the British of access to their trade and property there, and denying the New Calabar Africans of their only means of livelihood, which consisted in trade with the Europeans. It was on this river that most of the murders were committed and the 'masked men' operated, boarding boats and destroying property.

To put an end to these attacks Birch insisted on the inclusion, in the 1848 treaty, of a guarantee by Bonny 'to afford every protection

[1] F.O.2/3, No. 125, Misc. 80 and 65, Ward to Stanley, 9 July 1847.

[2] F.O.2/3, No 125, H.M.S. *Penelope*, Ascension, Hotham to Ward, 3 May 1847.

[3] F.O.2/3, No. 125, 5 Misc. Minutes on Admiralty letter of 31 Dec. 1847, Ward to Stanley, 2 Jan. 1849.

[4] F.O.2/3, 5 Misc. Encl. 14, C.O., Grey to Palmerston, 7 Feb. 1848.

in our power to the persons and property of British subjects trading in the River', and 'to send two trusty men, our subjects, in each boat trading between River Bonny and New Calabar for the purpose of guarding the said boats from attacks made on them by our people, but without our knowledge or approbation'. It was also stipulated that trading boats should not leave Bonny for New Calabar or vice versa, except by daylight, and that masters of British oil ships were at liberty to accept or reject the protection of Bonny guards, but that Bonny could not be held responsible for acts of piracy and murder incurred by ships without guards unless incontrovertible evidence of the identity of the attackers could be produced. This commercial treaty was followed by the slave-trade treaty of 1848 in which King Pepple was induced to accept the 2,000 dollars subsidy of 1839 in place of the 10,000 dollars of 1841.[1]

During his mission to Bonny and throughout the negotiations which led to the conclusion of the 1848 agreements, Birch pointed out that King Pepple 'more than once referred to the bad faith the English Government had kept with him, and at last accused it of defrauding him of 50,000 dollars', the amount of compensation agreed to be paid to him by the treaty of 1841. The king 'declared most solemnly Captain Tucker informed him that immediately the Treaty was signed by him . . . it was in full force, never explaining that it had first to be ratified by our Government'.[2]

The lessons learnt from these upheavals were not lost, and although the events described belong to Delta history their influence on British foreign policy had a West African significance. Palmerston came to realize that the Government had no clear policy towards the Delta states and that the amount of British property involved was large enough to warrant the appointment of a resident official, since the intermittent 'gunboat rule' provided by officers of the naval squadron was clearly inadequate. That this need was urgent can be seen from the fact that between 1844 and 1849, the date of Palmerston's appointment of the first British Consul to the Bights of Benin and Biafra, the naval authorities had themselves employed on nine different occasions the services of an English merchant, John Beecroft, who had unrivalled experience of local affairs, to aid them in their political work. In May 1844 Beecroft accompanied Lieutenant Blount

---

[1] F.O.2/3, 5, Misc. Encl. 6; also Hertslet, *Commercial Teaties*, vol. viii.
[2] F.O.2/3, Misc. 5, H.M.S. *Penelope*, St. Helena, Hotham to Ward, and its enclosures, 11 Nov. 1847.

to Old Calabar to ratify the treaty made with that city-state. In June of the same year he followed Commander Brisbane to Bimbia on a political mission to the chief of that place. During 1845 he was employed on three occasions, first with Commander Gooch 'to visit the Chiefs of Calabar, Bimbia, Cameroons to see that they were fulfilling the treaties they had entered into for the suppression of the Slave Trade'. On the second occasion, 'in consequence of the report that the Chiefs of Bimbia were carrying on the Slave Trade an expedition composed of H.M. Frigate *Actaeon*, and Her Majesty's Steam Vessels *Hydra* and *Styx* were despatched there, at the request of Captain Mansell, I accompanied him to investigate charges which were proved groundless'.[1] During 1847 Hotham instructed him 'to accompany Captain Mansell . . . to the mainland for the purpose of communicating and making treaties with the native chiefs', and in August of the same year he diplomatically prevented the French from concluding any treaties with Old Calabar 'having witnessed in the River Gaboon the prejudicial effects to British Commerce of the interference of the French authorities'.[2] For his work as a political agent John Beecroft received fees totalling £477 from the Government.[3]

When, therefore, in 1849 Palmerston decided to appoint a consul the need for such an official was clearly overdue: there was, moreover, little doubt who the official would be. John Beecroft had become something of an institution in the Bight of Biafra. His connexion with the Delta began in 1829 when Nicolls, Governor of Fernando Po, brought him out to take charge of the Department of Works. Beecroft stayed on after the settlement was evacuated in 1834 and was connected first with the firm of Messrs. Tennant & Co. of which he was a partner, and when that business went bankrupt in 1837[4] he was employed by Robert Jamieson of Glasgow on various scientific explorations up the Niger in the steam vessel *Ethiope*.[5] In 1836 he had explored the Delta above Abo and was well known to African chiefs beyond the northern Delta.[6] Between 1841 and 1843, when the controversy over the ill-fated Niger expedition brought the Delta and the Niger valley to the notice of Europe, Spain was careful to reassert her sovereignty over Fernando Po, and it is a measure of Beecroft's

---

[1] F.O.84/775, London, Beecroft to Palmerston, 16 July 1849, and its enclosures.
[2] Ibid.   [3] Ibid.
[4] Geary, op. cit., pp. 74–75.   [5] Jamieson, op.cit., pp. 3–6.
[6] F.O.82/9, F.P., 779, Beecroft to Nicolls, 28 Feb. 1836.

influence and ability that Spain appointed him Governor of the island.[1] Among Africans his reputation was great and it was mainly owing to his friendship with the chiefs of Old Calabar that that city-state remained consistently pro-British throughout the thirties and forties. On the whole, then, the first Consul was a fortunate appointment. Throughout the Delta, wrote a contemporary, 'he is well-known, highly respected, and possesses influence such as no man on the coast has ever obtained'.[2]

On 30 June 1849 Beecroft was officially appointed Her Britannic Majesty's Consul for the Bights of Benin and Biafra, an area covering not only the Niger Delta and Lagos, but also the kingdom of Dahomey. It is interesting to note that the following paragraph which denied any territorial ambitions on the part of Great Britain in making this appointment was crossed out in the original draft in Palmerston's own hand: 'H.M.'s Government in establishing this Consulate in the Bights of Benin and Biafra, have no intention to seek to gain possession, either by purchase or otherwise, of any portion of the African continent in those parts, nor of any neighbouring Islands.' During this period Palmerston was the only Foreign Secretary who appeared to have an intelligent grasp of the meaning of events in the bights of Benin and Biafra. He was convinced that with the growth of equitable traffic British interference could no longer be delayed. It was he who had attempted to purchase Fernando Po after its abandonment in 1834, had urged the payment of slave-trade subsidies to Bonny, and two years after making his appointment of the first Consul to the Bights in 1849 had ordered the occupation of Lagos.

His purpose in pressing for the payment of slave-trade subsidies was to make effective treaties which alone could give legality to energetic measures pursued towards the African states. He stood for action in this area where a semblance of non-interference could no longer be maintained. Between the months of February and May 1850 more than half a dozen new major projects for furthering British political and economic interests in West Africa were brought to the notice of the Consul with instructions to aid them actively. On 12 February Beecroft was instructed to lead a mission to Dahomey to induce its powerful potentate to establish 'commercial relations

[1] Scotter, op. cit., f. 95.
[2] F.O.84/549, Encl. 1 in (Admiralty to F.O. letter of 12 June 1844) Nicolls to Barrow, 5 June 1844.

with the British Government and abolish the slave trade'.[1] On the 25th of the same month he was directed to forward a report on the recently founded republic of Liberia, giving details of its population, the extent of its authority, and the state of its agriculture and commerce.[2] In another dispatch of the same date, Lord Palmerston proposed that he undertake a mission to Abeokuta, the chief city of the Egbas (50,000 inhabitants) which was connected by the River Ogu to Lagos. 'The establishment of commercial relations with the Interior of Africa through the Yoruba Tribe would materially contribute to the suppression of the slave trade',[3] and if he could make navigation of the Ogu 'free and safe' a vital link between the sea and hinterland would be forged.

Three months later Palmerston wrote to Beecroft.

I have to inform you that several eminent Mercantile and Manufacturing firms in this country have combined for the purpose of testing by practical experiment the possibility of procuring a supply of cotton from the West Coast of Africa and that the parties in question have purchased two vessels, the *Firefly* and *Georgiana*, and are about to send them out from Liverpool. ... I have to instruct you to give every assistance in your power to this Expedition, and to promote, by exerting your influence with the King of Dahomey and other Native Chiefs, the object which it has in view.[4]

These instances serve to illustrate the responsibilities thrown on the Consul and the Palmerstonian attitude to West African affairs which cannot be described as that of an absent-minded Minister, even as early as 1850. The Foreign Secretary was prepared to face to the full the implications of legitimate commerce. His support of missions to establish direct trade contact with the interior was proof that he saw the Niger Delta in true perspective—as the key that would open the door to West African trade.

[1] F.O.84/816, F.O., Palmerston to Beecroft, 12 Feb. 1850.
[2] Ibid., 25 Feb. 1850.
[3] Ibid.   [4] Ibid., 18 May 1850.

CHAPTER VI

The Development of the Oil Trade

THE disorders which characterized the ten years period of treaty-making did not altogether interrupt the growth of legitimate commerce. A phenomenal rise in the palm-oil exports in the thirties led many observers to predict a continued increase in the forties. This hope was not fully realized. Between 1837 and 1854 there were constant fluctuations:[1]

1834	1837	1845	1846
13,945 (tons)	11,000	25,000	18,000

The view that increased slave-trading activity was responsible for every decline in the oil trade was general in the nineteenth century. Indeed, the tendency to make the slave trade the scapegoat for all the evils that afflicted Africa, a tendency as misleading as it was characteristic of that time, has come to be accepted by modern writers.[2] So far as the Niger Delta is concerned that view is, to say the least, inaccurate. The trade figures, to be understood, must be studied in the closest relation to conditions in the coastal states since the Delta economic organization was dependent on the state of the alliances with the hinterland producers.

An examination of the facts will reveal that contrary to Dr. Madden's assertion that 'an increased demand for slaves in 1837 took the natives away from their former occupation and the quantity of oil exported from Africa was considerably diminished', there was little slaving at the port of Bonny that year.[3] Simultaneously with the initiation of the slave-trade treaties, the naval methods of suppression altered. From 1837 it may be said that the blockade system was initiated in preference to the cruising system. The new tactics entailed sudden concentrations of the squadron at various notorious ports.[4] Thus the most important slaving areas were almost sealed off

---

[1] Parl. Pap. 1854, LXV (296), Quantities of Palm Oil imported into U.K., 1844–53.
[2] Stilliard, ch. v. Cf. Hancock, op. cit., ii, pt. 2, 160.
[3] Parl. Pap. 1842, XII, Pt. II, Appendix, pp. 33–36.
[4] Lloyd, op. cit., pp. 89–103.

by close blockade, and the field left free to the protagonists of equitable traffic. Such was the case with the Delta ports. Captain Denman showed that even before the Equipment Treaties in 1835, Bonny, 'the stronghold of the slave-trade was constantly watched, and being a river, every vessel could be seized coming out; and in fact for a number of years no slave vessel escaped capture. The slave trade in that river was a losing concern, and was therefore abandoned.'[1] Captain Bailey, master of a palm-oil ship trading to Bonny between 1827 and 1837, said that in 1827 he had seen 16–20 slavers 'in the River [Bonny] at one time', but that on his last visit in 1837 there was not one to be seen. Instead sixteen British vessels were taking oil.[2] All available evidence showed that the Navy's close blockade of Bonny river was effective.

The records plainly indicate that from the thirties to the fifties Bonny was the centre of the oil trade in West Africa. Mr. William Hutton, a merchant with more than thirty years' experience in the African trade, declared: 'Bonny exports from 15,000 to 20,000 tons of palm oil, and we think it a good deal if we can get 300 to 400 from Popo. I suppose the single river of Bonny exports as much as all the rest of Africa put together.'[3] Dr. Madden in a passage already cited showed that in the thirties Bonny produced more than three-quarters of the whole African supply. The reduction in oil exports at this time therefore could not reasonably be attributed to an increase in the slave trade. Any remnant of that illegal traffic had been completely diverted to the underground smuggling confined to the Brass river. The real cause for the 1837 decline must be sought elsewhere.

It was in that year that news of the usurpation of kingly power in Bonny by Alali the regent reached the interior markets. The hinterland producers, who were devoted to the Royal House of Pepple, in retaliation closed the oil trade. The quantity of palm oil which reached the port during the months of disorder, boycott, and stagnation must have been very small. It was not till Britain intervened in April 1837 that the regent fell and trade with the hinterland was reopened. That was why in their letter thanking Craigie for the part he played in the deposition of the regent, the British supercargoes said: 'We conceive the produce of the inland country, will, when his [the regent's] fall is generally known, arrive in great abundance.'[4] In

---

[1] Parl. Pap. 1848, 1st Report, XXII (272), Q. 240.
[2] Parl. Pap. 1842, XI (551), Pt. I, QQ. 1868–79.   [3] Ibid., Q. 3811.
[4] F.O.2/1, Encl. 7 in No. I, Supercargoes to Craigie, 11 Apr. 1837.

the repercussions of that dispute lay the cause of the decrease in palm-oil exports for 1837.

Another year often cited is 1846. At this date the slave trade could not have been responsible for the decline in oil trade. A merchant who had been in the Bonny trade from 1825 to 1842 stated that within his experience the number of oil ships had risen from eight to fifty and where there had been three Liverpool Houses by 1840 there were twelve.[1] This gentleman who had seen fifteen or sixteen slavers in the twenties, saw none in 1842.[2] A naval officer, Captain Vidal, said there were many slavers in 1826, but heard (in 1842) 'from officers in the station that the slave trade is now broken up'.[3] Commander Broadhead declared in 1842 that 'the slave trade at Bonny, and Calabar had been done up these three years; it was not carried on at all'.[4]

Yet whereas in 1845 oil exports reached the 25,000 tons mark, in the following year they fell to 18,000 tons.[5] 1846 was the date of the famous Bonny–Andoni war. By that time palm oil had replaced the slave trade as the economic mainstay of the city-state and King Pepple knew it. To safeguard the Ibo oil markets which his father, Opubu, had patiently built up, he attacked and annexed Andoni in a highly successful campaign in 1846.[6] Like most wars it had an adverse effect on trade and did not improve the economic health of the victor. In 1847 the king himself admitted to Birch that the reason why large debts were owing to British supercargoes and why trade had declined was due 'to the great expense and loss of time he had been put to by the war with Andoni just settled'.[7]

The Delta production, which averaged 15,000 to 20,000 tons in the forties, was worth approximately £500,000 and in peak years like 1845 was nearly £750,000[8] at £34 a ton. Throughout the forties

[1] Parl. Pap. 1842, XI (551), Pt. I, Q. 1645.
[2] Ibid., Evidence of Clegg, Q. 1590.
[3] Ibid., Evidence of Vidal, Q. 357.
[4] Ibid., Evidence of Broadhead, Q. 2557.
[5] Parl. Pap. 1854, LXV (296), Quantities of Palm Oil imported into the U.K. 1844–53.
[6] See Appendix B for copy of the Treaty signed between Bonny and Andoni at the conclusion of this war.
[7] F.O.2/3, Birch's Report to Hotham, in Hotham's letter to Admiralty No. 338, 20 Mar. 1847.
[8] Parl. Pap. 1842, XII, Pt. II, Appendix and Index, Palm Oil Trade, pp. 33–36, cf. Parl. Pap. 1842, XI, Pt. I, Appendix and Index, No. 7, pp. 574–84, Memorandum on British Trade with Africa. Also Parl. Pap. 1842, XI (551), Hutton's Evidence, Q. 3811.

and early fifties the Delta held this lead over the rest of West Africa. After the record figure of 1845 the position was fairly steady with a slight fall to 21,723 tons in 1850. But in the next three years there was marked improvement, from 29,000 tons in 1851 to 30,000 tons in 1853.[1]

The rise in the fifties can be explained in part by the comparative peace in the city-states from 1849, and in part by the growth of the trade in the Bight of Benin, centred around Lagos and the Benin river. Since the capture of Lagos in 1851 and the diminution of the slave trade in that quarter, the increase in the oil trade was fairly rapid, reaching 21,592 tons in 1857.[2] But in spite of the challenge from this rival, beginning from the middle of the century, the Delta held its own. Moreover, in the oil rivers slave traffickers were in retreat, for even their traditional stronghold, the Brass river, was by this date invaded by the legitimate merchants. In 1857 Lieutenant (later Şir) John H. Glover witnessed a bustling activity in the oil trade in Brass ports. He saw 'five English vessels taking palm oil, and the English cask houses on shore, dotted among the splendid foliage, give an air of life and movement'. At Tuon, a village on the river, he saw 'as many as a hundred Brass River Canoes come down [from the interior] each carrying six puncheons of palm oil'.[3] Mr. T. J. Hutchinson on his first consular visit to that river in the same year testified that the Spanish–Portuguese dominance had collapsed and 'the ruin of an old slave-trading establishment constitutes the only relic of this traffic in the Town [Nembe]'. There was one deserted house formerly tenanted by a Spaniard named Madjine whose last visit to the river was made 'in a small schooner, about three and a half years ago'.[4] Whatever criticism might be levelled against the naval tactics in the suppression movement, beyond any doubt their blockade of Delta ports, maintained throughout the forties, led to the ultimate decline and fall of the slave trade in the fifties. With the destruction of the Brass slave trade, the success of the Navy was complete.

The entire African production of palm oil in the years 1855–6 averaged between 40,000 and 42,000 tons. In the same period the

[1] Parl. Pap. 1854, LXV (196), Quantities of Palm Oil imported into U.K.
[2] Stilliard, ch. v. Cf. Allan McPhee, *The Economic Revolution in British West Africa* (London, 1926), ch. ii, which was the first general study of the palm-oil trade in West Africa.
[3] Hastings, op. cit., pp. 66–75.
[4] F.O.84/1030, No. 41, H.M.S. *Trident*, Hutchinson to F.O., 20 July 1857.

principal Delta trading centres—Brass, 2,280 tons; Bonny and New Calabar, 16,124 tons; Old Calabar, 4,090; Cameroons, 2,110 tons; Fernando Po, 360; and Bimbia, 96 tons—totalled 25,060 tons, over half the African production. These figures represent only the British trade, which accounted for the bulk of the Biafra supply. 'Independent of this, in the Rivers Malimba, Boreah and Kampo, palm oil is bought by coasting vessels, chiefly, American and French.'[1] Ten years later, in 1864, Richard Burton, then British Consul, reported that the palm-oil trade had not altered very much from the position in the fifties. The annual product of Brass varied from 2,000 to 2,800 tons; Old Calabar, 4,500 to 5,000 tons; Bonny and New Calabar 16,000 to 17,000 tons, although in one year these two rivers reached the 22,000 tons mark; and approximately 20 tons came from other trading stations. Bimbia had ceased to be a centre of trade in 1864. The 26,000 tons Delta total was worth £800,000 out of a total African oil trade of £1,500,000, again slightly over half of the entire production.[2]

Palm oil was not the sole commodity of trade, but it was by far the most important. In 1842 the ivory produced in the Delta was worth about £17,000 per annum; camwood and other dye-woods were worth between £10,000 to £15,000 per annum.[3] The timber trade, although at the time increasing, was unimportant. In 1856 Consul Hutchinson reported that 'from all the Rivers, Ivory, Ebony, and Redwood are brought home in nearly every ship'. The centre for the ivory trade was the Cameroons where 'from six to ten tons are annually exported'; a small trade in ivory was also carried on at Old Calabar and Campo, and 'from Benito, Redwood, India-Rubber, Wax, Ivory and Ebony' were exported.[4] But the main object of every white merchant remained the trade in oil.

The palm oil exported from Africa was paid for in manufactured goods. In the thirties the average value of British exports to West Africa stood at £234,000 but rose to £492,000 in the forties—the main increase was in cotton goods which rose from £75,000 to

[1] Hutchinson, *Impressions of West Africa*, pp. 252–3.
[2] F.O.2/45: Confidential, F.P., Burton to Russell, 15 Apr. 1864, Private, Printed for the F.O.
[3] Memorandum on British Trade with Africa, Parl. Pap. 1842, XI, Appendix and Index, No. 7, pp. 574–84.
[4] General Report on the Trade of Biafra, quoted by W. N. M. Geary, op. cit., p. 83.

£261,000 while the sale of spirits declined from 209,000 gallons to 132,000.[1] The commodities of the import trade varied of course from year to year depending largely on the current demands of the African market—a market that was notorious for its fickleness. The Delta trade was done largely with Liverpool Houses, who accounted for over 12,000 tons of oil valued at £400,000 exported annually from Africa.[2] Of this quantity about nine-tenths came from the oil rivers. The Liverpool trade with the Delta employed between 12,000 to 15,000 tons of shipping annually; in 1840 the 'List of Bonny Trading Ships' totalled 13,170 tons, employing 736 Englishmen.[3]

The English manufactured goods were exchanged for Delta oil through a system of barter trade known locally as 'trust', a peculiar form of credit. Goods were trusted to the Delta middlemen by the British merchants for periods of from six months to a year or, in some rare cases, to two years during which time the African recipients were required to trade them for interior produce and pay back their European customers the equivalent in oil, ivory, timber, &c. This system was not new to the African for it was certainly prevalent during the slave trade. It was another strut in the framework of Delta commerce which was carried over from the old trade to the new. John Adams who wrote when the oil trade was still in its infancy noted: 'The natives of Bonny are expert traders and obtain from masters of [palm oil] vessels very extensive credits, who grant them this indulgence, in order to bind them to their interests, and the great secret of the trade, both here and at Old Calabar, where credit is even more extensively given, is to discriminate properly in whom you place confidence.'[4] Throughout the period under survey this system prevailed.

Commander H. J. Matson declared in 1848 that the £500,000 or £600,000 of manufactured goods which went out from Britain had to be trusted to the natives before the oil which eventually reached England could be bought. In some of the Delta ports individual traders received from between £3,000 and £5,000 worth of credits.[5] In 1851 Consul Beecroft reported that in Old Calabar 'the amount of property entrusted to them [the Calabar middlemen] for carrying on trade with the interior is startlingly enormous to those unacquainted with the system. At this time there must have been at least £70,000

---

[1] Stilliard, ch. iii, pp. 31–35.   [2] Ibid.
[3] Parl. Pap. 1842, XII, see Appendix.
[4] Adams, op. cit., pp. 112–14.   [5] Stilliard, ch. vii.

in their actual possession, besides £130,000 more in their power', that is, vested in property on shore.[1] Four years later another consul declared that British goods given on trust to Bonny traders were over £80,000 and that the value of property in the river including shipping and shore establishments amounted to £800,000.[2] These figures might have been a little exaggerated yet they clearly indicate the growing British property in the Delta and bore out Hotham's forthright statement during the Bonny disturbances in 1848 that 'the trade of Africa is founded on credit' and that to understand the right and wrong in the credit system amounted to probing the whole structure of African commerce.

The credit system was a West African phenomenon. The practice varied in some important details from one trading area to another. In the Gold Coast where there existed infinite gradations of middlemen, the goods given on credit to African agents and entrepreneurs were in comparison with the position in the Delta never large. Besides, whereas in the Gold Coast the white traders themselves either took goods in the interior for sale or else employed agents to do it for them,[3] in the Delta the middleman was his own master and capitalist and never permitted intercourse between Europeans and producers. This practice obtained down to the seventies. Consul Livingstone writing to the Foreign Office on this issue stated in 1872: 'The black brokers [Delta middlemen] are strict protectionists, and allow no trade with white or black except what passes through their hands, at their own price; and each tribe on the river or coast, does the same with its next inland neighbour.'[4]

Even in the Delta itself credit was given, as a rule, only to the great merchant princes, heads of the old established Houses, or to young traders recommended by them and for whom they stood as guarantors. In its early stages and before abuses and corruption crept in, the system worked well and depended solely on mutual confidence for its operation and success. Responsible chiefs did not fail to warn European merchants against giving credit to the unprincipled among their countrymen, 'and when they see a captain too liberal in lending or giving, advise him to be more circumspect, or, to speak in one of their metaphors, to keep his hand shut'.[5]

---

[1] F.O.84/858, No. 70, Beecroft to Palmerston, 27 Oct. 1851.
[2] F.O.84/975, No. 80, Bonny, Lynslager to Skene, 12 Sept. 1855.
[3] G. Cruickshank, *Eighteen Years on the Gold Coast* (London, 1853), ii. 31–34.
[4] Stilliard, ch. vii.   [5] Adams, op. cit., p. 112.

In its origins trade by barter was of course necessitated by the lack
of a universally accepted currency. The credit system closely associated with it can be traced partly to the fact that the manufactured
goods used in the barter trade—particularly the cotton goods—
incessantly altered with the changing fashions of West Africa. Since
these barter goods served the role of capital, the Delta middlemen—
capitalists of the oil trade—were forced to depend on their white
customers. The changeability of the West African market meant that
the middlemen could not accumulate trade goods which though in
vogue in one season may be outmoded in another. Besides during
the pioneering stages (1807–30) the opening up of new markets at
first provided infinite scope for capital investment in the interior,
but with the development of the available oil resources the demand
for capital and therefore for credit was correspondingly curtailed.
The effect of this on the working of the credit system will be discussed
in due course.

Every Delta community had its mode of fixing prices on barter
goods. In Brass, New Calabar, and Bonny the standard medium of
exchange was the 'bar', every manufactured article being valued at
so many bars. A bar was worth approximately 5s.,[1] and a piece of
cloth, regardless of its quality or cost in England, was generally
valued in the Delta at 5 bars. Similarly, a gun, a puncheon of rum,
or half a barrel of gunpowder, would be priced at so many bars.
The 'bar' was not a circulating currency but merely an accepted
standard for valuing trade goods and had its equivalent in the other
rivers.

At Old Calabar the standard mode of reckoning was the 'copper-
bar'. Its value fluctuated from $4\frac{1}{2}d$. to 1s. In the Cameroons the
'crew', worth about 20s. sterling, took the place of the bar and
the copper-bar. Their values fluctuated from time to time and the
figures quoted are approximate for the 1850's.[2] The type of goods
in demand at any given time also varied from river to river as the
following tables A and B, compiled by Adams at the beginning of
the nineteenth century, will illustrate.[3]

[1] Adams, op. cit., p. 111.
[2] Cf. Hutchinson, General Report on the Bight of Biafra; quoted from Geary,
op. cit., pp. 80–84.
[3] Op. cit., pp. 97–119.

TABLE A

Merchandise suitable for barter for palm oil and ivory at Bonny

Names of the various goods	Remarks	Cost price in England	Value in Africa
		£ s. d.	Bars
Bafts, blue	India, best	18 0	4½
Chelloes	India, small pattern	16 0	4½
Bejutapauts	India, deep red	18 0	4½
Neganipauts	India	17 0	4½
Photaes	India	10 0	3½
Niccanees	Manchester	15 0	3½
Cushtaes	Manchester	10 0	3½
Romals, Bonny blue	India	10 0	3
Romals, tape	India	10 0	3
Romals, common	Manchester	18 0	3
Bandannoes	India, yellow	1 10 0	4½
Pullicats	India	1 5 0	4½
Chintz, English, large pattern, blues best		12 0	4½
Iron bars, 160 bars to the ton		2 0	1
Guns, soldiers' muskets, best		15 0	4
Guns, French and Spanish		10 0	4
Gunpowder, 70 kegs to the barrel		3 3 0	1½
Neptunes		1 5 0	3
Manilloes, 40 to a bar		5 0	1
Copper rods (in boxes)		..	4½
Ox horns, rough		..	1

He added that beads (China, black points, birds' eye, barley corn, and guinea-guinea), flints, hardware (assorted in razors, scissors, knives, &c.), brandy (English, in puncheons), hats, and worsted caps were also in great demand at Bonny.[1]

At Calabar, in addition to goods in Table B, the following goods were also in demand: flints, hardware (assorted in scissors, knives, razors, locks, &c.), earthenware (assorted in mugs, jugs, basins, &c., mugs with covers always sold well), stone jars, brandy, rum (Leeward Islands in puncheons). Salt, an important article of trade, sold in tubs of 36 lb. for 4 coppers.[2] These two tables illustrate very clearly how the manufactured goods used for barter were first reduced to the local currency before they were used for the purchase of oil.

There were two items in the barter trade that remained constant: alcohol and guns. Both in the days of the slave trade and throughout the nineteenth century rum was one of the most important items of

---

[1] Adams, op. cit., p. 111.   [2] Ibid., p. 113.

trade on the coast. In the eighteenth century distilleries were established at Liverpool for the express purpose of supplying ships bound for Africa.[1] In 1770 New England exports of rum to Africa represented over four-fifths of the total colonial exports of that year.[2] It was profitable to the slave-traders to spread a taste for cheap liquor on the coast, not only because it provided a means of giving little for the men but also because it was a convenient form of currency; a bottle of rum was much easier to transport than a bag of salt.

TABLE B

Merchandise suitable for barter at Old Calabar

Names of goods	Remarks	Cost price in England			Value in Africa
		£	s.	d.	Coppers
Photaes	India, in great estimation		18	0	30
Allijars	India, in great estimation and of good colour		10	0	24
Sastra cundies	India, in great estimation and of good colour		12	0	. 24
Carry darries	India, in great estimation and of good colour		12	0	24
Romals, tom coffee	Always in demand, best				
Asshantee	Always in demand, best				
Bonny blue	Always in demand, red borders, best				
Broad tape	Always in demand, red borders, best		10	0	24
Quaducker	Always in demand, red borders, best				
Danes, red	Glasgow, best		10	0	24
Bafts, blue	India		18	8	24
Lungees	India	1	5	0	24
Pullicats	India	1	5	0	24
Chintz	English, large pattern		18	0	24
Gunpowder	Barrel	3	3	0	300
Guns	Soldiers' muskets in great demand		15	0	40
Guns	Common		11	0	
Beads			2	6	30
Iron bars	160 to ton		2	0	
Lead and copper rods	A box				

Another unchanging item in the barter trade was the musket introduced into West Africa in the sixteenth century. The English

[1] Donnan, op. cit., ii. 529.
[2] E. R. Johnson and others, *History of Domestic & Foreign Commerce of the U.S.* (Washington, D.C., 1915), i. 118.

guns came mainly from Birmingham and the 'Black Country'. The growth of Birmingham is to some extent closely linked with the rise of the African trade in guns, cheap trinkets, mirrors, toys, pots and pans, and other metal goods. The best guns originally came from Denmark, hence the trade name 'Dane gun'. European rivals, however, soon copied the Danish model and flooded the market with guns. The impact of this new weapon on West African society must have been great: the importance of the musket is preserved for us in the Benin bronzes of the sixteenth century in which the trading European and his gun are closely associated. In the Delta and Dahomey its advent dates the overwhelming military superiority of coastal tribes over the hinterland people. But for this the few thousands in the Delta could not have maintained their privileged position in the Atlantic trade and played the role of economic dictators to the millions in the hinterland. Even as late as 1864 when Delta society was comparatively peaceful, Burton reported that in the case of a fight at Bonny each House would be able to raise 2,500 musketeers and that the city-state possessed 'abundance of ammunition, ships swivels and carronades and when hostilities break out they will be equally bloody to the natives, and injurious, if not dangerous, to the Europeans'.[1]

Trade was not limited to the barter and credit systems. A measure of direct trading obtained through the use of cowrie shells and manillas as circulating mediums. The manilla was made of copper and was worth about threepence. The cowrie was a currency widely used throughout West Africa and was introduced from the coast of India, it would appear, early in the nineteenth century.[2] Its value in the Delta and the hinterland fluctuated greatly but the following table compiled by Burton in the sixties will serve to illustrate the nature of the currency:

40 cowries = 1 string = $\frac{1}{4}d$. to 1d.
5 strings   = 1 bunch   = 3d. to 6d.
10 bunches = 1 head   = 1s. $9\frac{1}{2}d$. to 2s.
10 heads   = 1 bag   = 18s. or 4 dollars.[3]

Cowrie shells and manillas being cumbersome, their use was almost entirely confined to petty trading in the tribal areas and in domestic transactions between Africans.

One currency, however, gained wide circulation in the dealings

[1] F.O.2/45: Confidential, Printed for the F.O., Burton to F.O., 8 Aug. 1864, pp. 8–12.   [2] McPhee, op. cit., p. 234.   [3] Burton, op. cit., pp. 40–45.

between Africans and Europeans—Spanish doubloons and dollars.
The dollars were first imported by slave-traders from the Americas,
Spain, and Portugal. They soon became very popular with the
middlemen and were the one form of European currency with which
African traders were thoroughly conversant. As an illustration, the
subsidies paid to the Delta states by Britain were reckoned in dollars.
During the British occupation of Fernando Po that settlement
depended for its food supplies on the Delta states. In April 1828
Owen bought 80 bullocks from Old Calabar at a cost of 18 dollars
each.[1] In November 1830 Beecroft purchased for the settlement 35
oxen, 5 casks of salt provisions, 5,200 yams, and 20 goats; in
December of the same year he bought another 194 oxen at 20 dollars
each, 78 sheep at 3 dollars each, a total of £891. 7s. 4d. and all were
paid for in dollars.[2] Most of the dollars in this transaction were
issued by the Sierra Leone Government and were worth 4s. each.[3]
Their use began to fall off with the diminution in the slave trade.[4]
Even so direct trading and the use of circulating currency were
never important features of Delta trade; trade by barter and its
attendant credit system largely prevailed, although increasing resistance to that mode of trade was to come from the African side.
Because this resistance was bitter and prolonged and was at the roots
of Afro-European conflicts throughout the nineteenth century, its
origin must be traced.

From its inception the Liverpool pioneers sought to monopolize
the trade in palm oil and thereby eliminate competition. It is noteworthy that during the Napoleonic and Revolutionary wars, when the
British Government decided to convoy merchant ships trading to
Africa, a Liverpool merchant, George Case, wrote to the secretary
of the African Company in September 1814 to express the objections
of European merchants in the Delta, particularly those at Old Calabar,
who pleaded that it would increase competition in the trade. The

[1] C.O.82/1, Fernando Po, Owen to Hay, 28 Apr. 1828.
[2] C.O.82/4, Fernando Po, Beecroft to Nicolls, 17 Nov. and 11 Dec. 1830.
[3] C.O.82/1, No. 6, Owen to Hay, 28 Apr. 1829.
[4] R. Chalmers, *History of Currency in the British Colonies* (London, 1893).
'The remedial legislation of 1838 for the West Indies was extended to the West
Coast of Africa by two Orders-in-Council of 10th June 1843 . . . the second
Order-in-Council laid down the following rates for the current circulation of
foreign coins with sterling:—Doubloon of Spain, Mexico, or the States of South
America £3. 4s. 0d. Twenty franc piece 15s. 10d. Dollar of Spain, etc. 4s. 2d. 5
franc piece, 3s. 10½d.'

supply of palm oil, he claimed, was limited and the institution of a convoy would mean that many more ships might enter the scene of their operations.[1] As Case had anticipated, the concentration of competition tended to drive up the price of oil. From 1822 to 1826 the average price per ton was about £12, falling as low as £5 in the less-frequented rivers.[2] In the middle of the century it had risen to £19.[3] To keep the Delta trade to themselves the old supercargoes resorted to all sorts of devices. Of these the most successful was their clever manipulation of the credit system.

'Trust' introduced an element of monopoly in the transactions. Once the pioneer oil merchants had given goods on trust to the principal oil brokers in their respective trading ports and by the peculiar operation of the system managed to keep the middlemen perpetually in their debt, every new white trader was, in effect, an interloper since he could not freely 'open trade' with Delta middlemen already indebted to his compatriots. In the Cameroons river every British supercargo had his African customers whom he kept in his debt from year to year by means of trust and, their economic interests being closely knit, they supported each other 'in all palavers' in the river.[4]

In practice this meant that Africans were no longer free to trade with all comers. But new white traders could not sanction an arrangement which virtually excluded them from a profitable trade. Such an intolerable situation was bound to end in conflict and even in the thirties the attempt to break the monopoly of the old hands had begun. To gain a footing in the trade the new men had to tempt Africans with better terms and this encouraged the latter to evade debts owing to their old customers and trade with the 'interlopers'. The receiving of 'double trust', as the practice came to be designated, became a common feature of the trade, particularly at Bonny. To counter the threat to their monopoly the old supercargoes replied by 'chopping oil', an expression meaning the forcible seizure by established merchants of oil intended for the vessels of the newcomers. This practice naturally led to violence. In the many fights that ensued the Delta middlemen invariably allied themselves with the white interlopers to save their oil from being 'chopped'. In March 1837 Lieutenant Huntley described 'oil chopping', which he defined as 'the

---

[1] Parl. Pap. 1850, IX (53), QQ. 3077–80, quoted in Stilliard, f. 25.
[2] Adams, op. cit., p. 111. Cf. Owen, op. cit., pp. 343–61.
[3] F.O.2/45: Confidential, Burton to Russell 8 Aug. 1864.　　　[4] Ibid.

indiscriminate seizure of oil, that may be in canoes coming off because some native of Bonny is indebted to the ship so seizing the oil. The result is first, a conflict between the boats of the ship seizing, and the ship for which the oil was embarked (this indeed I witnessed only yesterday). Secondly a stop is put to the trade by the Native Powers, because a canoe with oil has been forcibly carried by an English boat, to an unintended destination; and thirdly a general suspicion of the English character, is engrafted upon the Native.'[1]

The reference to the stoppage of trade by the 'Native Powers' is important. In the Delta there was no method by which individual members of the white community could be tried for crimes committed against the African states or their subjects. The native authorities therefore instituted collective punishment as a means of obtaining reparation in cases of gross injustice. The usual practice was to cease trade with the British, a measure the white traders dreaded to a man, knowing from experience that Africans obeyed promptly any order 'to stop trade' issued by their Government. The intolerable delay this entailed was sufficient to force the white community to put pressure on the offender to redress his wrong. Usually the effect would be to restore instantly the 'chopped' oil to the rightful owner. To regularize proceedings of this sort and prevent the imposition of collective punishment by the Africans, a species of international court (the Court of Equity) was instituted at Bonny in the middle of the century, as we shall see.

In the nineteenth century cut-throat competition was the common feature of European trade with the Niger Delta. When competition became acute, however, European traders combined to keep prices down. This tendency—intense competition alternating with attempts at combination—persisted until the foundation of Sir Taubman Goldie's gigantic monopoly, the National African Company in 1879. Invariably European combinations were defeated by the Delta middlemen's consistency and unanimity in withholding their produce when threatened with a price agreement. Hence the combines only succeeded when the consuls, in the name of the British Government, forced their terms on the African community. It was a regular complaint of the consuls that whereas unanimity was easily achieved by the African merchants, British traders never trusted each other. Down to the seventies this tendency persisted. In April 1870 Consul Livingstone informed Lord Granville that the British traders in the

[1] F.O.2/1, No. 1, Encl. 3, Huntley to Craigie, 27 Mar. 1837.

Benin river combined 'to lower the price of oil'. At the end of three months' struggle in which both sides refused to yield, one of the British merchants 'saved the blacks, by opening trade at the old high price, which of course compelled others to do the same. Native traders are united, and almost always win. The whites cannot trust one another, and lose; and some begin to doubt whether these whites are the superior race.'[1] Two factors worked consistently against the success of European combinations in the Delta: in the first place the white 'interloper' was ever present to undercut the combines. Secondly, while the foreign trader dreaded a long sojourn on the coast with its dangers to health and capital, the African merchant could survive without the aid of European imports—most of them luxuries—and he had in consequence far less need to barter his produce for European manufactures.

The generation of Africans who had grown up with the new trade in oil was coming of age thirty years after the Abolition Act of 1807. With the development of trade, new men and new ideas were making powerful inroads into the Delta abstentionism of the slave-trade days. Against these new forces the old at first held its own but inevitably, and particularly on the material plane, increasing contact with the world outside was beginning to make some impression on the younger generation. With the Niger expeditions came emancipated and educated Africans from Sierra Leone and the West Indies (men such as Simon Jonas, an Ibo ex-slave and Christian)[2] who expounded to the eager ears of youth the ways of the western world. The missionaries followed in the wake of the expeditions and in the forties the Baptist Mission was founded at Fernando Po and the Scottish Presbyterian Mission under Hope Waddell at Old Calabar. Their schools came to be powerful instruments of change in the Delta. Old Calabar, the city-state from which the export slave trade first disappeared, took the initiative in founding schools after the western pattern. Even before the establishment of the missions, she had become to the invading Europeans the centre of the new civilization in the Bight of Biafra. Writing between 1786 and 1800 Adams observed that at Old Calabar 'the natives write English, an art first acquired by some traders' sons, who had visited England, and which they had had the sagacity to retain up to the present period. They

[1] F.O.84/1326, No. 37, Livingstone to Granville.
[2] Allen and Thomson, op. cit., i. 221.

have established schools and schoolmasters, for the purpose of instructing in this art the youths belonging to families of consequence.'[1] The oil trade was making for changes not only on the economic and political planes but also in the sphere of knowledge and culture.

One of the effects of this growing contact with the outside world was the rapid change in the type of consumer goods demanded in exchange for the valuable oil. Formerly white supercargoes had managed to convince Africans that articles of clothing, such as old soldiers' jackets and cocked hats bought at little cost at Monmouth Street, were a fair exchange for their raw materials. 'One of our skippers trading down the Coast told me he got rid of a quantity of inferior silks, by assuring the native merchants that the Queen of England and all the great people never wore anything else.'[2] It was natural that in their isolated world the middlemen should depend on the white merchants for their notion of what was precious and respectable amidst the endless flow of novelties that descended on them from the treasure houses of Europe. The supercargoes of course exploited this ignorance for their own ends and reaped handsome profits in return. 'I have seen it written by a hand which sets down the truth in all things that supercargoes then could make their £6,000 a year in commission and yearly fortunes besides for the far-off owners of the time, and in a few years set up as merchants in their turn. A hundred pounds laid out in beads and coloured cloth brought thousands in the value of the oil, and no wonder that they called them the golden days of prosperity.'[3]

But times were changing and Delta opposition to the credit system and the cheap goods associated with it grew in strength. King Pepple's treaty with Britain in 1838 was designed to abolish it and to institute direct trading, but Admiral Elliot backed the white traders and successfully resisted its ratification on the plea that the supercargoes favoured the system. In 1839 the same gentleman warned the home Government, after the slave-trade treaty with Bonny, that they should be circumspect in sending out the first year's subsidy (2,000 dollars) because he feared that if goods worth that amount were sent, Africans might discover the real value of the articles in England and as 'the

[1] Adams, op. cit., pp. 40–43.

[2] T. Kehoe, *Some Considerations in Favour of Forming a Settlement at the Conference of the Niger and Tchadda* (Watford, 1847), p. 13.

[3] Hastings, op. cit., pp. 217–18.

price usually put on English goods in Bonny is very high' this discovery 'might create great difficulties with the traders'.[1] This supports
the persistent African contention that they were grossly overcharged
and shows that many had good grounds for their refusal to pay
'debts' they attributed to the exorbitant prices put on barter goods.

In the early stages of the conflict the Navy supported the supercargoes against the middlemen and the 'interlopers'. In 1841 Captain
Tucker proposed to blockade the Bonny river, not to keep out the
slavers but to prevent fresh palm-oil vessels from entering until
the 'debts' owed by Africans to the old traders had been paid.[2]
Opposition to the continuance of the system was reflected in the
attack on British life and property in 1848. It coloured every aspect
of Anglo-African relations. After the treaty of 1841 Pepple asked that
the 10,000 dollars annual subsidy agreed upon be paid to him in
dollars, obviously afraid that he might be defrauded if goods were
sent in lieu of cash.[3] It was usual to pay these subsidies in goods, as
when the Cameroons, after its conclusion of the slave-trade treaty of
1841, received the first year's subsidy comprising 60 muskets, 100
pieces of cloth, 1 scarlet coat with epaulets, 2 barrels of powder,
2 puncheons of rum, and 1 sword as the equivalent of 2,000 dollars.[4]

African discontent was widespread, and apart from the question
of overcharging they were beginning to reject the types of goods
previously foisted on them. The supercargoes complained that New
Calabar prohibited the giving of trust in her territory: 'The chiefs',
they protested, 'arbitrarily name the goods they want for barter and
if any ships have not got these, it cannot trade.'[5] In 1842 King Eyo
Honesty of Creek Town, Old Calabar, in agreeing to accept the
slave-trade subsidies for that year in goods warned Raymond that he
wanted 'proper India romorle . . . I no want fool things',[6] alluding to
the ridiculous articles of clothing which the supercargoes had formerly
passed off on them as the attire of the nobility in Europe. In 1856,
when Liverpool monopoly was on the wane, John Tobin—head of
Messrs. Tobin and Horsfall, the biggest importers of palm oil in the
United Kingdom—admitted before a parliamentary committee that
'Formerly, it was the custom of white men to fancy that anything

[1] F.O.84/340, No. 142, Simon's Bay, Elliot to Ward, 5 Nov. 1839.
[2] F.O.84/384, vol. ii, No. 18, H.M.S. *Iris*, Tucker to O'Farral, 23 July 1841.
[3] F.O.97/432, Treaties Concluded with Native Chiefs 1818–66, Encl. 3.
[4] Ibid.
[5] F.O.84/816, Bonny, Supercargoes to Beecroft, 1 Oct. 1850.
[6] Johnson, op. cit., p. 261. See letter from King Eyo to Raymond, 1 Dec. 1842.

was good enough for a black man, and they attempted to impose upon them. (Now) they are as well able to distinguish between genuine articles and fictitious as any person in this country.'[1] It is a matter for reflection that little of permanent value came to West Africa from the 400 years of trade with Europe. In return for the superior labour force, the palm oil, ivory, timber, gold, and other commodities which fed and buttressed the rising industrialism, they received the worst type of trade gin and meretricious articles. When the Old Calabar chiefs demanded capital equipment for sugar manufacture and cotton culture, we have it on Owen's authority that the West India interest successfully resisted these 'legitimate aspirations'.

In 1852 a new factor emerged to aggravate a situation already highly charged. The British Government advertised for a firm to carry mails to West Africa, and largely through the efforts of a single individual, MacGregor Laird, the African Steamship Company (precursor of Elder Dempster Lines) was founded to undertake the contract.[2] The steamers of this company which carried passengers and goods as well as mails were three in number—the *Armenian*, *Athenian*, and *Ethiope*, 600 tons each—and were the first steamers to run a regular service from Europe to the west coast. The company received a government subsidy at the rate of '£2,500 per sailing, with a contract speed of only 8 knots per hour'.[3] Great success attended this venture. The tonnage of mail steamers which stood at 1,800 tons in 1852 rose to 124,262 in 1853, whilst the sister company had a further tonnage of 43,000 tons.[4]

The regular appearance of these steamships had an electric effect on West African trade. It led directly to the influx of new small traders who, availing themselves of the cheap freights provided by the steamers, set up on their own in rivalry with the old monopolists. Before 1852 the tendency throughout West Africa was for big firms to monopolize the trade of each region, as did the firms of Messrs. Forster and Smith, Messrs. Swanzy, and Messrs. T. Hutton in the Gold Coast, and Messrs. Tobin and Horsfall and a half-dozen others

[1] Parl. Pap. 1865, V (412), Report of Select Committee on West Africa. Evidence of Mr. Tobin, QQ. 5356–7.
[2] Parl. Pap. 1852, XLIX (284), Correspondence Relating to the Conveyance of H.M. Mails to West Coast of Africa.
[3] Parl. Pap. 1857, XVL, Hutchinson's Report on Bight of Biafra Trade. Cf. J. Pinnock, *Benin: The Surrounding Country, Inhabitants, Customs, Trade* (Liverpool, 1897), pp. 12–14.   [4] Ibid.

in the Delta. Writing to Lord Stanley on the state of the Delta trade in the sixties, Consul Livingstone pointed out that the Liverpool merchants' large capital in ships and goods had given them a monopoly of the trade and enormous profits, but that the mail steamers had broken their hold. 'Business was formerly conducted on the principle of large profits and slow returns', but the small traders worked on the principle of moderate profits and quick returns. 'Shrewd African chiefs like those of Bonny, will soon begin to ship oil themselves by steamer direct to Liverpool.' In that way they would get '50% more for their oil and yet be able to sell it in Liverpool 50% cheaper than it is now sold'.[1]

According to a former director of the African Steamship Company the number of firms in the West African trade increased from 'very few' to 'upwards of 200' in 1856.[2] In 1869 a second steamship company appeared and further lowered the freight, thus leading to an influx of small firms and unlimited competition. Since this occurred at a time of general trade expansion the newcomers tended to swamp the monopolistic firms and the result was a savage trade war lasting till the eighties. It was in the Delta, the centre of West African trade, that this competition was seen at its worst. To fight the threat to their monopoly Liverpool merchants on more than one occasion approached Laird, the chief owner of the mail steamers, and offered to charter regularly all the vessels on their homeward voyages in the hope of preventing the small traders, Africans and Europeans, from shipping oil. He turned down their offers 'because he considered it good policy to encourage the natives'.[3]

Laird himself was responsible for this revolution in the trade. Ever since his 1832 expedition he had come round to the view that West Africa could never be saved by 'European agency' alone. The African must be made an active partner in the work of development, Christianity, and civilization. This view he expressed throughout the forties and fifties in the many papers he submitted to parliamentary select committees, in contemporary journals, and in public speeches, notably the one he delivered before the Anti-Slavery Convention in

[1] F.O.2/7, F.P., Livingstone to Stanley, 1 Oct. 1866, Report on Trade of the Bight of Biafra.
[2] C.O./96/40, No. 4530, C. W. Gregory to C.O., 19 May 1856; quoted by F. Wolfson, 'British Relations with the Gold Coast, 19th Century' (unpublished thesis in the University of London). Also McPhee, op. cit., pp. 71–73.
[3] F.O.84/1001, 183, Memorandum on Hutchinson's No. 76, F.O., 20 Aug. 1856.

1843.[1] He held that there were two types of Africans with whom the European must co-operate. The tribal inhabitants, men who though ignorant were not 'degraded' like the Delta middlemen, formed the first group. The other, and from Laird's point of view the more important, were Negroes from the West Indies and from Sierra Leone, men who would act as intermediaries between their 'benighted brethren' and the new Europeans (as opposed to the 'degraded' white men of the coast) in their attempt to develop and civilize Africa.

This belief in the regeneration of Africa through African agency was central to Laird's thinking. History, he repeatedly affirmed, had shown 'that the Employment of European agency in the improvement' of West Africa, 'can be but subsidiary and the main reliance must be placed on African blood'. The 'importation of improved African blood' became to him the *sine qua non* in the development of inland trade and the elimination of Delta ascendancy. 'The power of the Tribes in the Delta to impede the navigation of the Stream [the Niger] is owing to their command of arms and ammunition procured from the Coast. This superiority will speedily cease with the opening of trade above them, and the introduction of free Africans who in Sierra Leone and the West Indies have been in contact with a superior race and have acquired European habits and wants.' He argued that before the exploitation of the West African hinterland could be rendered profitable, these men must be introduced to act as retail dealers in British goods, collectors of produce, and purveyors of 'civilization'.[2] This belief in the superiority of their acquired culture and religion divorced the returned African from the indigenous peoples, and although they became the pioneers of education and other beneficent movements of the nineteenth century, few were leaders of tribal thought, which they despised and misunderstood.

When the African Steamship Company was founded Laird encouraged and assisted the emigration of Africans from Sierra Leone to the Delta and its hinterland. The African middlemen and the white coast-traders were the enemies of inland trade and so of African civilization; both must go and in attacking them Laird never faltered. In 1853 a mission led by the Rev. E. Jones, an American Negro and Principal of

[1] Johnson, op. cit., pp. 238–63.
[2] F.O.2/23, 1856 and 1857, Baikie's Second Expedition up the Niger, Laird to Hammond, F.O., 4 Dec. 1856. See also Laird to Secretary of Admiralty, 12 Feb. 1856.

Fourah Bay Institution, was dispatched from Sierra Leone to the Niger Delta to advise on ways and means of effecting the projected emigration of 100 liberated Ibos, who had 'long pondered' over the efforts made in resettling the Yorubas at Abeokuta, and pleaded to be sent back to their own country in the hope that they might introduce Christianity to their people.[1] This request was made with the knowledge that Laird and the Church Missionary Society had offered to aid those who were desirous of returning to the land of their birth. At Bonny the reception of the party was cold and the middlemen viewed the scheme with hostility. King Eyo Honesty of Old Calabar, however, welcomed the idea and was prepared to receive them. 'Let them come', Eyo declared, 'I will be glad to see them and give them land. I will look on them as white men because they have learnt white men fashion. Let them come and teach my people. Nobody will trouble them.'[2] The avid desire of the nineteenth-century Efiks for Europeanization was demonstrated once again. The Presbyterian Church of Scotland operating among them since 1846 lent its support to the scheme and was instrumental in housing the first emigrants. Thus was introduced into the Delta the 'educated African' of the nineteenth century. Once the first emigrants were successfully planted others followed in their wake and almost every mail boat added to their number.

It was natural that the coast monopolists, European as well as African, should view these schemes with intense hostility. It was the Liverpool supercargoes, however, who were directly affected and the Delta middlemen sided with the interlopers to break the stranglehold which the credit system had imposed on their freedom of trade. At Old Calabar, where the new men were most numerous, a violent struggle developed. The African interlopers were accused of encouraging the chiefs to ship their oil direct to England. Accordingly the supercargoes singled them out for attack.

When Consul Lynslager arrived in 1855 to investigate the complaints, he found that the middlemen in alliance with the Sierra Leone immigrants were shipping their oil direct to England before they had paid the 'trusts' owing to the old traders.[3] The supercargoes claimed that by this practice King Eyo and his subjects were detaining the

[1] *Church Missionary Intelligencer* (London, 1853), iv. 253–8.
[2] Ibid.
[3] F.O.84/975, Journal of Proceedings in Old Calabar, Lynslager to F.O., Oct. 1855.

British vessels. The Consul decided that 'the natives of Creek Town [King Eyo's Town] were inclined to be insolent' and that a show of force would bring them to their senses. He determined to dispel their belief that their position high up the river through a narrow creek kept them safe from the guns of the warship, and accordingly H.M.S. *Minx* was safely negotiated[1] to the town.

In the meeting which followed Lynslager pointed out to King Eyo that he was 'defrauding' the 'supercargoes and English merchants who had so long been his friends, in sending oil to England and transacting business with perfect strangers'[2] (the interlopers). The king replied that he had been trying to meet the needs of both parties. He defended the right of the newcomers to trade because like the old merchants, they had given 'trusts' to him, and 'had also paid Duke Town and himself comey [customs dues] the same as the vessels'. In other words, having conformed to the trade laws of the country, they were as free to trade as the other merchants. The king maintained that the non-payment of some of the trust was due not to the presence of the Sierra Leone men but to 'a very dry season for oil, in consequence of which he had not been in a position to liquidate his debts'. He complained 'that the white men bothered him too much, that he had no peace from them day or night from their repeated calls on him for oil'.[3] The Consul was not convinced by the king's plea, and warned him that he had no right to ship oil to England till his debts and those of his subjects were paid and that 'he as King ought to protect the white men, who paid him comey for that protection'.[4]

In the same year Lynslager destroyed Old Town, Old Calabar, by naval bombardment. This town maintained a missionary settlement and had little trade. According to his own accounts Lynslager destroyed the town to punish the inhabitants for indulging in human sacrifice. The white missionaries who knew the facts of the case stated that it was a veiled measure, designed to intimidate the natives. Protests were raised in Parliament and in the English press at the time.[5]

In 1856, while admitting that the average produce of the Old Calabar river had never 'exceeded 4,500 tons' a year, the super-

[1] F.O. 84/975, Journal of Proceedings in Old Calabar, Lynslager to F.O., 8 Oct. 1855.
[2] Ibid.   [3] Ibid.   [4] Ibid.
[5] F.O.84/975, F.P. Ag., Lynslager to Clarendon, 31 Oct. 1855, and its enclosures.

cargoes gave out trust to the value of 9,030 tons of palm oil in the following order:—

Ships	Palm oil on trust
	tons
Calabar . . .	1,000
Thornhill . . .	750
Abeona	1,000
Clan George . . .	900
Lady Head . . .	1,000
Parramatta . . .	1,200
Africa	1,300
Petrel	130
Eendragi (Dutch) . .	1,000
Hantz	750
TOTAL	9,030

Their spokesman, in a letter to the British Consul, claimed that 'the produce of this river is now purchased by us for 2½ years in advance'.[1] Meanwhile more Sierra Leone men had arrived and settled at Duke Town near the missionary location. As soon as their trading operations began, the Europeans levelled all sorts of accusations against them and often attacked them bodily. On 1 November 1855 sixteen puncheons of palm oil bought by a Sierra Leone man, Peter Nicoll, were seized by an English trader, Captain Cuthbertson, on the beach at Old Calabar where it had been placed to await the arrival of the mail packet, *Candace*. Cuthbertson alleged that the oil belonged to King Eyo, who was indebted to him in trust.[2] The Consul reported, 'Cuthbertson in my presence threatened to break Nicoll's head, if he again came trading to Old Calabar'.[3] In 1856 Captain Davies, a Liverpool supercargo, seized the oil of Daniel Hedd, a Sierra Leone man, and refused to release the oil on the grounds that Old Calabar being a 'trust river', all oil produced there belonged to the English ships.[4] Seizures such as these occurred frequently.

In their attack on Sierra Leone men, the supercargoes stopped at nothing. They incited Duke Ephraim, the African ruler of Duke Town, to expel the interlopers from his territories, saying 'that if they

[1] F.O.84/1001, No. 126, Encl. 4, Davies to Hutchinson, Old Calabar, 17 June 1856.
[2] F.O.84/1001, Minutes in F.O., Clarendon to Hutchinson, 15 Jan. 1856.
[3] F.O.84/1001, No. 23, F.P., Hutchinson to Clarendon, 12 Mar. 1856.
[4] F.O.84/1001, Encl. 4 in No. 126, Davies to Hutchinson, 13 Oct. 1856.

did not do so, these will eventually expel the chiefs and take possession of their country'.[1] This propaganda campaign was not without
effect. Ephraim issued a proclamation forbidding his subjects to have
any dealings either with the missionaries or the Africans from Sierra
Leone. It was the intervention of King Eyo that saved the situation.[2]
The supercargoes nearly succeeded in making Old Calabar untenable
for the immigrants. In 1856 the Foreign Office received a 'Memorial
from nine liberated Africans' resettled at Duke Town which stated
that they lived in 'fear of being persecuted by the Native Chiefs at the
Instigation of certain British Traders' who resented their intrusion
in the oil markets. Lord Clarendon affirmed that the Government
would continue 'to take a warm interest in the Welfare and Safety'
of liberated Africans. He instructed the Consul to make it clear to
the native chiefs that the Government would not 'tolerate the persecution with which these persons appear to be threatened'.[3]

The white merchants, having considerably weakened the opposition
from the small traders, directed their attacks against the native people
of Calabar. Quite often, in order to recover trusts owing to them,
some of the white traders visited the middlemen's homes and attacked
them if they refused to pay their debts. In 1856 Duke Ephraim wrote
to the new Consul, Mr. T. J. Hutchinson: 'I beg you to do something
to stop white men from going into the House of Calabar men and
knocking them. You white men have fashion to bind men to keep
the peace, so I beg you to do this, and no let palaver come up again.'[4]
The incident which gave rise to this letter may serve to illustrate the
rude justice characteristic of the gunboat politics of the time. Cuthbertson was reported to have attacked a lame African, Henshaw, 'in
his own house and struck him both with his fist and his stick', on
four different occasions, and for no other reason than that Henshaw
had publicly expressed his disapproval of Cuthbertson's act in maintaining as his mistress a woman belonging to the Henshaw House.[5]
'One great aggravation of Captain Cuthbertson's conduct in the eyes
of the Calabarese is that Henshaw is not in his debt, "does not owe
him a flint".'

Calabar young men therefore felt that this was the limit, and out
of sympathy for the injuries suffered by their kinsman attacked

[1] F.O.84/1001, Encl. 2, Old Calabar, Anderson to Hutchinson, 17 June 1856.
[2] F.O.84/1001, No. 71, F.P., Hutchinson to Clarendon, 24 June 1856.
[3] F.O.84/1001, S.T., No. 29, F.O., Clarendon to Hutchinson, 19 Oct. 1856.
[4] F.O.84/1001, No. 115, Encl. 8, Duke Ephraim to Hutchinson, 15 Sept. 1856.
[5] F.O.84/1001, No. 115, Encl. 6, Missionaries to Hutchinson 27 Aug. 1856.

Cuthbertson and 'inflicted several smart blows on his person'. Instantly, as was the custom when Africans tried to defend themselves against attacks from the supercargoes, and in spite of the offer of the Calabar chiefs to settle the affair with the European traders, the latter 'prefer sending for you [the Consul] and a man-of-war'.[1] Although there was no doubt about Cuthbertson's culpability, the Consul fined him four puncheons of oil, while on his victim, Henshaw, a penalty of twenty puncheons of palm oil was imposed, with the provision that his Egbo titles should be taken from him. Justifying the proceedings in his report to the Foreign Office the Consul declared: 'I would not have made this latter so seemingly severe, had it not been deposed before me' that the young Africans who attacked Cuthbertson 'have threatened to murder white men, if they went to their houses demanding payment of debts. I deem it my duty to use every precaution to prevent loss to British merchants.' The missionaries, who were disliked both by the merchants and the Consul, did not fail to point out that 'from what we know of the state of matters generally' Europeans believed they had 'a licence to perpetrate any outrage they choose on the natives of Old Calabar' and at the same time 'prevent the natives taking any action whatsoever, even in self-defence'.[2]

Whereas the Liverpool monopolists held that all oil produced in that river for $2\frac{1}{2}$ years virtually belonged to them, the Foreign Office disputed their claims and condemned their trade practices as unjust. In a memorandum prepared on this issue the Foreign Office recognized that the established commercial Houses would deprecate any encouragement given to the native trader lest it diminish their own trade, though 'the community at large will benefit by the Opposition'.[3] Lord Clarendon was convinced that the African small trader must be given a chance, yet the question of aiding the native on the African coast was, of necessity, a matter of discretion on the part of the Consul.

The questions as to how these complaints of the Native Traders should be dealt with is one of some importance, for while on the one hand the Consuls have not the power to interfere effectually to restrain the supercargoes from arbitrary and illegal acts against the Native Traders, on the other hand it is submitted that both on commercial grounds and also with the view to the extinction of the slave trade, it would be good policy to

[1] Ibid.
[2] F.O.84/1001, No. 115, F.P., Hutchinson to Clarendon, 23 Sept. 1856.
[3] F.O.84/1001, No. 183, Memorandum on Hutchinson's No. 76, 20 Aug. 1856.

encourage as much as possible the independent class of traders just spring-
ing into existence, for in proportion as the Natives get interested in the
Palm Oil Trade, so they will become enemies to the Slave Trade.[1]

Although in theory the Consul had no 'magisterial powers' over
British subjects or the subjects of the Delta kings, in practice his
power over the latter was, in all essentials affecting Anglo-African
relations, complete. The Consul gave the impression in his dispatches
of striving to carry out his instructions in a very difficult situation,
while secretly aiding the monopolists against the best intentions of
the home Government. But the Foreign Office, as we shall see, was
not unaware of the direction in which his sympathies lay.

The African groups, on the other hand, having seen that they could
get much more for their oil by shipping it direct, used every means of
eluding the monopolists. In explaining the motive behind the Africans'
resistance to the payment of trusts, the Board of Trade cited the
following facts:

The prices at which European articles are pressed upon them in the first
instance are unnecessarily exorbitant. It is not to be wondered that the
native debtor, aware of the disadvantageous terms on which he had originally contracted his engagement, on returning to the coast, and bringing
with him the articles collected during his long circuit in the interior,
should hesitate to deliver them to the creditor, and should yield to the bait
of better terms offered by a rival European agent.[2]

In order to prevent severe disruption of trade the Government
decided to examine the system of trust and monopoly. The opportunity for this investigation came in 1857, four years after the
inauguration of the mail packets, and was provoked by what might
be called the 'Olinda incident', the biggest effort ever made by the
African community to break the Liverpool monopoly. The struggle
had come to a head. King Eyo and others not only shipped oil direct
to England in the mail packets, but on this occasion chartered a
whole vessel, the brig Olinda. According to the Consul the trust then
owed by King Eyo amounted to 400 tons, worth £18,000. Hutchinson
had informed the king that he 'could not permit him to load a ship
which he confessed to me to have been sent out according to his own
Order before he had paid his debts to the supercargoes. I could not
allow him trifling in this way, with British Capital'.[3]

[1] Hutchinson, Ten Years Wandering among the Ethiopians (London, 1861), pp.
189–95.   [2] Ibid.
[3] F.O.84/1030, No. 23, F.P., Hutchinson to Clarendon, 29 Apr. 1857.

Although the Consul implied in his report that no pressure was brought to bear on King Eyo, the owner of the *Olinda* gave a different impression. According to him Hutchinson had 'summoned the said King Eyo Honesty on board Her Majesty's Ship *Firefly* and by threats and intimidation compelled him to sign an undertaking not to ship oil in the *Olinda* until his debts were paid'. He declared that the Consul could hardly be considered an impartial judge of such matters since he had been informed that Hearn and Cuthbertson, 'the merchants on whose behalf Consul Hutchinson interfered, were formerly his [Hutchinson's] employers'.[1] Later it was revealed that the Consul received bribes and had a vested interest in the trade. Hope Waddell wrote in a book published in Hutchinson's lifetime, that Hutchinson 'had formerly been a surgeon in the River, and had not inspired all who knew him with a conviction of his super-eminent abilities for such a sphere of duty, we were prepared to receive him as an old acquaintance, without expecting too much from him'.[2] What is important, however, in connexion with the *Olinda* incident, is that the disparity between the views of the Consul and the Foreign Office was made unmistakable. On reading the dispatch dealing with the incident Clarendon wrote: 'Upon what ground does the Consul interfere at all? The Merchants know the risks they run by the credit system and would it not be better to let the supercargoes settle their own matter with the natives at all events until we enable the Consul to interfere with legal authority.' To this Stanley, the Under-Secretary, replied: 'I apprehend his argument would be "pro bono publico" for he certainly is invested with no powers to this extent, in other words—a very imperfectly qualified individual, connected apparently with the trade, exercises an authority exceeding any we know of in the Queen's Dominions.' The issue was so complicated that the Foreign Office transferred it to the Board of Trade for solution.

A lengthy memorandum was submitted to the Secretary of the Board by the Foreign Office, in which the general situation at Old Calabar was outlined. In a separate letter Lord Clarendon expressed the opinion 'that measures should be taken to place the important trade which is now established between this Country and the West Coast of Africa, on a more secure and satisfactory footing, but his Lordship doubts whether any representation made to the principal

[1] B.T.2208: General Department No. 1794 (Encl.), Schwerzensky to Clarendon, 2 Nov. 1857.   [2] Waddell, op. cit., p. 577.

firms engaged in the Palm Oil Trade would have the effect of inducing them to abandon the monopoly which they possess'.[1] The Board of Trade's main conclusions accorded with those of the Foreign Secretary,[2] yet they could not wholly condemn the action of Hutchinson. King Eyo had admitted, according to the Consul's report, that he owed trust, and as the Consul denied using any pressure other than that 'of reasoning and remonstrance', the Board decided that 'his action in that particular case may be generally approved'.[3] This decision should occasion small surprise: the Board knew little of the Consul's character, nor was its knowledge of Delta trade profound. A permanent result of the incident, however, was that it led the British Government to consider as urgent the need for investing consuls in West Africa with 'magisterial powers'. In a letter to the Liverpool Association of Merchants, the Board of Trade stated that 'measures will be taken to control the violent conduct, so frequently exhibited by supercargoes in the African rivers, that additional powers would be conferred [on the Consul] for that purpose'.[4]

The *Olinda* incident wrought no immediate change in Calabar society. The disorders continued, perhaps with less intensity in the sixties, but the improvement was gradual. The only difference was that the Government intensified its efforts to find a solution to a complicated situation and watched more closely, from 1857, the Consul's actions in favour of the supercargoes and Liverpool monopoly. In 1860 Consul T. J. Hutchinson was accused of receiving bribes from a Liverpool supercargo named Hearn and of aiding that gentleman in his disorderly and questionable dealings in the river. A Commission of Enquiry, headed by Commodore Edmonstone, reported unfavourably on the Consul, and Lord Russell, now the Foreign Secretary, warned Hutchinson that he would be dismissed unless he could vindicate his conduct.[5] Unable to do this, Hutchinson was replaced by the celebrated traveller and writer, Sir Richard Burton.

It is significant that the city-states in which these disorders were most intense were those where African polity was weakest. Thus we

---

[1] B.T. No. 1794, General Department, Minute Paper 701/57, F.O. to B.T., 5 May 1857.

[2] B.T. General Department, Minute Paper 701/57, 6 May 1857.

[3] B.T. No. 1794, General Department, Shelbourne to Clarendon, F.O., 11 Nov. 1857.

[4] Whitehall, Tennant to Secretary to the Association of Merchants, Liverpool, 28 May 1857, quoted from Hutchinson, *Ten Years Wandering*, pp. 189–95.

[5] F.O.84/1117, No. 112, Class B, F.O., Russell to Hutchinson, 4 Sept. 1860.

find that the most disturbed area was Old Calabar, with its four independent towns or, more properly, trading communities, precariously held together by the Egbo fraternity. Similarly the divided region of the Cameroons, where every river settlement had its king, witnessed disturbances which, if smaller in scale, were certainly more violent than those in Old Calabar. In their attempts to recover trust the supercargoes there murdered more Africans than anywhere else in the Delta. In 1862 one of the Cameroon chiefs, King Aqua of Aqua Town, writing to Consul Burton, complained bitterly of the manner in which British traders killed Africans for very trifling matters, and in his broken sentences conveyed an impression of disgust with the class of supercargoes that visited his river.

I beg to confess that the repeated oppression of the European on us this Bight of Biafra is heavily brewing in our mind. I shall now bring before you numbers of us that have been killed by British Trader[s] 1st Young Lindo was killed by one Mr. Hamington, 2nd Five men together was killed by one Mr. Jonathan Scott, 3rd My brother Ned Acqua was killed by one Walker, and my house was broken down by one Consul Hutchinson, 4th on the 15th April, 1862 one Captain Wm. Babington have comite the like crime is murdered one Mongar—by shooting him in the guts, and severely wounded, three other, in their own town, with his revoleing pistol and violent sword. We are led to presume, Sir, that industry, civilization, have sprung from Good England—and yet from this same country come a class of low adventurers who are trying to imped[e] the benevolent plans of their wise, and good country men.[1]

At New Calabar and Bonny, on the other hand, conditions were vastly different.

Of all the Delta states the Royal House of Amakiri, New Calabar, alone had never tolerated the credit system, and as this state was situated 16 miles away from the warships its sovereign power remained unimpaired even in the fifties. King 'Amakree is the most independent King to be met anywhere on the coast; and I believe he owes this reputation to the fact of his not taking goods on trust from any supercargo, nor allowing his people to do it, consequently maintaining his high position'.[2] New Calabar was a remarkable exception, and her prosperous state in the nineteenth and twentieth centuries[3] was undoubtedly due to rejection of the trust system and

[1] F.O.84/1176, Encl. 3 in No. 19, Cameroons, Acqua Town, King Acqua to Burton, 16 May 1862.

[2] Hutchinson, *Impressions of Western Africa*, p. 101.

[3] It is remarkable that this town which in the nineteenth century was less than a quarter of the size of Bonny is today far more important than the latter.

all its works. Even the Consul was moved to remark: 'In New Calabar the King and Chiefs walk on the deck of any ship with an air of independence, similar to that assumed by a wealthy capitalist on the Stock Exchange at home.'[1]

At Bonny, too, trade progressed in a comparatively harmonious atmosphere, but for a very different reason. After the first disturbance over trust and the anti-British measures of the forties, which followed the non-ratification of slave-trade treaties, the British merchants learned not only to act together in their own defence but to evolve a system of settling trade and other disputes between African and European merchants in a 'Court of Equity'. The usefulness of this institution, the part it played to save Bonny from bloody disorders such as characterized Old Calabar and the Cameroons, and its utility generally have been fully acknowledged by contemporaries. Of the inception of the Bonny Court, Dr. Baikie wrote:

A commercial or mercantile association was, by the exertions of Captain Witt and others, formed, the members being the chief white and black traders in the place, and the chair is occupied by the white supercargoes in monthly rotation. All disputes are brought before this Court, the merits of the opponents are determined, and with the consent of the King, fines are levied on defaulters. If any one refuses to submit to the decision of the Court, or ignores its jurisdiction, he is tabooed, and no one trades with him. The natives stand in awe of it, and readily pay their debts when threatened with it.[2]

Attempts by various consuls to initiate similar courts in the other trading rivers never proved wholly successful. 'I wish the Bonny Court of Equity to be considered the model', declared Consul Hutchinson in 1856, 'after which all institutions of its kind are formed in the Bight of Biafra.' But it was not enough for Bonny to provide a model. Men of the right kind had to be found to work it in other Delta ports. Trade rivals were slow to trust one another and men able to command the respect of the leading merchants of both races were not forthcoming. At the Cameroons, where Burton repeatedly urged upon the merchants the necessity of a Court of Equity, 'all signed the agreement but no one adhered to it'.[3] The Consul had previously protested that the merchants frequently sought his active assistance in retrieving their debts and asked the Foreign Office to

[1] Quoted from Geary, op. cit., p. 83.
[2] Baikie, op. cit., p. 356.
[3] F.O.2/45: Confidential, Burton to Russell, F.P., 8 Aug. 1864, pp. 2-3. Private, Printed for F.O.

approve his proposal to let them settle such matters themselves—
'unanimity would do more than a dozen gunboats'.[1]

So far as the Liverpool monopoly was concerned, the recall of
Consul Hutchinson was the beginning of the end. True, it remained a
powerful force till the seventies, but for a brief spell at least, the
small trader indulged his natural propensity to 'traffic and exchange' without fear of the monopolists supported by the Consul
and the warship.

The British Consuls to the Bights of Benin and Biafra were a mixed
lot. Some of them, such as John Beecroft, Dr. W. B. Baikie, and Sir
Harry Johnston, were zealous and clear-headed imperialists religiously dedicated to the service of Great Britain in West Africa;
others, Dr. T. J. Hutchinson for example, were drawn from the bar-
barians of the Western world. Charles Livingstone, an eccentric and
sickly man, but a brother of the great explorer, owed his appointment
almost entirely to his great name. The impediment to the recruitment
of satisfactory consuls was the evil reputation—greatly exaggerated
by generations of travellers' tales—attached to the West African
climate. When Captain R. F. (later Sir Richard) Burton was appointed Counsul to the Bight of Biafra his dread of the West African
climate was expressed in his statement against the Foreign Office
officials who posted him to this part of the world: 'They want me to
die, but I intend to live, just to spite the devils'.[2]

[1] F.O.84/1176, Cameroons Mountains, Burton to Russell, 14 Jan. 1862.
[2] Burns, op. cit., p. 152, footnote 1, quoted from T. Wright, *The Life of Sir
Richard Burton*, p. 176.

CHAPTER VII

The Rise of Consular Power

JOHN BEECROFT'S contribution to the growth of British power in Nigeria rests mainly on two achievements. Until his appointment as Consul in 1849 British intervention in Nigerian politics was desultory. With the sole exception of 1837, when she interfered to restore to King Pepple the power he had lost to the regent—an action made imperative by the threat to British life and property in that quarter—Britain abstained totally from the domestic politics of the African states.

Beecroft reversed this policy. Twenty years' experience of Delta life had taught him that European occupation of West Africa could not long be delayed, and from the date of his assumption of office his activities were guided by that awareness. In him Palmerston found an enthusiastic ally who launched a forward movement marked by bold intervention in the internal politics of the city-states. The period of his consulship, 1849–54, saw the end of non-interference and the inauguration of empire building in Nigeria.

Secondly, long before the Partition of Africa had become a subject of practical politics in European capitals, Beecroft, in his peculiar way, had succeeded in making British rule familiar to the native states under his consular jurisdiction. Not unnaturally he encountered long and bitter opposition. But in time Africans came to look on the British Consul as the *de facto* Governor of the Bights of Benin and Biafra. This position of power which Beecroft won for himself passed on to his successors and enabled Britain to enjoy the authority of a protecting power before the Berlin West African Conference had legalized that status in international diplomacy. Beecroft therefore initiated the politics which were to characterize the consular period of Nigerian history.

In 1850, despite Lord Palmerston's calls on him to attend to business in other parts of West Africa, the Consul visited all the states within his jurisdiction, from Lagos in the west to Bimbia in the Cameroons. In each state he read aloud his commission to demonstrate to the native powers that he was the accredited representative of Great Britain and 'to acquaint them by whose authority' he interfered in their affairs. He went further. Recognizing that the African chiefs stood in great dread of the warship, he invariably visited them in such a vessel and introduced the practice of settling the lengthy 'palavers' on the spacious decks of the men-of-war instead, as of old, in the courts of the native potentates. In September 1851, when the supercargoes at Old Calabar petitioned him to settle the dispute between 'the Omun and Acoona-Coona people' which was holding up trade, Beecroft reprimanded them for not bringing up the matter during his last visit, when he had an armed force at his command comprising H.M. ships *Jackal*, *Archer*, and *Bloodhound*. 'Without sufficient force at hand to compel a settlement of the dispute I fear we can obtain no satisfactory result.'[1]

The smaller states soon recognized consular authority and tried to work with it. Particularly was this the case with Old Calabar. Beecroft was always at home there and not without reason. Calabar and the Cameroons were consistently pro-British from about 1815, and led the way in the introduction of legitimate commerce, Christianity, and education—according to Beecroft 'the greater part of the adults here can read and write'[2]—and its rulers from the 'Great Duke Ephraim' to Eyamba, Eyo Honesty, and King Archibong were personal friends of the Consul. Consequently the chiefs needed little persuasion to accept the new order. When King Archibong died in 1852 Beecroft presided over the election of the new king and his right to do so was never questioned. He in turn reciprocated the confidence of the chiefs and allowed them to install a man of their choosing. The event ended in great rejoicing with the Consul inviting the new king and 'his principals' to dinner on board a warship. They drank Her Majesty Queen Victoria's health and that of King Duke Ephraim, after which the latter and his suite 'retired into their canoes'.[3]

From Calabar he repaired to the Cameroons and there deposed 'the present King Aqua' and placed 'Prince Jim to reign in his stead'. The deposition of the king, whom the Consul described as 'a drunken imbecile, a liar and a great rogue', was justified on the grounds that it was for the good 'of the people of Acqua town, and the great and grand object was the welfare of Legitimate Trade'.[4] The truth was that he would tolerate no chief who took an independent line or showed signs of an anti-British attitude in trade or

---

[1] F.O.84/816, No. 66 and its enclosures, Beecroft to Palmerston, 9 Oct. 1851.
[2] F.O.84/886, Beecroft to Malmesbury, 30 June 1852.
[3] Ibid.   [4] Ibid.

politics. It became the conscious policy of the Consul to remove
African rulers who challenged the supremacy of Great Britain in the
Bights.

A study of John Beecroft's methods and ideas will reveal that
although he was a consummate diplomatist, he was above all a man
of the nineteenth century. That is to say, consciously or uncon-
sciously, his political activities were guided by general principles.
Nigerian kings who favoured slave abolition, embraced Christianity,
encouraged legitimate commerce, and supported missionary enterprise were good kings. Those who stood for the old abstentionist
policy and resisted encroachment, whether they dealt in slaves or not,
were to him enemies of 'progress' and 'civilization' and were singled
out for attack. This policy was sometimes cloaked by his diplomatic
manœuvres, his efforts to discredit in the eyes of the Foreign Office
African rulers who dared to defend their 'savage independence'. But
he adhered to this pattern of behaviour during his tenure of office.

Opposition to the Consul crystallized round the more powerful
and established kingdoms. His visit to Dahomey in May 1850 convinced him that nothing short of a major war could bring that kingdom into line with British policy.[1] It was therefore against the kingdom
of Lagos that he planned his first major assault on a native power.
The event occurred in 1851, but he had begun to formulate his plans
in September of the previous year when he had been unable to accede
to an urgent call from the supercargoes of Old Calabar to settle a
paralysing trade dispute as his 'presence was required in the vicinity
of Lagos on matters of weighty importance'.[2]

The oft-repeated story of the capture of Lagos in 1851 shows in
plain relief the elements of Beecroft's diplomatic finesse. As the
stratagem he adopted there was in all essentials similar to the one he
employed at the deposition of King Pepple of Bonny in 1854, an
examination of the earlier incident will shed some light on Beecroft
the politician. Knowing that Kosoko, the anti-British and slave-
trading king of Lagos, could not be persuaded to change his ways,[3]
Beecroft approached the ex-king Akitoye, an uncle of the reigning
monarch who had deposed him in 1845. Akitoye was then living in
enforced retirement at Badagry and welcomed British alliance in the
hope of regaining his throne. Beecroft proposed 'to make a treaty

[1] F.O.84/816, F.P., Beecroft to Palmerston, 4 May 1850.
[2] F.O.84/816, No. 66 and its enclosures, Beecroft to Palmerston, 29 Sept. 1851.
[3] Geary, op. cit., pp. 25–26.

with him for the suppression of the slave trade, and place him at Lagos, his former seat of Government'. This, he claimed, 'would release the people of Abeokuta [a pro-British centre of missionary work] from the jeopardy that they are continually in, and from the fear of the King of Dahomey'.[1] Beecroft's employment of the 'classic imperialist technique of replacing the usurper with a docile, and in this case, legitimate ruler'[2] met with complete success. Akitoye acquiesced in his demands and promised to 'carry on lawful trade, especially with the British merchants'.[3] With the capture of Lagos in 1851 Beecroft turned his attention to Bonny, the centre of resistance to his authority in eastern Nigeria as Lagos had been in the west.

At Bonny King Pepple appeared to be contemplating anti-British measures similar to those of the forties. The cause of his discontent was the Government's failure to honour the treaty of 1848 which was to have superseded the unhonoured slave-trade treaties of the early forties, but by a curious accident had remained unratified by the home Government. The Foreign Office officials acknowledged that the fault was entirely theirs. In a dispatch to the Consul, Palmerston asked that the regret of Her Majesty's Government be conveyed to King Pepple for the two years' delay in honouring the treaty and pleaded that it was due 'to accidental circumstances'.[4] Beecroft grudgingly admitted that he was 'only sorry that the fellow [King Pepple] has not received his presents [subsidies]', but protested that the king should not be allowed to make it an excuse for 'any mal-transactions that himself or his people may commit against British property'.[5] In spite of the Foreign Minister's apologies, the Consul was in no mood for appeasement and did not disguise his hostility to Pepple. The difference between the position in the forties and that in the fifties must be noted. At the time of the first conflict there had been no Consul to protect British interests: when Beecroft was caught in the disturbances of 1844 he had protested that it was 'highly necessary that there should be a Consul' to deal with Pepple's persecution of British traders.[6] In 1850 he was that authority himself and determined to use his power to the full.

The first letter received by the Consul after his appointment was

[1] Burns, op. cit., pp. 123–6.
[2] Lloyd, op. cit., p. 157.   [3] Ibid.
[4] F.O.84/816, Palmerston to Beecroft, 16 Aug. 1850.
[5] F.O.84/816, F.P., Beecroft to Palmerston, 13 Aug. 1850.
[6] F.O.84/549, Encl. 2 in Admiralty letter of 12 June to F.O., F.P., Beecroft to Nicolls, 2 Feb. 1844.

from Bonny supercargoes detailing their persecution at the hands of the king who 'is now doing all in his power to obstruct and annoy us in our trade—and constantly upbraiding us with the fact that several of Her Majesty's Cruisers have called and promised him a compensation for suppressing the slave trade'[1] (and yet though he had carried out his obligations, the British had failed to honour theirs). 'In the meantime all trade is suspended, and we urgently call your attention to these facts.'[2]

The king had real cause for anger. The slave-trade treaties concluded with the smaller states like Calabar and the Cameroons had been ratified and the subsidies paid. The state of New Calabar only 16 miles away was still openly dealing in slaves, believing herself to be inaccessible to warships. In 1850 the master of H.M. brig *Contest* had 'captured a schooner, with 152 slaves' from that city-state.[3] That King Amakiri could do as he pleased, yet he, the legitimate heir of Opubu the Great, should be compelled by means of unhonoured treaties to carry out the behest of naval officers, deepened Pepple's rancour. The supercargoes affirmed that 'Since a slave vessel was loaded in the Calabar this ill feeling [of Pepple against them] seems to have increased.'[4] As late as 1855, while exiled at Ascension, in explaining to Clarendon his reasons for making war on New Calabar in 1854—a war which Beecroft used as a pretext to force his removal—Pepple declared: 'New Calabar wishing to trade in slaves, and I being made acquainted with the fact instantly forbade such a direct violation of the treaty existing between myself and Her Most Gracious Majesty, Queen Victoria; and finding peaceful measures would not avail prepared to make war upon New Calabar in case she should persist in so flagrant an outrage.'[5]

When Beecroft arrived to settle the differences between the king and the supercargoes, he let it be known that he would not sanction liberties such as Pepple enjoyed during the forties in his relations with the British and immediately summoned the king and his chiefs to come on board H.M.S. *Jackal*, and hold a conference relative to the complaints made to him by the supercargoes. Pepple refused the invitation, pointing out that it was not 'customary for him to go on board vessels to settle palavers', but said he would be happy to

[1] F.O.84/816, Bonny River, Supercargoes to Beecroft, 27 June 1850.
[2] Ibid.   [3] F.O.84/816, F.P., Beecroft to Palmerston, 4 May 1850.
[4] F.O.84/816, Bonny River, Supercargoes to Beecroft, 27 June 1850.
[5] F.O.84/1161, F.P., Encl. in No. 17, Pepple to F.O., Ascension, 5 Nov. 1855.

receive the Consul and his retinue 'at his House at 3 o'clock'. After some hesitation, Beecroft went ashore to meet the king and both he and the British party were well received. At the end of the conference the Consul insisted that the king visit the man-of-war. Pepple, who thoroughly distrusted Beecroft, consented on condition that three of the leading English traders were kept as hostages with his people. This condition being met, he went on board, but as no business of any kind was transacted it was plain that the Consul's sole purpose had been to impress him with the power at his command.[1]

Alarmed though he was by this show of strength, Pepple began to perceive the significance of Beecroft's appointment: intermittent naval intervention had left him long periods in which to enjoy his sovereignty, but a consul resident at Fernando Po was an ever-present menace. Indeed, the location of the consular post on that island meant that British authority was only a day's sail from the kingdom of Bonny. Unlike the regent Alali on a similar occasion in 1837, Pepple did not resort to any warlike demonstrations, for his experience in that crisis had taught him how much could be effected through diplomatic channels. Realizing that his independence was threatened by the Consul's *de facto* power, he sought an interview with Beecroft at which he 'quietly expressed a desire to cancel the treaty [of 1848]' and revert to the *status quo* ante 1837. Beecroft indignantly rejected this and accused him of desiring to resume 'the abominable traffic of selling your fellow men, which of course he strongly denied, but it was too obvious his motive, he is a subtile rascal not to be trusted, and must not be dealt with on mild terms'.[2]

Of evidence to support the Consul's accusation there is not a shred. Perhaps it was written as propaganda against Pepple and designed for Foreign Office consumption, since Beecroft well knew that Pepple could easily carry on the slave trade by way of the Brass river without being detected. This point was even made in June 1850 by the supercargoes in a letter to Beecroft. 'Whether he [King Pepple] has or has not done so [abolished the export slave trade] is perfectly unknown to us, as there are many indirect ways of carrying on the trade, without our knowledge.'[3] Moreover, by 1850 the rapid growth of the oil trade in Bonny had virtually rendered the slave traffic obsolete, and Pepple himself had a good share in the profits brought

[1] F.O.84/816, F.P., Beecroft to Palmerston, 15 Oct. 1850.
[2] F.O.84/816, Beecroft to Palmerston, 14 Oct. 1850.
[3] F.O.84/816, Bonny River, Supercargoes to Beecroft, 27 June 1850.

by the new commodity. His strong denial, as reported by the Consul, is more likely to be nearer the truth than Beecroft's imputation. Pepple plainly discerned that by his adherence to the one-sided treaties with the Navy, the Consul, and supercargoes, he was signing away his sovereignty. The cancellation of the treaty of 1848 for which he asked was part of a bigger question: he was seeking a release from obligations to which he had never been a willing partner. The surprise is that he was so naive as to have imagined that the Consul would acquiesce in such a proposition and that Beecroft, a mere agent of the home Government, could of his own volition alter the policy of the nation. It is only fair to add that Pepple made this proposal when he was in a difficult state of mind: at a time when he was faced with the crisis of his country's independence.

The king faced a challenge to his authority from the outside in addition to the beginnings of slave insurrection at home. The party led by the ex-regent Alali, whom he antagonized by his pro-British measures in 1837, was as bitterly opposed to him as were the British, his former allies. With British support he might have been able to control his African enemies and through the ancient government of the country have maintained the peace so necessary to legitimate commerce. But his opponents tended to unite as time went on, and came to regard the monarchy he represented as their common enemy. These two forces—British power and the power of the ex-slaves— which emerged with the rise of equitable traffic, threatened the existence of the only government available. The gravity of the situation can only be grasped when the place of the monarchy in the Bonny constitution is appreciated.

William Dappa Pepple, whatever his faults as a man, occupied an all-important position in the constitution. He was a divine king who had inherited an autocratic system of rule which served his forebears well in the semi-military society of the slave-trade days. There was no evidence in 1850 that that constitution had altered one iota from its eighteenth-century form despite the far-reaching changes in the economic sphere. Religion and politics remained indivisible. The priests, who owed their high rank to the central position of the monarch in the constitution, were careful to see that by the propaganda directed from their headquarters at Ju Ju Town the religious sanctions and powerful sentiment built around the king were kept alive. The result was that Pepple, like his ancestors, became 'Ju Ju', a sacred king whose power, however despotic, no freeman—much less slave or ex-slave—could attack without, it was supposed, calling disaster on himself and the country at large. This belief in the king's divinity was for three centuries the mainstay of the Pepple dynasty; it became an essential part of that unwritten constitution and was accepted by all classes, even by those who suffered under the king's despotism.

There is ample evidence that the Consul and the supercargoes failed to appreciate the place the king occupied in the Bonny oligarchy. They did not foresee that his removal would mean the end of all government, or that at a time when Britain was unready to install her own administration, as in Lagos, the authority which Pepple exercised was indispensable to the existence of the oil trade. European contemporaries who knew little of the source of his power felt that the king had 'exaggerated notions of his own importance'. Yet viewed against the background of Bonny history, the king's attitude was not without explanation. Throughout his boyhood (he was born in 1817) he had known no other power but that of his family over the Bight of Biafra. His father Opubu till his death in 1836 was not only master of the greater part of the Delta but exercised unbounded influence over south-eastern Nigeria. Hence the young king's high notion of his office was in the tradition of the Pepples. It is necessary to appreciate that the Pepples believed themselves and their kingdom to be great and saw others in terms of their own world. They had an intense attachment to their country and its historic associations, no matter how crude these might appear to the foreigner. Waddell narrated how during his visit to King Pepple in 1846 'I asked him about a very rude image of a man in a squatting posture, made of clay, that stood in his yard. He said it was a statue the same as we had in England, and seemed to value it less for its beauty than for its antiquity. "Old people made it long ago," he said, "and it do no harm".'[1]

Any estimate of the reaction to conquest of the House of Pepple in the nineteenth century without reference to its past is bound to do injustice to its character, and leave unexplained many acts of the king. The city-state of Bonny was a creation of the Pepples. It originated with the Atlantic trade and attained the zenith of its power in the hey-day of the traffic in men. Bonny became, in Adams's words, 'the wholesale market' for slaves on the West African coast.

[1] Waddell, op. cit., p. 272.

The despotism of the Pepples was tolerated because it brought the country wealth, power, and glory abroad.[1] From Perekule to Opubu, its kings were soldier-statesmen who won universal respect by their sheer ability and efficiency in government. Dappa Pepple appears to have inherited the despotic elements of his ancestors without their greatness of heart and ability to utilize the talents within the kingdom. He chose his chief advisers from weak and docile men, like Yanibo and Ishacco, men who dared not question his authority since they owed everything to him. The ex-regent and his experienced advisers Pepple contemptuously ignored, and he tried to rule without the active co-operation of the great majority of the most able and industrious elements in the population.

Pepple was, in fact, in his home policy a little man, dangerously ignorant of the bitterness he stirred in the hearts of the emancipated classes by his constant refusal to recognize their new status. Blinded by his overweening pride as heir to the Pepples, he carried his personal rule to extremes regardless of the consequences. The strong sentiment for the monarchy and his own courage sustained him for over a decade, but the opposition against him was growing daily, and even at a time when his power over his people seemed complete, shrewd observers could sense the coming storm. In 1846 an eyewitness commented: 'He [Pepple] regarded the people of Bonny and its "colonies", as he called outlying villages, as all his slaves, himself alone as really free. He carried his ideas on that subject too far, however . . . when the Chiefs rebelled against him.'[2]

The ill-fated rule of Dappa Pepple was partly a tragedy of character, and partly one of circumstance in home and external relations. At a time when the city-state was faced with the issue of its independence, the nation was irrevocably split between the party of the king and that of Alali. The ex-regent had never forgiven Pepple for engineering his public humiliation in 1837 and naturally exploited any event which would weaken the position of the king or discredit the monarchy whose magic hold on the people he fully recognized.

During his years of opposition to Pepple, Alali had by skilful organization advanced his House to the foremost position in the land. In the process he absorbed a great number of the smaller Houses. According to Bonny sources, King Pepple watched him closely and enacted laws which made it illegal for any House to surrender its independence to another. In all matters of trade and local

---

[1] See Appendix B.   [2] Waddell, op. cit., p. 273.

affairs the Houses were to function as separate units. So formidable was the structure which Alali had built up that the king dared not demand the restoration of the freedom of the Houses he had already absorbed. Such a demand would have led to a declaration of war. This internal conflict had a direct bearing on the state's external relations and the events leading up to Pepple's exile in 1854.[1]

In February 1853 Palmerston curtailed Beecroft's consular jurisdiction and 'limited it to the Territories within the Bight of Biafra, lying between Cape Formosa, and Cape St. John'. Thus his sphere of duty was restricted to the Niger Delta. Palmerston explained that the Government had made the change 'not because they undervalue in any degree your capacity and services, but because this arrangement has been necessary in consequence of the altered state of affairs in Lagos'.[2] Mr. Campbell was appointed to the recently conquered island of Lagos and Beecroft, relieved of duty in that area, was able to devote his energies to the affairs of the Delta.

'In the latter end of May 1852, King Pepple was attacked with paralysis, since which time he had remained in almost imbecile state, and quite unable to conduct the business of the country.'[3] This sudden illness of the king precipitated the crisis of the next two years and brought the whole internal conflict to a head. Filled with hatred and contempt for the party of the ex-regent, he completely ignored that powerful section of the kingdom and appointed two of his favourites, Yanibo and Ishacco, 'to administer the Government in his name as Regents'.[4] Alali's party 'took umbrage at the choice, and did not obey the mandate given in the name of the King. This was the bone of contention.'[5]

Pepple's tactics on this occasion were characteristic. Realizing that the appointment of Yanibo and Ishacco as regents during his illness would be unpopular with the opposition, he sought to associate the British community with his decision and so 'requested the masters and supercargoes of the various vessels to call a meeting of his Chiefs

[1] The struggle between King William Dappa Pepple and the ex-regent, Alali, is very well known in Bonny history as also in the history of Opobo, the city-state founded by Jaja in 1870, when the party of Alali had to leave Bonny and found the new community and named it after the great Opubu himself.
[2] F.O.2/9, Palmerston to Beecroft, 19 Feb. 1853.
[3] F.O.84/920, Encl. 3 in No. 62, Bonny River, Supercargoes to Beecroft, 31 Aug. 1852.
[4] F.O.84/920, F.P., No. 3, Beecroft to Palmerston, 4 Feb. 1853.
[5] Ibid.

to appoint two competent persons as Regents', and, particularly 'at his own request', Yanibo and Ishacco were chosen.[1] That the king should have associated the supercargoes in the settlement of this purely internal affair angered the ex-regent and his followers, but Pepple's strategy in his hour of trouble can be explained. It was an opportunist move which he had no intention of repeating after the trouble was over. His plan was simple. If, as was likely, Alali and his party rejected his nominees, they would then not only be defying the king's authority but also the new authority of the Consul and super-cargoes. It worked out just as the diplomat had hoped. The opposing party boycotted the meeting and writing to the Consul the super-cargoes declared: 'We, in conjunction with King Pepple, convened a meeting of the Chiefs to take such measures as would be thought advisable in the present confused state of affairs, when the authority of the King and ourselves was set at defiance by the parties refusing to attend, although they had twenty-four hours notice.'[2] The Consul added his authority to that of the supercargoes, and 'intimated to the Chiefs Assembled, that it was their bounden duty to attend to the wishes of the two Regents as they would now be properly appointed, during the King's pleasure, or as long as he continues indisposed'.[3]

The opposition persisted in its refusal to recognize the regents and argued that the British community had no right to decide an internal affair of Bonny. Tempers ran high because Pepple, who opposed British interference on other occasions, always called on them when it suited him to do so. This was in line with his tactics in 1837. The man was nearly without principles. In the critical period of Bonny history, the weakest spot in Pepple's character was his unreliability. For this reason neither side trusted him. But the king's apparent success was short-lived. The problem was too deep-seated to be solved by an adroit diplomatic manœuvre, however brilliantly executed. And Pepple knew it. Beecroft reported that at a meeting in the king's House at which the opposing faction met him on the question of the appointment of the regents, he received 'a note from King Pepple requesting me to excuse him not appearing at a public conference. He did not wish to be present at a meeting of his Chiefs, not being able to speak as he wished.'[4]

[1] F.O.84/920, F.P., No. 3, Beecroft to Palmerston, 4 Feb. 1853.
[2] F.O.84/920, Encl. No. 3 in No. 62, Bonny River, Supercargoes to Beecroft, 31 Aug. 1852.
[3] F.O.84/920, F.P., No. 3, Beecroft to Palmerston, 4 Feb. 1853.
[4] Ibid.

The regency did not, however, last very long. At the end of November 1853 Pepple was able to take control of affairs. His recovery was followed by a dramatic turn of events, culminating in his deposition the next year. In his measures to lessen what he considered the abnormal influence of the ex-slaves in trade and politics, the king indirectly injured the interests of the British supercargoes. He not only initiated laws prohibiting the continued amalgamation of Houses and advanced other domestic measures designed to split and weaken the new classes, but he carried these tactics to the sphere of trade. In 1852 it was decreed that no Bonny merchant would be permitted to trade in the interior markets unless they took trusts from Pepple. The law hit the supercargoes. They complained to the Consul about the 'injury done to trading interests here by the King compelling individuals to take trust from him at exorbitant and ruinous prices before they can be allowed to trade at any market in the interior and knowing the said parties have trust from the ships, in all probability of older date than his own'.[1]

Indirectly the king's policy of attacking the active commercial classes in the kingdom was an assault on the European interests since the latter depended on them for their trade commodity. The African traders pointed out that in Pepple's attempt to control hinterland trade, 'he had sent goods to all the markets at such prices as we are totally unfit to compete with and seriously injuring the whole trade of the country. On several occasions when representations have been made to him about the high prices his boys [traders] have been paying at the fair [markets], the parties complaining have been imprisoned by him and mulcted in heavy fines.' They stated that the king 'has frequently expressed his determination to suppress and ruin every House in the country in order that he might have sole and uncontrolled power'.[2] Thus Pepple's repressive domestic measures antagonized the African and European traders to the point of conflict.

His tactics were to exploit his people's anti-foreign sentiment, but to defer to it when it suited his purpose. An astute and shrewd politician and a master in the art of prevarication, he did not scruple to use the foreigner against his opponents at home as the occasion demanded. Yet the supercargoes protested that he used 'insolent and

[1] F.O.84/920, Encl. 4 in No. 62, Bonny River, Supercargoes to Beecroft, 31 Aug. 1852.
[2] F.O.84/950, Encls. 1 and 11 in No. 57, Bonny River, Chiefs to Beecroft, 17 and 31 Dec. 1853.

uncourteous language' when talking to them and that they were sometimes attacked by his chiefs. 'On the 14th October, 1853 three gigs were chased by an armed war-canoe, one Master struck at most violently by a native and the whole party only enabled to escape a severe assault by the speed of the boats.'[1] They reported 'repeated attacks' on their employees at their trading establishments on shore, 'their implements stolen and themselves beaten by parties who cannot be detected—but whom we believe to be instigated by Jew-Jew Peterside', the new High Priest and successor to Awanta. Meetings called by the supercargoes 'for the better regulation of trade'[2] were boycotted by the chiefs. The British community believed these attacks and the attitude of non-co-operation to have been secretly engineered by Pepple.

The king was therefore distrusted by the white merchants as he was by the new classes, but for very different reasons. Alali and his party saw no hope of political emancipation so long as Pepple enforced despotic and unenlightened laws. The British shunned him because at a time when the Consul was looking for docile puppets to toe his line of policy, Pepple by nature, habit, and conviction was ill-suited for such a role. No one knew what side he would support from year to year in the constantly disturbed political chessboard of Bonny. When the king perceived that he could no longer play the supercargoes against the new classes or vice versa he sought a new outlet in which to canalize the growing discontent within the kingdom. To this end he planned his *coup de main*.

In November 1853, soon after he recovered from the attack of paralysis, King Pepple ordered his chiefs to mobilize and 'equip all our war canoes to the number of forty-three' on the pretext that he was going to pay a state visit to the birthplace of his mother.[3] There was nothing unusual in this since it was the custom for anyone delivered from death or serious illness to return thanks to the spirit of his ancestors and carry out sacrifices according to the directions of the priests. In the case of a king it was usually a great occasion. While preparations for this journey were being made, Pepple sent a strange letter to the supercargoes, strange because anyone acquainted with the traditional feud existing between King Pepple and King

---

[1] F.O.84/920, Encl. 4 in No. 62, Bonny River, Supercargoes to Beecroft, 31 Aug. 1852.   [2] Ibid.
[3] F.O.84/950, Encls. 1 and 2 in No. 57, Chiefs of Bonny to Beecroft, Nov. 1854.

Amakiri of New Calabar would hardly believe that that letter was as innocent as it seemed:

King's House, Bonny, November 9th, 1853.

Gentlemen:

I am anxious to pay a visit to Billa Country—and I shall feel much obliged if two or more Captains or Supercargoes will go with me in their boats as far as Calabar River, to invite King Amachree on board my canoe as I wish to see him and make him a small present.

This is a perfectly friendly invitation on my part, and if Amachree will not accept of it I beg that one Captain will remain at King Amachree's as a guarantee that he may come back safe—I intend to leave Bonny in 4 days time. The Billa is the native country of my Mother.

(Signed) Pepple.[1]

What he thought of doing had Amakiri entered his canoe, we shall never know. It is clear that he had instructed his trusted commanders about the nature of the operations, but the vast majority of his chiefs and warriors, although equipped for war, were told their destination was the Billa country. There is small doubt, however, that his opponents, who knew their king, had their own suspicions. The European merchants surmised that his intention was to make war on New Calabar which would entail 'stoppage of trade' with all its consequences. They therefore wrote to Beecroft asking for protection and pointed out that when they tried to reason with Pepple not to go to war he 'treated our advice with the greatest contempt and proceeded to equip his canoes'.[2]

'Upon arriving there' (New Calabar), he ordered his fleet of war-canoes to blockade the river channel separating that city-state from the trading quarter occupied by the foreign merchants and their shipping. More than half of his war-canoes refused to carry out his orders and returned to Bonny in protest. As the chiefs said in their letter to the Consul, 'we refused to proceed, seeing too that we had no cause for going to war. On our return to Bonny the whole voice of the country called for his removal, and we accordingly declared him no longer King'.[3] This last sentence must be read with discrimination. It was written by the supercargoes for the party led by the ex-regent, Alali, and though signed by the latter and his supporters, not a single chief of the king's party signed the document. The supercargoes

---

[1] F.O.84/950, Encl. 3 in No. 57, Pepple to Supercargoes, Bonny, 9 Nov. 1853.

[2] F.O.2/9, Bonny River, Supercargoes to Beecroft, 15 Dec. 1853.

[3] F.O.84/950, Encls. 1 and 2 in No. 57, Chiefs to Beecroft, Nov. 1854.

embodied their own wishes in the letter and gave it the appearance of being the pronouncements of all the Bonny chiefs. The dispatches dealing with Pepple's overthrow were the work of the white merchants who had by this time openly allied themselves with the ex-regent against his king and exploited the chiefs' legitimate grievances in furthering their own purpose of removing a strong and inveterate foe from the control of their trade.

It was in line with Pepple's diplomacy to seek external outlets for internal grievances; unfortunately on this occasion the trick did not succeed and rather than help his cause its failure brought the city-state to its greatest crisis. But the ex-regent and his followers knew their limitations; there were customary, constitutional, and religious restraints which made it impossible for ex-slaves to call 'for his [Pepple's] removal' and declare 'him no longer king'. There is ample evidence that in 1854 these restraints had lost none of their validity at Bonny. Missionary teaching at Old Calabar, which tended to undermine these restraints by spreading the Christian and Western ideas of God and of individual freedom, did not penetrate Bonny until the late sixties. It is necessary, in using the consular reports on the issue of Pepple's exile and deposition, to recognize the different voices recorded in the documents: to differentiate between the voice of the chiefs and those of the supercargoes and the Consul.

The view still widely held is that Pepple was deposed and exiled at the request of his chiefs and the white merchants, and that he followed Beecroft to Fernando Po to escape with his life.[1] The truth is that his chiefs were opposed to his exile and deposition, and that in their eyes those two steps, which were really instigated by the Consul and supercargoes acting through the Court of Equity, were unconstitutional from the standpoint of Bonny law. The Consular records in which Beecroft attempted to make it appear that the king was deposed by his people contain incontrovertible evidence that the chiefs were unwilling partners in the act to the very end. When Pepple was deposed by the Court of Equity, a court in which Beecroft presided, the chiefs did not fail, according to the Consul's own reports, to make their position clear. 'Shortly afterwards', wrote Beecroft, 'the whole of the Chiefs said that sooner than Pepple should be taken away, they would let him be King again . . . they also said they thought that if he was taken away the Ebo [Ibo] men would not pay either his debts [i.e. the trusts they held in the interior markets] or

[1] Burns, op. cit., p. 147. Geary, op. cit., pp. 86–87.

theirs ... that it was contrary to their Jew-Jew' to depose their king.[1] These views were unequivocal, and the last point that Pepple's removal was 'contrary to their Jew-Jew' is the key phrase. The Pepples were divine kings and any attempt by freemen, much less by ex-slaves, to tamper with their divine rights was an infringement of the fundamental laws of the country. Left to themselves, the chiefs could never have carried their hostility to the king to that extreme; there were other methods open to them for redressing their grievances. In fact, as Beecroft again explained, he had to find means of disarming their fears and quieting their consciences, and strove to make it appear that 'he was not taking him [the king] away, but allowed him to go at his own request',[2] thus placing the responsibility for the act not on the shoulders of the chiefs but on Pepple himself. As for Beecroft's assertion that the chiefs did not want the king to go because they were unwilling to be saddled with the trusts he owed to the super-cargoes, that point is easily answered by the fact that Pepple was declared immensely rich by the chiefs themselves, who said that he was able to undersell them at the interior markets through the vast wealth he accumulated by usurping all public funds for his private use.[3] Not quite a year after he was deposed, one of his trading agents alone paid the 300 puncheons of palm oil Pepple owed in trust to the supercargoes.[4]

There was no difficulty in finding a puppet to succeed Pepple. A young member of the royal family, 'Prince Dappo, the son of an elder brother than Pepple and rightful heir', was proposed, 'and on January 23rd Pepple was pronounced deposed and Prince Dappo elected King, under the title of "King Dappo"—British warships fired 21 guns in honour of Dappo (or 'of Prince Dappo'). According to Beecroft's accounts, which Pepple later disputed, on the accession of Dappo, Pepple 'claimed the protections of the Consul and begged to be removed to Fernando Po—to which the Consul consented'.[5] It is inconceivable that Pepple would have offered himself willingly to Beecroft to be taken to Fernando Po had he known that once in Fernando Po he would become a prisoner in exile. Bonny opinion that Pepple never recognized the accession of Dappo and that the Consul managed to convince him that a few days' absence from his

---

[1] F.O.84/950, Encl. 1 in No. 57, Beecroft to F.O., 20 Feb. 1854.   [2] Ibid.
[3] F.O.84/950, Encl. 2 in No. 57, Bonny Chiefs to Beecroft, Nov. 1853.
[4] F.O.84/1161, Journal of Proceedings at Bonny, Lynslager to Clarendon, 27 Jan. 1855.
[5] F.O.84/950, Encl. 1 in No. 57, Beecroft to F.O., 20 Feb. 1854.

kingdom would suffice for things to calm down so that he could then return to a peaceful and contented people, seems nearer the truth. In 1855, writing to Lord Clarendon from Ascension, Pepple declared:

Upon my embarkation from Bonny in H.M.S. 'Antelope' for Fernando Po it was rumoured that I was forced away from my dominions by the voices of my Chiefs—this is at total variance with the truth as is certified by letters (which I still have in my possession) from the late John Beecroft and other Englishmen, which distinctly states that I left against the wishes of my chiefs and people . . . who would not be pacified until assured by Mr. Beecroft that I should return among them whenever I thought proper, that I was going a free agent and not a prisoner.[1]

During Pepple's exile his case was taken up in London by Quakers 'of some standing', including Mr. Ayrton, M.P., Mr. Gurney (solicitor), and Mr. Thwaites. A memorandum issued by Mr. Ayrton and delivered to the Foreign Office on behalf of King Pepple plainly states the king's version of the events leading up to his deposition and exile. According to this account Pepple traced the origins of his disagreement with his chiefs to his alliance with Britain in 1837. By this alliance the chiefs 'lost considerable advantages' through the suppression of the slave trade. They expressed their dissatisfaction at his abolishing half comey (customs dues) 'in favour of British Traders and granting them Customs' rights'. This was, of course, only part of the story of the domestic conflict already described. In a passage which is fully corroborated by Bonny sources the king showed that his deposition was the work of Consul Beecroft and not that of his chiefs. 'Being persuaded by Mr. Beecroft that it was better to go and return in a few days the King left. When Mr. Beecroft had thus got the King away he induced the Chiefs to set up a new King who was not appointed as represented by Mr. Beecroft whilst the King remained. There can be no doubt that after the King was entrapped into placing himself in Beecroft's hands he was most wrongfully and dishonourably detained as a prisoner for a long period.'[2] The 'few days' turned out to be seven years, which Pepple spent first at Fernando Po, then at Ascension, and finally in London.

If the treaty following Pepple's deposition is examined it becomes clear that the reasons for his removal were his trading activities and the clash between his own authority and the authority of the Court of Equity in which British influence was predominant. This treaty

[1] F.O.84/1161, Ascension, Pepple to Clarendon, F.O., 5 Nov. 1855.
[2] F.O.84/1162, vol. ii, Memorandum, Ayrton to F.O., July 1857.

forbade the new king to engage in trade of any kind and his income
was to be derived from customs dues and other public revenue; the
Court of Equity replaced the king as supreme authority in all matters
relating to trade; the king could not go to war without the approval
of the British section of the community; finally, all future meetings
on matters of common interest would be held, not as formerly in the
king's House, but in the building of the Court of Equity. In short,
the treaty subordinated the authority of the king to that of the Court
of Equity.[1] The year of Pepple's exile was also the year of Beecroft's
death. There was some unity between the events. The first Consul
to the Bights of Benin and Biafra had in 1851, soon after his assumption of office, brought to an end the reign of Kosoko, king of Lagos,
and put in his place a man favourable to British interests. Shortly
before his death he had removed from his throne the greatest of the
African rulers in the Bight of Biafra.

Contemporaries have left a comprehensive picture of the exiled
king which testifies to his intelligence, arrogance, and duplicity.
Waddell, who saw him at Bonny in 1846, left this impression: 'King
Pepple was a young man, of no apparent pretensions. He received
us civilly, spoke English tolerably, and had a rather plausible expression of countenance, with occasionally a look of deep conning.' He
refused Waddell's invitation to breakfast on board 'in a blunt way'.
When told that King Eyamba of Old Calabar (at the time the most
important chief in that river) 'sometimes breakfasted with us on
board', Pepple, who thought no African king could be his equal,
exclaimed with wrath and scorn, 'Eyamba be—Whom him be?
Eyamba be boy slave.'[2]

Dr. W. B. Baikie interviewed him during his exile at Fernando Po
in 1854. He described Pepple as 'a tall, intelligent-looking person,
but with a rather cunning eye. His remarks were extremely shrewd,
and he avoided making any very strong statements. His acquaintance
with the English form of Government, and his general fund of information much surprised me; he knew the names and offices of all
the Cabinet Ministers, and often referred to Wellington and to
Napoleon. "Why", said he in his peculiar way, and pointing to a
print of Bonaparte, "why your gubberment keep me here, I no do
bad like he, I be free man, I be King".'[3] Baikie noted that 'the

[1] F.O.84/950, Encl. 3 in No. 57, Treaty with Chiefs of Bonny, Jan. 1854.
[2] Waddell, op. cit., pp. 270–4. [3] Baikie, op. cit., pp. 332–5.

Revenue derived of late by Pepple from the increased palm-oil trade, must be little short of, if it does not equal, that made in the palmiest days of the slave trade. His income from shipping dues and other sources, I have heard reckoned, on sound authority, at from £15,000 to £20,000 a year.'

On his return from exile in England, then a broken old man, he was interviewed by Winwood Reade. The meeting took place in 1863 at Pepple's house. 'There sat Pepple, who had lived so long in England. I asked him whether he liked England or Bonny best. He gave me the Irishman's answer, by asking me which of the two I preferred. I replied enthusiastically, Bonny! But he only laughed incredulously, and remarked, wisely enough, that every man liked his own country best.'[1] The reference to the look of 'cunning' in his eyes and statements elsewhere as to his lies and unreliability should be treated circumspectly. On another occasion when a Delta king was described by a British consul as 'a deliberate liar', a European merchant, Count C. N. de Cardi, commented on the word 'liar' when applied to African politicians. 'This failing', he wrote, 'is called diplomacy in civilised nations.'[2]

Pepple's exile had a West African significance, and its place in history will be missed unless it is viewed as part of a larger pattern. In 1855 Beecroft's successor at Lagos, Consul Campbell, strongly advised against Pepple's restoration: 'the impression out here is, that Pepple's removal was absolutely necessary to prevent the valuable trade of Bonny from falling into the greatest confusion and causing most serious loss to the merchants engaged in it.' The value of that trade he assessed at nearly a million pounds per annum with capital invested in shipping and merchandise worth half that figure. 'To intelligent persons on the spot it appears impolitic in the highest degree to allow the same to be jeopardised by a single individual, although he may hold the rank of King. It will be a great relief to legitimate commerce when all such old cedevant slave trading Chiefs as Pepple are removed from the stage of life.'[3] Pepple was not a slave-trading king at the time of his removal. But politically and commercially the position he held was inconvenient to the Consul and supercargoes, and throws interesting light on the relationship between political and trade frontiers, between commerce and govern-

[1] W. W. Reade, *Savage Africa* (London, 1864), pp. 57–63.
[2] Kingsley, *West African Studies*, p. 547.
[3] F.O.84/1161, No. 10, Lagos, Campbell to Clarendon, 21 July 1855.

ment. The capture of Lagos in 1851 and the exile of King Pepple in 1854 marked the end of the British policy of *laissez-faire* in modern Nigeria. This forward movement was largely dictated by the development of trade. In the Delta the logical development of the humanitarian advocacy of equitable traffic—although few realized it at the time—meant political penetration. It was to protect 'legitimate trade' and eliminate its enemy the slave traffic that Fernando Po was occupied from 1827 to 1834. The same consideration necessitated the initiation of the commercial and slave-trade treaties, all of which embodied coercive political clauses designed to protect the growing British interests in the oil rivers. The appointment of a consul in 1849 followed hard on Pepple's threat to European traders in 1848. The process of political penetration, as the success of inland trade will reveal, grew apace with commercial expansion. This is not to say that the sole motive of British penetration of Nigeria was trade. The men who led the great missionary movements of the time were undoubtedly inspired by genuine idealism. Only a cynic could read the journals of the missionaries and explorers and remain unconvinced as to the sincerity of their motives. With trade expansion, however, economic and political issues dominated the Nigerian scene, both on the coast and in the vast interior.

The downfall of King Pepple did not give the supercargoes and their Court of Equity the ascendancy they desired in Bonny affairs. Events were to prove that the Pepple monarchy and government were irreplaceable and that with their destruction went the stability and unity of the state. The king was seen to be merely a symbol of something bigger than himself, and his banishment only increased the confusion it was designed to dispel. The young puppet, King Dappo, whom events had conspired to place on the throne, was a figurehead without ability or the capacity to learn. With the removal of his rival, Alali determined to regain the position he had lost in 1837. In January 1855 Consul Lynslager reported that the ex-regent had very strong influence with the king, who, 'being a young man, was very easily led astray, and it was greatly to be feared that if he (King Dappo) continued listening, and acting to Anna Pepple's advice, there would be serious disturbance'.

The ex-regent sought not only to control the king. He was determined to eliminate the party of the exiled Pepple and, acting in the name of the weak Dappo, he arrested Yanibo, the ablest leader of the royal party. The European community, alarmed at the way he was assuming control of Bonny affairs, summoned the Consul and in a public meeting demanded that Yanibo be released. In complete defiance of the Court of Equity, Alali rejected the demand and 'rose up and left the room, the other chiefs following him. The King was the last to leave.'[1] Following this incident anti-European demonstrations reached fever-pitch. 'Captains Wylie and Cahill [supercargoes], on going into the town, shortly after, saw many people armed and on entering the market place, they were assailed by a number of women, who yelled and hooted at them and treated them with the greatest contempt—the assailants were all of Anna Pepple's party.'[2] The Consul lodged a vigorous protest and warned the ex-regent 'to alter his ways, as long as he had yet time, and not to run on, to the degree the ex-King had done, or the same fate would await him'.[3] But Alali was an impetuous character, impatient of diplomatic processes, and where the exiled king would negotiate and reason he would act regardless of the consequences.

Pepple's removal did not, therefore, fulfil the hopes which the white community had entertained of running the city-state through the Court of Equity. In September 1854, barely three months after the death of Consul Beecroft, the supercargoes complained that: 'The Royal Court of Equity, established by the late Consul, the chiefs refused to attend when summoned.'[4] 'They look upon the Court and treaties with contempt, and violate them whenever it suits their purpose so to do.'[5] Within a year all that was gained by the deposition of Pepple had been lost. The ex-regent's hostility to the king had been mainly on grounds of domestic politics. In foreign relations he personified the opposition to the British at Bonny and attacked Pepple precisely because the latter sought to appease the Consul and supercargoes.

In August 1855 news of the death of King Dappo, successor to the exiled Pepple, was announced. According to the report of Dr. Stiles, an English doctor in the river, his death was the result of an 'inflammation of the chest' incurred during his fourteen days' expedition to

---

[1] F.O.84/1161, Journal of proceedings of Consul Lynslager, Encl. 1 in No. 65, Lynslager to Clarendon, F.P., 27 Jan. 1855.
[2] Ibid.   [3] Ibid.
[4] F.O.84/1161, Encl. 3 in No. 65, Bonny River, Supercargoes to Acting Consul Lynslager, 23 Sept. 1854.
[5] F.O.84/1161, Encl. 5 in No. 65, Bonny River, Supercargoes to Captain Adams, 22 Nov. 1854.

the interior oil markets to strengthen, as was usual with the Pepples, the covenant between Bonny and the inland states. During this tour 'he was . . . exposed very much to the weather which at the time was very bad, there being several days of incessant rain'. The cause of death was therefore plainly established. During his illness everything possible had been done to save his life, but due no doubt to native suspicions, 'the medicines prescribed and remedies proposed by Dr. Stiles were unattended to'.[1]

In spite of this evidence Alali and his supporters refused to believe that his death was due to natural causes and accepted the explanation of a 'Jew-Jew man resident in the Eboe country' that the late king had been poisoned by Yanibo and Ishacco. These two men were described by the Consul as followers 'in whom the ex-King had an unlimited confidence. They were therefore likely parties to be suspected by those who wished to exterminate the ex-King's People'.[2] By eliminating them Alali hoped to secure his party's dominance. 'These two men were at once condemned as the murderers of the King, although they were at some distance from Bonny at the time of the King's death.'[3] It was evident to disinterested observers that the ex-regent and his group were using King Dappo's death as a pretext to eliminate what was left of the so-called free classes. Yanibo and Ishacco refused to give themselves up and took refuge in the ship of an English supercargo, Mr. Witt. The chiefs demanded their surrender so that they could be tried according to the laws of the land. This was refused. Alali and his party promptly accused the supercargoes of interfering in Bonny affairs and declared the trade of the whole country closed.[4] Thus it was that the victorious party of ex-slaves came to direct their attack not only on the monarchists but also on the white community. Attempts by the supercargoes to pacify the chiefs had no effect. 'All further communication with us [Europeans] was forbidden unless these two men were returned, nothing besides would pacify or appease them, and they were distinctly seen dragging guns into position to bear upon the ships, and making other demonstrations sufficiently convincing of their warlike

[1] F.O.84/975, Encl. 1 in No. 80, F.P., Journal of Proceedings, Lynslager to Clarendon, 2 Sept. 1855.

[2] F.O.84/975, F.P., Lynslager to Clarendon, 5 Oct. 1855.

[3] F.O.84/975, Encl. 1 in No. 80, F.P., Journal of Proceedings, Lynslager to Clarendon, 2 Sept. 1855.

[4] F.O.84/975, Journal of the Proceedings in Bonny and New Calabar, Lynslager to Clarendon and its enclosures, 2 Sept. 1855.

intentions.' As there was little hope of effecting a revocation of the trade-closure, the supercargoes decided that they 'must demand them [Yanibo and Ishacco] to be given up in whosoever custody they were and that we should hold that party responsible who refused to comply with our request'.[1] It was only the determination of Witt not to surrender the men that saved their lives.

Meanwhile civil war had flared up. According to the reports of the Consul, on Captain Witt's refusal to surrender the men 'the firing of musketry commenced in the Town and continued almost uninter- ruptedly for three days; several heavy explosions of Gunpowder were heard, and many houses seen on fire'.[2] There

commenced a massacre among the people belonging to or friendly to the family of the ex-King Pepple and the town was in a state of civil war. Stray shots sometimes struck the vessels lying at anchor which had been removed from the position they formerly were in to a greater distance from the Town—fearing the natives might forget themselves and endeavour to seize upon the shipping. Many loud explosions of gunpowder were heard and the last remnant of the ex-King's people who had defended themselves until the means of subsistence were totally exhausted, ignited some gunpowder and thus ended their miserable existence.[3]

Baikie reckoned that the number of the king's supporters who ended their life in 'this awful tragedy' was about 300.[4] The Bonny monarchy, with all its material assets seized or destroyed, suffered a defeat from which it was never to recover. From 1854 the ex-slave classes were the undisputed masters of the city-state. The restless king pined away in intolerable exile at Ascension, while his trusted lieutenants Yanibo and Ishacco, who owed their lives to the unexampled stand of Captain Witt against both Alali and the supercargoes, settled at Fernando Po. The Pepple monarchy perished when the trade in oil displaced the trade in men. The civil war therefore marked the end of an epoch in the history of the Niger Delta.

When the Consul Lynslager arrived in H.M.S. *Philomel* to look into the state of affairs he knew that the ex-regent and his victorious party were in no mood to be dictated to. As a matter of fact they were preparing, if need be, for a show-down with the British. They

---

[1] F.O.84/975, Bonny River, Supercargoes to Hutchinson, 6 Sept. 1855.
[2] Ibid.
[3] F.O.84/975, Journal of Proceedings . . . Lynslager to Clarendon, 2 Sept. 1855.
[4] Baikie, op. cit., p. 357.

had in their possession by way of trust £80,000 worth of British goods which, according to the Consul's report, Alali and his party stated 'would do to purchase clay and bamboo mats to rebuild their town should the British men-of-war destroy it. The natives had been for several days engaged in removing their property to a place of greater security,[1] anticipating war with the British.' Lynslager therefore proceeded cautiously. 'On consulting with Commander Skene', said the Consul, 'we considered it advisable to open negotiations with the chiefs by letter, to be carried on shore with the Flag of Truce.' A supercargo, Captain Stowe, volunteered to deliver this letter to the insurgents. Contact was made with Alali, but it was not until after two days' parley and the dispatch of a bigger mission headed by a naval officer (Boger) 'who was in full uniform, according to the request of the Chiefs', that permission for the warship 'to come up the River'[2] was granted.

The Consul and Commander Skene, accompanied by the leading British representatives, arrived at the market place which had been prepared for the meeting—the impressive brick building of the Court of Equity having been razed to the ground during the civil war.[3] 'In a short time the Chiefs assembled, and a great number of the natives standing around sullen. When all were seated and quietness obtained, I addressed them saying that I had come in a man-of-war but not for the purpose of going to war with them.' The Consul emphasized that his aim was peace and that he shared their sorrow at King Dappo's death. He outlined the efforts the British had made and were making to bar the exiled king from his kingdom and from influencing the course of events in the interior markets. Pepple, he said, 'had now gone to Ascension and would never be seen again'.[4] In short the Consul assured the victorious party that Britain would do nothing to threaten the victory they had won in internal affairs by restoring the banished king. This amounted to an unconditional acceptance of the *fait accompli*.

It was apparent to all that some sort of government was needed to fill the place left vacant by the death of King Dappo. A form of Regency Council was installed. Four regents were appointed to take charge of affairs, one from each of the leading Houses, until a new

[1] F.O.84/975, Lynslager to Clarendon, 5 Oct. 1855.
[2] F.O.84/975, Journal of Proceedings . . . Lynslager to Clarendon, 2 Sept. 1855.
[3] Baikie, op. cit., p. 356. 'The new Court-house of brick' which Baikie saw being erected in 1854 was destroyed in the civil war in 1855.
[4] F.O.84/975, Journal of Proceedings . . . Lynslager to Clarendon, 5 Oct. 1855.

form of government could be arranged. Lynslager assured the chiefs 'that I would not interfere in that election; the chiefs must elect their own Regents as no white man had any right to interfere in any of their country affairs'.[1] The Consul must have studied the situation very closely, for he conceded to the chiefs the very point which had been Alali's main opposition to the European community since 1837, and was conciliatory in all matters that would lead to a reopening of trade. It was an astute political manœuvre which instantly achieved its purpose. The chiefs were completely satisfied with these assurances and although they still demanded the surrender of Yanibo and Ishacco and complained of past injustices suffered at the hands of the Consul and supercargoes, it was plain they had been won over. Alali and his party could well afford to relent, and in the joy of victory to forget for the moment the calamity and distress which the conflict had brought on the city-state itself. After ten days' hard work the Consul reported agreement on all points and before he left 'a great many canoes with oil was afloat and the River again resumed its former busy appearance; the shipping were again dropping into their old berths'.[2]

It is significant that of the four chiefs appointed to lead the city state, three belonged to the class of ex-slaves and only one represented the freemen. Alali, the delegate of the Anna Pepple House, was their undisputed leader. But the rise of the new classes was not a pheno-menon peculiar to Bonny. Similar uprisings were experienced in almost every city-state as the oil trade replaced the trade in men. In the next chapter we shall see how the city-state fared under its new rulers, and whether the Consul's assertion that 'no white man had any right to interfere' in Bonny affairs, in face of the immense British interests involved in the trade of the Niger Delta, had any validity in practical politics.

[1] F.O.84/975, Journal of Proceedings . . . Lynslager to Clarendon, 5 Oct. 1855.
[2] Ibid.

'has been the advance of civilization in Old Calabar, that, at present, though retaining many of the old forms, they [the Egbos] have lost their old influence, and no act of oppression can be committed through its agency without notice being taken thereof. The influence of the Christian missionary fast supersedes that of the Egbo.'[1]

The first conflict between the two orders was provoked by the arrest of some members of the Blood Men at Duke Town in 1851 by Egbo law. The slaves retaliated by ravaging the plantations and invading Duke Town, threatening to destroy the town if their imprisoned members were not released. The arrested men were instantly freed. The insurgents were joined 'by many free and half-free people of Duke Town for their own ends'. All those whom the small clique of Egbo dictators oppressed joined hands with the slaves. The rebellion united many diverse elements;[2] but it was predominantly a slave revolt.

As was to be expected, British persons and property were involved. The supercargoes called a meeting 'for the purpose of taking into consideration certain alarming symptoms of revolt among the slaves'. They stated 'that a large number of slaves had renounced the authority of their owners, had plundered various plantations, and had this morning come in an armed body to the town and made demands of money from various chiefs, threatening further ravages in case of refusal. In consequence of this outbreak, our lives and property are endangered.' They summoned the Consul and the warships.[3] On this occasion, it is notable that Beecroft, who knew Old Calabar and its institutions more intimately than those of Bonny, and had no prejudice against the native rulers such as that he entertained for Pepple, took the view that whatever the grievances of the insurgents, they must seek redress along constitutional lines. He did not seek to abolish Egbo authority as he did that of Pepple. Instead, as the treaty which was concluded through his mediation between the masters and the insurgents shows, he sought to reform the existing authority rather than destroy it.

The arrival of two warships, the release of the slaves imprisoned by Egbo authority, and the influence exerted on the insurgents by men whose authority they still respected, brought about a temporary truce and they retired in order to their stronghold on the Qua river.

---

[1] F.O.84/858, No. 70, F.P., Beecroft to Palmerston, 27 Oct. 1851.
[2] Waddell, op. cit., pp. 476–9.
[3] F.O.84/858, Encl. 1 in No. 4, Supercargoes to Beecroft, 31 Jan. 1851.

The Consul, on arrival, 'desired the King to send a Messenger . . . desiring the Insurgents to send in delegates' to the peace conference he called at Duke Town, and after ten days' hard work 'we succeeded in conciliating the Insurgents, and amicably settling the Palaver'.[1]

The treaty which followed was the work of Consul Beecroft, and showed his strong support of Egbo authority.

> It is, hereby enacted and agreed to
>
> 1st That the Ancient Egbo Law of the country be strictly respected and adhered to within the jurisdiction of Duke Town.'
>
> 2nd That no armed bodies of men come into the town on any pretence whatsoever.
>
> 3rd That no slave who has a master living shall chop blood with other slaves without special permission of the said Master.
>
> 4th That in the event of any slave belonging to any person in the Town running away to the plantations he or she shall be given up when demanded.
>
> 5th That all combinations among slaves for interfering with the correction of any domestic servant by his or her master be henceforth declared illegal.
>
> 6th That the Law abolishing human sacrifices be hereby confirmed and that the said law be not so interpreted as to interfere with the action of the Criminal Law (native) of the country.[2]

On receipt of this treaty, Lord Palmerston viewed with disfavour Articles 2, 4, and 5, which he denounced as an attempt on Beecroft's part to suppress a genuine movement among the lower orders for self-emancipation. In reply the Consul stressed that he had 'no desire to aid the slave powers to subdue an attempt at self-liberation'; but argued that there must be a government, and that such a government must be protected against all forms of disorder and insurrection. 'The "Egbo" is at once the Legislature, and Police Establishment of Old Calabar. At present no government, or order, can exist in Old Calabar, without Egbo in its present form.' Beecroft claimed that it would have been fatal to British interests to have allowed the insurgents to carry out 'their threatened proceedings' and that by preventing the insurrection and yet remedying the principal grievance of the rebels he served all parties well. 'Thus I treated them, my Lord, not as slaves, nor the higher powers as slave masters, but the whole as a community, a part complaining truly of a barbarous and inhuman custom held by the more powerful division. I took advantage to do away with a law that had been a disgrace to a partially civilized place,

[1] F.O.84/858, F.P., Beecroft to Palmerston, 21 Feb. 1851.   [2] Ibid.

and all Europeans connected with the Trade. It saved the loss of an immense sum (£200,000) to English merchants, and allayed the storm in a manner which could have been done only by myself, for no one else knows so well how to deal with African character.'[1]

Beecroft's treaty stipulations did not tempt the slaves to believe in the good faith of their masters. All that was achieved by it was merely a truce. The insurgents maintained and strengthened their power of combination and used it whenever their hard-won liberties were threatened. The Consul's settlement is capable of detailed criticism not only because he failed to appreciate that the slaves could no longer be bullied into submission but because, apart from his abolition of human sacrifice (in which the slaves were directly affected), he surrendered to the masters on all points in dispute. But the principle behind Beecroft's action must be grasped. In the Delta Britain was not ready to take over the responsibilities of government. Yet the valuable trade carried on by her subjects in these parts needed peace and it would have been bad politics to remove the sole protection that trade enjoyed by destroying Egbo power. To govern at all the Consul must make the existing government the instrument of his policy. Failure to recognize this principle in the treatment of the Pepple monarchy led to serious loss of British property at Bonny.

A permanent result of the slave revolts must be noted. The British abolitionists who advocated 'a just and equitable traffic' with Africa, had their eyes fixed on the destruction of the export or Atlantic slave trade. They could do nothing to effect the abolition of domestic slavery. This study reveals that the domestic slaves won their freedom entirely by their own struggles in which their power of combination was their strongest weapon. In Old Calabar, the Cameroons, and to some extent in Bonny, the slave revolts brought full emancipation to thousands of the domestic slave hierarchy and made for great improvements, socially as well as economically, among the slave masses.

Consul Hutchinson, who took office soon after Pepple's exile and the assumption of power by the four regents at Bonny, declared:

The experience of five years has taught the British as well as the Native Traders that this government [of the regents] has been no more than a mockery and delusion, its paternal care of the country, and its protective guardianship over British life and property, being alike deceptive. The four Regents never lived in amity or unanimity; they had their little

[1] F.O.84/858, No. 70, F.P., Beecroft to Palmerston, 27 Oct. 1851.

jealousies of trade as well as their domestic social bickerings; they took the money (customs dues) but never joined in concert to expend it in obtaining peace in their immediate circle, or in the interior markets; consequently civil war was ever rife around and about them as there existed in Bonny territory no strong-handed man like Pepple to put down such disturbances, leading to immense loss of British property. It is sad to be obliged to confess that despotism is the only form of government which is calculated to preserve law and order in the present social degradation of the native Africans.[1]

In 1858 the very supercargoes who intrigued to effect King Pepple's exile now discovered that the measure, instead of advancing their self-interest, was militating against it. They suddenly awoke to the fact that legitimate commerce could not thrive without protection and admitted to Hutchinson: 'The present Government of this country we unanimously consider to be quite unfit for the management of its own affairs and altogether inadequate for the protection of the lives and property of British Subjects.' As they knew of no one 'here capable of holding the reins of Government', they, supported by 'many of the principal chiefs', requested the Consul to petition the home Government 'to send out the ex-King Pepple and reinstate him as the sole ruler of this Country'.[2] One of the regents 'even expressed himself satisfied to have Pepple returned, though conscious that from the loss of all the ex-King's property [during the civil war] he could only possess a shadow of authority in Bonny at the present time'. In order to remedy the main weaknesses of what the Consul described as the 'Quadruple Regency', he decided to elevate one of them to the position of head regent.[3]

From the moment of his appointment the head regent realized that the stigma attached to his former slave status was a grave handicap in his new role. He therefore approached the Consul asking for British backing in cleansing him from this stigma. 'I savey very well,' he said, 'English Queen want to do good for all Blackmen and I come for Man of War to ask you for give me book to make me free, and then no man can call me slave, for Queen of England make me free. I remain, Consul, you good friend and friend of all English men. Manilla Pepple.'[4] A Consul's decree at Bonny followed this letter,

[1] Hutchinson, *Ten Years Wandering*, pp. 176–8.

[2] F.O.84/1061, Encl. in No. 19, Bonny River, Supercargoes to Hutchinson, Mar. 1858.

[3] F.O.84/1061, No. 2, F.P., Hutchinson to Clarendon, 22 Jan. 1858.

[4] F.O.84/1061, Encl. in No. 9, Bonny River, Manilla Pepple to Hutchinson, 4 Jan. 1858.

declaring the head regent manumitted and asserting that anyone who made reference to his slave origins during his administration of the country would incur the 'displeasure of H.B.M. Government and of suffering such penalty as Government may attach to such a step',[1] but it impressed no one. Bonny political ideas were not made or unmade by consular decrees. This Delta version of the caste-system derived from 300 years' experience in governing a predominantly slave society. Even the Consul admitted that the new head 'is one of that class who however they may rise in worldly condition by their exertions are still prevented by reason of the natural position of serfdom in which they are born, from rising into any state of influence amongst their people'.[2] The reasons why the new classes failed to provide a government after Pepple's exile must be sought for not only in the conflicts and rivalries among the regents but even more in the realm of political ideas.

The impact of western European commercial enterprise on the Delta states after three centuries of continuous contact was more evident on the material than on the ideological plane. European institutions and dogma had remarkably small influence, and traditional religious and political beliefs, though unwritten, still dominated the daily life of the nineteenth-century Africans. The city-states looked to the African interior rather than to Europe for their inspiration. Bishop Crowther noted, ten years after the foundation of Christianity at Bonny, that the chiefs who sent their children to mission schools stated quite frankly that they 'did not want religious teaching, for that the children have enough at home; they teach them such themselves; that they want them to be taught how to gauge palm-oil and other like mercantile business as soon as possible'.[3] The children were sent to mission schools for one purpose only: that they might learn the business methods of the West. Instances of this abound in contemporary records.

Even European merchants recognized the power of the indigenous institutions. 'The master of a vessel belonging to Liverpool purchased what is called "Egbo" [Egbo orders are usually bought], that is making himself a partner in the exhibition of some disgusting mummeries which they have to their deities there. This man dressed up, and danced, and all that kind of thing, and went through all this

---

[1] F.O.84/1061, F.P., No. 2, Hutchinson to Clarendon, 22 Jan. 1858.
[2] Ibid.
[3] *The Church Missionary Intelligencer*, 1875, xi. 249–50.

just for the purpose of getting in a cargo of oil quickly.'[1] In 1875 Bishop Crowther wrote: 'Strange things are done by some European merchants in Africa, which Christian friends in England could hardly believe were possible. Some three months ago an intelligent, well-educated Englishman degraded himself so far as to conform to the idolatrous practices of the heathens at Bonny; to join their secret club, he performs all the idolatrous rites required on the occasion. This, it was said, cost him about £300.'[2] If these prove nothing they indicate that African religions and political ideas had lost none of their validity so far as the city-states were concerned. Even the foreign merchant was not entirely unaware of their power in Delta society.

The Consul saw no solution for the lack of a stable government other than the restoration of King Pepple. 'Some of the people wish to have King Pepple back, because they are more willing to endure a despotic rule, [such as they confess his to have been towards them] than to suffer under a condition of insubordination, which must ever exist during the present regency—constituted, as it is, of men, who being of the slave [ex-slave class] class, can have no authority.'[3] In 1859 the supercargoes were 'perfectly aware that none but one of the Royal Blood [*Ama-nya-nabo*] will be accepted or recognized by the natives [as king], and therefore it is our individual opinion, together with that of the majority of the Bonny men, that nothing but the reinstalment of the deposed King, can possibly meet the exigencies of the occasion'. Only by this measure could they 'recover their property from the hands of the natives' and prosecute 'the trade with any possible chance of success'.[4]

There is some irony in the reflection that the supercargoes who were foremost in advocating the removal of Pepple in 1854 were in 1859 the most zealous in demanding his restoration. But the damage had been done; it will be seen that even the restoration of the king in 1861 could not repair the ravages of the civil war of 1855, nor the permanent harm done to that city-state during the seven years of the king's exile. In 1861 the British Government ultimately consented to Pepple's return to Bonny, but rejected the large sum he claimed as compensation for his illegal detention at Fernando Po, Ascension,

[1] F.P. 1842, XI (531), Pt. I, Q. 5899.
[2] *The Church Missionary Intelligencer*, 1876, i. 475.
[3] F.O.84/1087, No. 19, F.P., Hutchinson to Malmesbury, 4 June 1859.
[4] F.O.84/1087, Encl. 5 in 19, Supercargoes to Hutchinson, 25 May 1859.

and London. They paid him only £4,520 compensation and £3,003 for legal expenses, a total of £7,523.[1] All was now set for the king's restoration, but Pepple was not returning to a united people. The party led by the ex-regent would never yield to a king whose return might mean their death. Hence although a majority of the Houses stood for Pepple's restoration, Alali and his followers were irrevocably set against him. The new leader of the movement in support of the monarchy was another powerful ex-slave, Oko Jumbo. He was known to be a fanatical advocate of constitutional methods, and although a young man was in direct opposition to the revolutionary movement of the anti-Pepple party.

On 18 August 1861 King William Dappa Pepple arrived in Bonny waters in a privately chartered vessel, the *Bewley*. He did not, however, land until 15 October.[2] His reluctance to land, according to Bonny sources, was due to the fact that he was endeavouring to unite the warring factions, and to make his assumption of office the signal for unity in the land. This gesture was of little avail. Every attempt to get Alali to meet the king on board failed. It appeared, according to one account, that he had fled from the town when an armed band acting on the king's orders tried to arrest him. 'He had hemiplegia of the left side, shortly afterwards, and died probably poisoned.'[3] Thus ended the revolutionary career of the ex-regent, Alali. He, more than any other Bonny man of his day, fought to destroy the Pepple monarchy. His death did not mean the end of the formidable House he had built up nor of the opposition against the monarchy which his prolonged attacks had inspired.

The restored king soon discovered that the economic basis of the monarchy had been wiped out in the civil war of 1855. There was no banking system at Bonny; the hoard of dollars and doubloons buried in the rooms of the king's House had been looted by the revolutionaries. The vast wealth and property preserved by successive generations of Pepples during the slave trade and after was almost entirely lost. As Pepple's trusted lieutenants Yanibo and Ishacco had fled the country during the insurrection, his trade, the main support of a Delta king, was, after seven years' interruption, non-existent. Just as the social stigma attached to the status of the well-to-do ex-slaves barred them from the exercise of political power, so the poverty of

[1] Geary, op. cit., pp. 86–87, based on F.O.84/1164.
[2] F.O.84/1176 Cameroons Mountains, Burton to Russell, 14 Jan. 1862.
[3] Burton, op. cit., ii. 274–6.

Pepple at his restoration proved the greatest impediment to his government of the Bonny country. A poor king, though of royal blood, could not hope to command respect in a society built on trade. Those who visited Bonny at this time averred that the king had not the power which was his before 1854. He had lost it within the state to the ex-slaves, and externally to the Consul and the warship. 'King Pepple never regained his ancient sway over the Bonny people, and after lingering in very indifferent health a few years . . . passed away at Ju Ju Town [in 1866], where he had been living almost ever since his return to his native land.'[1]

William Dappa Pepple was succeeded by his first son Prince George Pepple. King George, as he came to be known, had followed his father to exile in London. 'This young man had been educated in England, and I must say did credit to whoever had had charge of his education. He both spoke and wrote English correctly, and had his father been able to hand over to him the kingship as he received it in 1837, he might have blossomed into a model king in West Africa; . . . the only thing he inherited from his father beyond the kingship was debt—King only in name, receiving only so much of his dues as the principal chiefs liked to allow him, not having the means of being a large trader, looked upon with scant favour by Europeans, and owing to his English education lacking the rude ability of such men as Oko Jumbo and Ja Ja to make a position for himself, he became but a puppet in the hands of his principal chiefs.'[2] Far more important, the new king, through his eight years' education in England and long absence from Bonny, did not quite belong to the society he came to rule. Unlike his father he was a thorough convert to Christianity and in other respects a typical westerner. At Bonny these attainments disqualified him in the eyes of his subjects. 'Few people can understand the reason for this. It is simply another proof of the wonderful power of Ju-Ju amongst these people,' declared an eyewitness with over thirty years' experience of the Delta trade, 'for it is to that occult influence that I trace the general ill-success of the educated native of the Delta in his own country—unless he returns to all the pagan gods of his forefathers, and until he does so many channels of prosperity are completely closed to him.'[3]

'The present King of Bonny,' said a French traveller in the seventies, 'George Peppel, was brought up in England; he dresses in

[1] de Cardi, op. cit., p. 521.   [2] Ibid., pp. 530–1.
[3] Kingsley, op. cit., p. 531.

European fashion, trades in oil, and devotes to it a little steamer of which the English have made him a present. In fact, George Peppel is rather an English Agent than a King.'[1] The new king was a nonentity. In the coming struggle for power the Bonny chiefs came to treat him as such and his accession made little difference to the dying power of the Pepples.

[1] A. Burdo, *The Niger and the Benue* (London, 1880), p. 87.

CHAPTER IX

Background to the Parliamentary Select Committee of 1865

It is a commonplace of West African history to assume that the recommendations of the Parliamentary Select Committee of 1865 advocating partial and gradual withdrawal from the settlements represented the British Government's attitude to West Africa in the sixties. So far as the Niger territories were concerned, nothing can be further from the truth. This document can rightly be claimed to embody the views of those members of the House who were not merely sciolists in West African affairs but reflected in their opposition to expansion a widespread view of imperial policy; in the mid-nineteenth century the dominant note in British colonial policy was withdrawal whenever possible and retrenchment of expenditure everywhere. This tendency underlies Cobden's speeches on Indian policy and motivated the withdrawal of the colonial garrisons in the sixties. In the Niger territories, however, the reverse was the case. Here the British Government and her traders launched a vigorous policy of expansion during the sixties. This statement, if not true of all West Africa, certainly applies to modern Nigeria.

The background to the committee's recommendations cannot be fully grasped without reference to the trade of the Niger Delta in relation to the rest of West Africa at the time. All contemporary evidence showed that the greatest volume of British trade was done in that part of West Africa (the Niger Delta) where 'we have no government agents, forts or settlement'. The 'Free Traders' attributed this state of affairs to the competition which has always existed in the Delta trade and its 'Freedom as yet from all extraneous interference'. Thus in contemporary writings generally and in parts of the report the Delta was held up as the model to which the rest of West Africa should approximate. Free traders looked forward to the emergence of 'a commercial intercourse' between Africa and England such 'as that which now flourishes on the Delta of the Niger'.[1]

---

[1] Robert Jamieson, op. cit., pp. 19–26.

The important point was that the emphasis was not so much on withdrawal as on economy. The Niger Delta had proved that commerce had no need for protection. Therefore the cost of running the forts and settlements ('protectors of commerce') should be lowered. No one suggested that commerce—the chief end of British enterprise overseas—should be abandoned. So far from Britain ceasing to be interested in West African territories and their trade she was merely altering the focus of her interest: the free traders were showing that the benefits of the territories could be had without incurring administrative responsibilities.

The inquiry itself was precipitated by events in the Gold Coast closely connected with the expense of administering the settlements and the cost of the Ashanti invasions which threatened the area of the forts. The annual cost to the Imperial Treasury of the Gold Coast forts had risen from £5,000 in 1850 to about £12,000 in 1863 without corresponding increase in revenue. Increasing involvement in West African politics during 1863–4 meant further increase in expenditure and in 1864 Colonel Ord was appointed Special Commissioner to West Africa, one of his instructions being to recommend how this expenditure could be reduced without impairing the efficiency of the establishments. In its origin therefore the Select Committee was called forth largely by considerations of economy and not solely by the desire to abandon West Africa or her trade.

The committee's chairman was Mr. Charles B. Adderley, a free trader, and his anti-expansionist views undoubtedly influenced the final recommendations. Nor was he alone in this prejudice. Even the well-known palm-oil magnate Mr. (later Sir) John Tobin of Liverpool, testifying before the committee, declared himself against protection: 'I do not like to see commerce and men-of-war going together. I would rather trust to good conduct . . . on the part of the traders, than to any demonstration of force.'[1] Yet the supercargoes in the employ of this gentleman repeatedly called on the Consul and the warships for protection. Such is the measure of the extent to which men could become slaves to an economic doctrine; those whose mental horizon was bounded by the academic teachings of the Manchester School failed to perceive the political implications of a rapidly expanding trade.

Officials in control of West African affairs, however, had no illusions and their position must not be confused with that of the

[1] Parl. Pap. 1865, V (412), Evidence of J. A. Tobin, Q. 5304.

selfish merchant or the doctrinaire member of Parliament. National policies are rarely shaped by parliamentary debates and recommendations. During the sitting of the committee the official view was expressed by Mr. William H. Wylde who, as Head of the Slave Trade Department in the Foreign Office for ten years, was in possession of facts not available to the committee. Among other things he was asked:

> *Q.* Has it not been the case, and is it not almost inevitable, that a great power like England, assuming the Government in such a country like West Africa, must maintain certain native powers against the others?
> *A.* Exactly; you cannot help that.
> *Q.* Should you say that for the interest of commerce and civilization it would have been almost better not to have so interfered, but to have left the natives to fight it out among themselves so that the strongest would finally become predominant?
> *A.* Probably that might be the best thing; but if you have an (commercial) establishment in some place, you cannot help interfering in the politics of the country.[1]

Such was the clear appreciation of the issue at stake by those who made policy. Nor were they allowed, by reports from the consuls of the chronic 'palavers' that agitated the coast and memorials from the short-sighted merchants—who voiced their free-tràding prejudices when it suited them but sought the state's aid in time of trouble—to forget the protection which Her Majesty's Government owed to British subjects trading to West Africa. As a matter of history the recommendations of the committee appeared at the very moment when British merchants and statesmen were implementing a vigorous policy of expansion in modern Nigeria. Because the theories did not fit the facts the resolutions for eventual withdrawal were never carried out. The sixties, far from being the era of retraction, saw the rapid expansion of trade and empire in Nigeria.

The decade after 1850 marked the end of an epoch in Nigerian history. Repeated British attempts to penetrate the hinterland since 1832 by way of the River Niger—signalized by the well-known Niger expeditions—had failed disastrously after twenty-two years of continuous effort to accomplish their object. True, in these years the Niger was charted, the people on its banks studied, and its commer-

---

[1] Parl. Pap. 1865, V (412), QQ. 2713–15.

cial possibilities assessed; yet African opposition to penetration and the impediments posed by nature remained impregnable.

But in 1854, owing to the death of Consul Beecroft, whom the Foreign Office had ordered to take charge of operations, Surgeon Commander Dr. William Balfour Baikie[1] found himself at the head of the expedition of that year. In this voyage, and for the first time, he proved 'that the use of quinine, as a prophylactic or preventive, would enable the Europeans to withstand the influence of the African climate . . . and that quinine not only cures [African fever] but that it actually prevents (it), and that by taking this invaluable drug while in unhealthy localities persons may escape totally unscathed'.[2] This discovery has been said to be 'worthy to rank with Cook's conquest of scurvy'.[3] Baikie led his expedition as far as Hausaland and returned to the coast without the loss of a single life; in some of the previous expeditions over forty European lives had been lost. The event proved a turning-point in Nigerian history. From 1854 the British Government and the far-sighted among her traders looked to the Nigerian hinterland rather than to the coast for trade and empire. The connexion of Macgregor Laird with this successful expedition is very well known and his faith and vision which bridged the decade of disillusionment (1841–54) have been discussed. In the fifties the British Government recognized Laird as the authority on Niger questions and financed his schemes for the commercial development of the Niger valley. On 1 January 1857 a contract was entered into between Macgregor Laird and the Government by which he was to maintain a steamer on the river for five years at a subsidy of £8,000 the first year, diminishing annually by £500 to £6,000 in the fifth year.[4] Dr. Baikie led this expedition in the *Dayspring* and his

[1] W. B. Baikie: b. Kirkwall, Orkney, 1825. Graduated in medicine at Edinburgh. Entered Royal Navy 1848 and was Assistant Surgeon at Haslar Hospital 1851–4. Commanded the Niger expedition of 1854, penetrating 250 miles farther than any previous expedition. Published his *Narrative of an Exploring Voyage up the . . . Niger*, 1856. Commanded the 1857 expedition in which the *Pleiad* was wrecked and was left in the interior to carry on alone. Founded the first British Government post in the Nigerian mainland at Lokoja and entered into friendly relations with King Masaba of Bida. Later Lokoja became the headquarters of the British interior consulate and of the trading companies. Baikie's contribution in planting British power in the Nigerian hinterland compares with Beecroft's work on the coast. He died in 1864, having visited Kano and made British power generally known in the Hausa states.
[2] Baikie, op. cit., pp. 5 and 453.
[3] Lloyd, op. cit., pp. 137–8.
[4] Geary, op. cit., p. 158.

second in command was Lieutenant J. H. Glover;[1] both were to become men of the front rank among the makers of modern Nigeria.[2]

Just as 1854 marked the end of the era of exploration, so in 1857 the traders took over where the explorers left off. Seen in this light the voyage of the *Dayspring* marked the beginning of an era in Nigerian history. The progress of inland trade was stoutly resisted by the old coast traders, especially Liverpool supercargoes, who could not abandon without heavy loss expensive equipments designed for a lucrative coast trade. An economic war developed between the opposing factions.

Baikie attacked the African middlemen and European coast merchants unreservedly.[3] It was due to the Liverpool monopolists, he declared, that 'much less was known of the Gulf of Guinea than of New Zealand and of the far-distant groups of the islands of the Pacific. No person can visit the West African Coast without hearing of deeds performed by European Captains and supercargoes which are, although fully attested, almost incredible. I have heard admitted by perpetrators or been told by sufferers and by eyewitnesses, deeds and actions the relation of which I hesitate to commit to paper.'[4]

All this may be true, yet the denunciation of the Liverpool supercargoes and the Delta middlemen by Laird, Baikie, and their group must be read with discrimination. Like partisans in general the inland traders used every means to discredit their rivals. Divested of nebulous verbiage, the naked aim of the opposing factions was the control of Nigerian trade: so long as the coast economic organization continued effectively to tap the hinterland production all talk of inland trade was of little avail. To succeed the new school must break the firm grip of the Delta states on the palm belt. To this end the inland traders turned the full blast of their tirade against the coastal merchants when the successful expeditions of the fifties raised hopes of success.

This is not to ignore the real differences in method and philosophy separating the new from the old. The former spoke a language that conveyed little to the Delta merchants. 'The regeneration of Africa',

[1] Hastings, op. cit., an admirable edition of Glover's diary kept during the 1857 voyage.

[2] A. F. Mockler-Ferryman, *British West Africa* (London, 1900), pp. 175–94. It is the best account of the commencement of trade in the Niger valley. Cf. Geary, op. cit., pp. 158–70.

[3] F.O.2/23, Haslar Hospital, Gosport, Baikie to F.O., 11 Oct. 1856.

[4] F.O.2/23, F.P., Baikie to Under-Secretary, F.O., 10 June 1857.

the introduction of 'religion' and 'civilization', the 'redemption of the savage', the 'preaching of the Gospel on the Banks of the Niger', phrases which occur with tedious frequency in the writings of the new school, were Greek to their countrymen. The Liverpool merchants might have been 'ruffians from the start, ruffians wherever they might go; some went out clean and became dirtied by the life they had to lead'.¹ Even so they had legitimate reasons for attacking men who came not only to convert their consciences but to seize their trade and plot their elimination. The battle between the two groups was predominantly economic, not ideological.

From 1857 to 1859 Laird erected 'factories' (trading posts) at Aboh, Onitsha, and at Lokoja, situated at the confluence of the Niger and Benue. These places were above the Delta and chosen for their commercial importance. 'Onitsha', wrote Baikie in 1857, 'is well-placed on rising ground with a dry soil, it is the key to the extensive Igbo districts, and is the proper spot for a trading nucleus'² in the interior. The town itself was a market of the Brass city-state; its occupation was therefore a challenge to that coast community. Similarly, Aboh was an ally of Bonny and the most northerly of the Delta towns. Every step taken by the inland merchants constituted a menace to coastal trade. In 1857 'the value of produce collected at [Laird's] stations realized in Liverpool £1,800; in 1858 £2,750; in 1859 £8,000–£9,000'.³ 'Though these sums show that the existing trade cannot support a steam vessel upon the river', Laird declared, 'the rate of increase holds out a fair prospect of its doing so in the course of another three or four years. The great drawback is the hostility of the tribes in the Delta where the natives are armed with cannon as well as musketry, and where they are encouraged and stimulated to prevent steamers ascending by the chiefs and slave traders on the coast.'⁴ In March 1860 a deputation to Lord Palmerston claimed that 'vessels sent up by Mr. Laird between 1857 and 1860 had been attacked by marauding tribes of the Delta'. The middlemen, they asserted, were 'deeply interested in opposing legitimate commerce, for the sake of an illicit slave trade'.⁵

The reference to the 'slave trade' and 'slave-traders' at this time in

¹ Hastings, op. cit., pp. 218–20.
² F.O.2/23, Baikie to Clarendon, 28 Sept. 1857.
³ Hutchinson, *Ten Years Wandering*, pp. 156–7. Cf. F.O.2/34, London, Laird to Russell, 18 Feb. 1860.
⁴ Hutchinson, *Ten Years Wandering*, pp. 157–8.
⁵ Ibid., pp. 154–5.

the Delta was fallacious. It is a fiction to state that those who attacked Laird's steamships were slave-traders and the misleading nature of that assertion, then so prevalent, must be confuted. Africans attacked the vessels because inland traders were attempting to capture the palm-oil trade on which their survival depended. They fought Laird solely for the control of 'legitimate commerce'. The British Consul admitted that the ships were attacked 'but not by any persons having an interest in the slave trade . . . for such traffic in the Bight of Biafra is like that recorded at Angola by Dr. Livingstone, "a thing spoken of in the past tense". It was the palm oil native brokers, who dwell between the districts where that article is manufactured, and the British receiving-ships at the mouth of the Brass River, by whom these several attacks were made.'[1]

1857, when the potentialities of inland trade were first demonstrated, was the year when African and European traders on the coast joined forces to attack the common enemy. Vital economic interests proved more potent than notions of race and nationality. Since 1832 Delta interests had sought to destroy the commercial expeditions to the interior. The supercargoes grumbled incessantly about 'these fellows', 'strange creatures', 'the meddling explorers' who disturbed an age-long monopoly and a valuable trade. The African middlemen hated inland traders bitterly. Available evidence indicates that they attacked Lander fatally at Angiama in 1833 and committed the murders connected with the 1841 expedition. The white merchants lent their support and contemporaries had little doubt that some 'Christian traders' urged 'the villages in the lower course [of the Niger] to acts of direct hostility'[2] against Laird's commercial vessels. It was natural that the Liverpool merchants in attacking their own countrymen should work underground. Mr. Wylde admitted 'I know that it was founded on facts that in Mr. Laird's time the [British] traders in the Brass River induced the natives to commit hostilities on his vessels, because the vessels going up the Niger cut up part of the supplies of oil that came down to Brass. You cannot get proof of such a thing as that, but there is no doubt about it.'[3]

Inland penetration was delayed not only by the deadly malaria of the river valley but even more by determined African opposition. The 1854 expedition solved the difficulties set by nature; quinine removed the menace of malaria just as the invention of the steam-

[1] Hutchinson, *Ten Years Wandering*, pp. 154–5.
[2] Burton, op. cit., pp. 246–58.   [3] Parl. Pap., 1865, V (412), Q. 2914.

engine had facilitated river navigation. But the barriers set up by Delta opposition remained. It is customary to emphasize the first obstacle and to write as if the second did not exist. Yet contemporary records reveal that with the possible exception of one or two expeditions all were attacked by the Delta natives. Heavy guns were mounted on banks where the river channel was narrow and the trading steamers came under heavy fire on their ascent or descent of the river. In several cases the steamers were brought to a standstill and boarded by Africans from their war canoes; hand-to-hand fighting ensued. Lives and goods were lost in each encounter and although warships took reprisals, destroying the native fortified points, yet these were quickly rebuilt and the attacks on passing steamers resumed. The 'Hostile Villages', as these fortified areas—Hippoteama, Sabogrega, Angiama, and Agberi—were designated, became the dread of the British Navy and many an admiral resisted Foreign Office and Admiralty instructions to convoy trading vessels up the river. Papers relating to the Niger expeditions of the fifties and sixties testify to the energy, courage, and resourcefulness with which the Delta middlemen fought to prevent the success of their rivals.

In 1857 the schooner *George*, the largest of Laird's trading ships, was attacked by Delta natives who attempted to 'carry her by boarding'. In 1859, 'emboldened apparently by the impunity with which they had escaped efficient chastisement, they attacked the *Rainbow* and *Sunbeam* [both Laird's steam-vessels] together on their ascent, and separately on their return—with a degree of method, arrangement, and association which shows a determination on their part to prevent the passage of trading vessels up and down the River'.[1] Laird contended that these attacks were 'equal to the most efficient blockade [of the Niger], as it raises the rate of insurance to a prohibitive one, and makes it difficult to get the necessary number of Kroomen and others to man the steamers'.[2] In the attack on the *Rainbow* the second officer, Mr. Kirkpatrick, and a Portuguese seaman were shot dead. According to Lieutenant Glover, who was in the *Rainbow* during this attack, 'I attribute in a great measure the hostility of the [Delta] tribes to the influence which is exercised by the English traders in the Brass River who are antagonistic to the development' of inland trade.[3] Laird protested repeatedly that unless effective

[1] F.O.2/34, 3 Mincing Lane, London, Laird to Russell, Jan. 1860.
[2] Ibid., 18 Feb. 1860.
[3] F.O.2/34, No. 1, St. James' Street, Adelphi, Glover to Russell, 13 Jan. 1860.

convoys for his trading vessels were provided by the Admiralty, trade would be impossible in the hinterland 'and Her Majesty's subjects foully murdered while in the peaceful pursuit of their lawful calling'.[1] Instances such as these can be multiplied.

In 1860, when Laird had proved that inland trade would pay, the Government decided to give his trading vessels adequate protection. To the surprise of the Foreign Office and the Admiralty, the Commander-in-Chief on the African station, Commodore Edmonstone, pleading the Delta's superior opposition, failed to carry out his instructions. He wrote to the Admiralty expressing extreme reluctance to convoying Laird's vessels through the Delta. He knew from bitter personal experience the ruthless character of the opposition.

To attempt to drive a legal trade with people hundreds of miles in the interior, and having to pass through hostile tribes who require to be coerced in the meantime was impracticable. The Natives of the Delta of the Niger are some of the most warlike, treacherous, and cruel in Africa, the banks of the River are precipitous, affording sure shelter for their guns . . . while our people could not touch them even by rockets. I do trust and hope therefore that if these arrangements with Laird [to convoy his vessels] are not irrevocably settled, that we should pause before committing ourselves to what seems at present a most hazardous and fruitless expedition.[2]

In consequence Laird's vessels were unable to go up the river that year. His trade goods were auctioned in the Delta and he sustained heavy losses in capital. His interior trading posts were left unreplenished and cut off from all communication with the coast. In November Laird wrote to the Foreign Office demanding compensation for losses attributable to the Government's failure to provide the promised protection.[3] Worse still, Dr. Baikie reported to the Foreign Office through the overland route linking the Niger to Lagos, that owing to the non-appearance of Laird's steamers the natives were attacking and destroying his factories at Aboh and Onitsha, due no doubt to the instigation of the Delta inhabitants.[4] In the following year, 1861, Macgregor Laird, the pioneer of inland trade, died.

The political implications of interior commercial expansion were early expressed in the well-known activities of Dr. Baikie who led, so

---

[1] F.O.2/34, 3 Mincing Lane, London, Laird to Russell, Jan. 1860.
[2] F.O.2/34, Encl. in Admiralty letter of 3 Sept., H.M.S. *Arrogant*, Edmonstone to Dundas, 13 July 1860.
[3] F.O.2/34, Laird to Russell, 16 Nov. 1860.
[4] F.O.2/34, Lokoja Confluence, Baikie to Russell, 11 Oct. 1860. Cf. F.O.97/433, H.M.S. *Arrogant* at Princes Islands, Edmonstone to Admiral Waller, 29 Oct. 1861.

to speak, the political wing of Laird's movement for hinterland penetration. Baikie's activities belong properly to the history of the interior
and his gallant stand against privation and ill health following the
wreck of the *Dayspring* at Rabba in 1857 are chronicled in his absorbing dispatches to the Foreign Office describing the state of trade and
politics among the native powers. This gentleman installed himself
in the dominion of King Masaba as unauthorized British Consul at
Lokoja, and later received official sanction. The Lokoja consulate was
maintained by Dr. Baikie's successors, Lieutenants Bourchier and
McLeod, from 1860 to 1869. It disappeared with the wave of anti-
British activity that agitated the Delta and Niger valley with the
increasing success of inland trade.

The home Government was not slow to appreciate the exigencies of
the situation. In 1860, when inland trading came up for review, the
Board of Trade recommended that 'protection should be afforded by
Her Majesty's Government to the British Trading Interests' on the
Niger,[1] and on 12 April John Washington, Hydrographer to the
Admiralty, was appointed by the Foreign Office to examine the whole
problem. In his report he affirmed that the Government's aim of
opening up the Niger to trade had been achieved, but doubted
whether the use of force against the middleman, the sole remaining
obstacle, was the best policy.[2]

This report was widely circulated among government departments
and the leading statesmen of the day, including Lord Palmerston, who
commented:

It may be true in one sense that trade ought not to be enforced by
Cannon balls [Washington had said in his report: 'Trade enforced by
Cannon shot will take no root'] but on the other hand trade cannot
flourish without security. It might be said of an European Country that
trade ought not to be enforced by the Cudgels of a Police or the Sabres
and Carbinas of a Gendarmerie, but those cudgels and sabres and carbinas are necessary to keep quiet the ill-disposed People whose violence
would render trade insecure and thus prevent its operation.

As always on West African questions Palmerston was for action. He
advocated the use of armed ships to deal with those who obstructed
the road to the treasures of the interior. 'It is not easy to put a limit
upon the resources which Africa affords for advantageous commerce
with England. Cotton, Palm Oil, Ground Nuts, Coffee, Ivory, may

[1] F.O.2/34, Board of Trade to F.O., 10 Feb. 1860.
[2] F.O.2/34, Admiralty, John Washington, Hydrographer, to F.O., 12 Apr. 1860.

be obtained in immense quantities, and of course in exchange for the productions of British Industry. The advantages to be derived from a great increase of our Trade with Africa, would infinitely counter-balance the small expenditure necessary for protecting that trade in its infancy.' He further recommended that 'the occupation of Lagos would be a very useful and important step' in consolidating British power in the Niger territories.[1] Accordingly the Foreign Office persuaded Docemo, king of Lagos, to cede his kingdom. The treaty of cession was signed on 6 August 1861. Thus Lagos, which Great Britain had attacked and occupied in 1851, was made a Crown Colony in 1861. The Foreign Office, under Lord Russell, accepted Washington's report and Palmerston's recommendations for the subjugation of the Niger valley. 'It is indispensable that steps should be taken to put an end to obstructions raised to the passage of ships up and down the Niger', wrote Russell to the Treasury. He asked that the required subsidies be paid and thus advanced Laird's attempts to lay the foundations for the interior trade.[2] The Treasury accepted the recommendations and sanctioned the grant,[3] but pointed out that objections may be raised 'on principle to Grants of Public Money in aid of commercial undertakings and in converting what has hitherto been in the nature of an Exploring Expedition, into a subsidy to support trading posts'.

The salient point was that the Foreign Office, along with other Departments of State, decided in 1860 that the Niger problem had been solved, and that the opposition of the Delta states must be broken. 'It has been proved that the Niger can, at the proper season [May to November], be navigated freely for six months in the year and the natives of the countries have moreover shown a desire to engage in legitimate commerce.' The Government was therefore determined 'to establish and develop permanent commercial inter-course by this route with the interior of Africa'.[4]

At the time of this important decision Baikie had shown from his post at Lokoja that the Niger was the highway not only to the Ibo country but to Yorubaland and the Hausa states. The Niger basin was seen as the focal point of modern Nigeria. From his base in Nupe territory he dispatched Lieutenant Glover (later Governor of

[1] F.O.2/34, Minutes on Captain Washington's Report, Palmerston, 22 Apr 1860.
[2] F.O.2/34, F.O. to Treasury (Relative to the Niger Expedition), 9 May 1860.
[3] F.O.2/34, Treasury Chambers, 19 May 1860.
[4] F.O.2/34, F.O., Russell to Consul Brand, 18 June 1860.

Lagos) on repeated visits to that port, and when Delta hostility closed the river channel Lagos became their sole link with the outside world. Another of his assistants, Mr. May, visited Ilorin, Oyo, and Ibadan from Lokoja. Similar expeditions showed that by the Niger important Hausa towns could be reached.[1]

Acting on the Government's decision Lord Russell instructed Baikie on 22 June 1860 'to make known to the Chiefs inhabiting the Banks of the Niger that for the future their country will be visited regularly' by British merchants and trading vessels.[2] This important statement of policy is clear and unequivocal and guided the policies of successive ministers on Nigerian affairs. The apparent stagnation and frustration that occasionally attended this forward policy was due wholly to accidental circumstances, unpredictable factors that no government could control. That these greatly hindered the working out of clearly stated policies and retarded the development of inland trade for a decade cannot be denied.

With the death of Laird his unifying and enlightened influence disappeared; new groups emerged to exploit the resources his enterprise had opened up. As on the coast, unlimited competition was the rule. Moreover, African·opposition hitherto confined to the Delta began to spread to the inland states as the political implications of interior commerce unfolded. Early in 1858 Baikie reported that even in the dominions of the pro-British ruler, King Masaba of Bida, suspicions as to British motives in penetrating the country were prevalent. Some of the chiefs stated that 'our intentions were to seize a part of the country, and they brought up in support of their assertions some people who had been to Lagos [and] had learnt from Spaniards and Portuguese that we are a very dangerous and encroaching nation'.[3] Native hostility grew with each succeeding year and led directly to the closing of the Lokoja consulate in 1869. Yet events throughout the sixties show that traders and Government alike defied these obstacles and pushed on the frontiers of trade and politics.

The assumption that the destruction of Laird's factories at the various trading posts between 1860–1 and his death took 'the spring

[1] F.O.2/23, Encampment near Jeba, Baikie to May, River Kwora, 31 Oct. 1857. Also F.O.2/23, F.P., May to Clarendon, 24 Nov. 1857. Cf. F.O.2/27, Encampment near Ketsa, Baikie to Malmesbury, 5 July 1858.

[2] F.O.2/34. Russell to Baikie, 22 June 1860.

[3] F.O.2/27, Encampment near Ketta, Nupe, Baikie to Malmesbury, 5 July 1858.

out of [inland] enterprise' is not altogether accurate.[1] The ferocity
of native attacks was matched by the British power to retaliate.
For example, under Commander Douglass H.M.S. *Espoir* ascended
the Niger in 1861 and mercilessly destroyed the Delta towns that
had attacked trading ships in 1859.[2]

Fresh plans for further advance were afoot only two years after
Laird's death. His executor, Mr. Archibald Hamilton, headed this
movement. To find the necessary capital for commercial development a joint-stock company was formed[3] and a government subsidy
solicited. In July 1865 Hamilton wrote to Lord Russell enclosing
the prospectus of the newly formed 'Company of African Merchants'.
The founders of the company were 'so satisfied of the profitable
nature of the business that they have themselves subscribed £300,000,
leaving only £100,000 to be offered to the Public'. They asked for
a subsidy on the grounds that the trade would run at a loss for several
years and that those who undertook to open it were performing a
national duty in clearing a great commercial highway for others of
their countrymen.[4] While the Foreign Office was still considering the
question, another company appeared in the field. This was 'The
West African Company' headed by Mr. Clegg of Manchester, with a
subscribed capital of £100,000: it also demanded a subsidy. The
sixties was the era of company formation in West African commerce.[5]
The Foreign Office studied the position and decided that the 'Company of African Merchants' was the better of the two. 'It contained
the names of many eminent men who have the welfare of Africa at
heart . . . and they have ample funds to carry out whatever they undertake in a manner that will set at rest the question' of the Niger trade.[6]

[1] Dorothy Wellesley, *Sir George Goldie* (London, 1934), p. 13.

[2] Geary, op. cit., p. 164.

[3] The Companies Act, 1862, put company law on its modern footing: it established liability limited by shares and by guarantee.

[4] F.O.97/434, 8 Adelphi Terrace, Strand, Hamilton to Russell, 22 July 1863.
Cf. F.O.97/434, Company of African Merchants, London, to Russell, 24 Aug.
1863.

[5] The following companies were formed to exploit the resources of the Niger
basin in the sixties: (1) The River Niger Navigation and Trading Company.
(2) Company of African Merchants. (3) The Anglo-African Company. (4) The
African Merchants of Bristol. (5) The Merchants of London and Liverpool
trading to the West Coast of Africa. An examination of the records reveals that
they include the names of individuals and firms of long standing in the Delta and
West African trade: Chas. Horsfall & Sons; Stuart & Douglas; Alfred Aspinall;
Thomas Harrison & Co.; G. J. Cornish; David Clark; Hatton & Cookson;
Messrs. Forster & Smith; Banner Bros. & Co.; T. Morgan & Sons; &c.

[6] F.O.97/434, Memorandum by Wylde, F.O., 28 Apr. 1864.

Meanwhile, Liverpool coast monopolists got wind of what was going on and in a letter to Lord Russell expressed 'surprise and alarm' at the fact that 'a purely trading company', under the pretence 'of extending civilization' to Africa, was demanding public funds for its own selfish ends. Quoting from the prospectus of the Company of African Merchants, they declared that 'there is no slave trade to be lessened or entirely suppressed, that not a single slave has been exported from the Niger or any of its mouths for at least ten years'. The signatories, representing 'every House in Liverpool trading to the West Coast of Africa employing 66 ships of 30,228 tons register entirely in the African Trade', avowed their intention to fight against government subsidies to private companies. One of them, Charles Horsfall, had a monopoly of the Brass river trade. Petitions were also addressed to the Foreign Office by the merchants of Bristol and London at the instigation of the Liverpool group. There followed a protracted fight over the subsidy issue.[1] This clash was another manifestation of the coast versus hinterland trade conflict; it was the last attempt by Liverpool to stem a swelling tide.

The Foreign Office believed that 'Mr. Horsfall is the promoter of the opposition' and that the attacks on the steamers were largely instigated by his agents in the Brass river. 'We must expect that those whose interests will be injuriously affected will oppose by all the means in their power any scheme for navigating the Niger. Profits of the Oil Trade have been hitherto so great, that the few great merchants engaged in the traffic have been quite content to let matters remain in statu quo, and have not troubled themselves to push up the rivers.' The Foreign Office observed: 'We have laboured hard for some years past to break this monopoly, and if we can open up the Niger to the Trade of this country, it will be another and a considerable step in the right direction.'[2]

Lord John Russell recommended the Company of African Merchants, under the leadership of Archibald Hamilton, for a subsidy 'of £5,000 a year for five years'. His Lordship came to this decision because 'experience would seem to prove that no private individual or company is willing to incur the large expenditure necessary for navigating and establishing proper trading stations in the Niger'. As was to be expected, a second wave of Liverpool attacks followed this

[1] F.O.97/434, Enclosures in Memorandum of 28 Apr.: Memorials from Liverpool Merchants Trading to West Africa, 3 May 1864; from Bristol Merchants, 6 May 1864; and 'the Anglo-African Company', London, 12 May 1864.

[2] F.O.97/434, Memorandum by Wylde on Niger Subsidy, F.O., 28 Apr. 1864.

decision and Lord Russell's recommendations were held up by the Treasury. The vast correspondence from Liverpool on this subject shows how bitter was their assault on the inland traders. On their side the Company of African Merchants averred that Liverpool was not concerned with the 'principles' involved and that personal and selfish motives blinded them 'to general and Imperial interests'. Writing to Gladstone, Chancellor of the Exchequer, Hamilton offered proofs that the African Association of Liverpool, prime movers in the opposition, had informed Mr. Clegg of their intention 'to oppose the application of this company for a subsidy but would not oppose a similar application made by Mr. Clegg's Company [the West African Company] if he would engage not to go into the Oil Rivers'. Hamilton maintained that the unenlightened self-interest of a few 'ought not to interfere with an object of Imperial policy and importance'.[1]

Liverpool objections to a 'Niger subsidy' ultimately prevailed, and the numerous companies formed to exploit Laird's opening up of Niger commerce entered into cut-throat competition. From 1864 Liverpool attempts to prevent their progress were the death struggles, so to speak, of desperate men. The future clearly belonged to inland trade and the continuous 'running battles' were the rearguard actions of coastal forces in retreat. Because that retreat meant extinction to the African middlemen and European coast traders they fought with a ruthlessness and desperation typical of men struggling for survival. Soon Liverpool interests, finding no alternative, joined in the scramble for inland trade and the movement of European merchants to the Nigerian interior assumed a universal aspect. In fact at the very time when the 1865 Parliamentary Committee was sitting several British firms were energetically developing the commercial potentialities of the Niger valley. This pioneering movement lasted till the seventies and eighties when the Niger territories were thrown open to British commerce.

As further evidence that the precepts of the 1865 Select Committee were at variance with the circumstances, witness the alarm of the Gold Coast Administration when the growing class of educated Africans took the recommendations literally and agitated for their implementation.[2] Indeed, in 1867 James Africanus Horton (a Sierra

[1] F.O.97/434, London, Company of African Merchants to Gladstone, 12 July 1864.
[2] Wolfson, op. cit., pp. 69–73.

Leonean and an M.D. of Edinburgh University) published his book *West African Countries and Peoples,* in which he demonstrated that 'the requirements necessary' for carrying out 'that self-government recommended by the Committee of the House of Commons, 1865' were present in West Africa.[1] The dangerous belief of the 'educated native' that restriction of British rule should follow the findings of the committee was a factor in ending loose talk about withdrawal.[2] European traders throughout West Africa demanded more, not less, protection. The recommendations of the 1865 select committee were therefore hopelessly out of touch with events so far as Nigeria was concerned, for the sixties signalled the dawn of a new era: an era in which everything pointed to advance, not to evacuation.

Finally a study of the committee's resolutions would indicate that at the conclusion of the inquiry the facts of the situation forced them to recommend a guarded and much-qualified policy of withdrawal. In the first resolution they admitted that it is not possible to withdraw the British Government 'wholly or immediately' from the 'West African Coast'; in Resolutions 2 and 3 they recommended drastic reduction of the existing commitments, declaring that the 'object of our policy should be . . . ultimate withdrawal from all (West Africa), except, probably, Sierra Leone'. The conflict in the committee's mind on the issue of the retention of, or retraction from, the West African Settlements is clearly reflected in the fourth resolution: 'That this policy of non-extension admits of no exception, as regards new settlements, but cannot amount to an absolute prohibition of measures which, in peculiar cases, may be necessary for the more efficient and economical administration of the settlements we already possess.' Within a decade of the adoption of these resolutions by Parliament the logic of facts drove the British Government towards a vigorous policy of economic and political expansion not only on the coast but in the West African interior.

[1] Horton, op. cit., Part II, pp. 69–74.

[2] Horton described the British desire to withdraw as 'a grand conception' and eagerly looked forward to the realization 'of that great principle of establishing independent African nationalities as independent as the present Liberian Government'. Fearing that the British Government might not act on the recommendations of the committee, he reminded them 'that written resolutions without being carried out into practice, are worse than waste paper'. But he believed there was 'every hope that the contemplated reform will be happily carried into effect'.

CHAPTER X

The Rise of Ja Ja

SOON after his return from exile in 1864, financial stringency forced King William Pepple to grant concessions to foreign trading companies in what he still thought were 'his dominions'. The Foreign Office promptly warned him that he had lost the power to do so by the treaty of 1848.[1] After this Pepple knew that his rule was at an end. When Charles Livingstone[2] came to Bonny, Pepple 'took no notice of a message from the Chairman of the Court of Equity announcing the arrival of H.M. Consul'.[3] It was a prematurely old man that retired to Ju Ju Town in 1865, where the following year he died. His son and successor, George, from the moment of his accession leant heavily on British support. 'King George', declared Livingstone in 1867, 'wished me to bring a Man-of-War and compel his chiefs to do whatever I thought fit.'[4]

Within the city-state the ex-slaves angled for leadership. Of these the most outstanding were Oko Jumbo and Ja Ja. The former was a strong supporter of the late king. In the civil war of 1855 he had opposed Alali's attempts to assume the leadership and stood for the king's restoration. The Manilla Pepple House, of which he was a leading member, was among the most powerful in Bonny. King George Pepple was in internal affairs Oko Jumbo's puppet and carried out his behests as he did those of the Consul in external matters. Contemporaries described Oko Jumbo as a highly intelligent and civilized gentleman.[5]

[1] Parl. Pap. 1865, V, Select Committee on West Africa, op. cit., QQ. 2726–7.

[2] Charles Livingstone: brother of David Livingstone; b. Blantyre in Lanarkshire in 1821. In 1840 emigrated to the U.S.A. In 1850 graduated from the Union Theological College, New York, and later became the minister of an American church. In 1857 returned to England and joined the Zambesi expedition; invalided home 1863. In 1864, through the influence of his brother, obtained appointment as Her Britannic Majesty's Consul for the Bight of Biafra. As a Consul he was a failure, being eccentric and strongly individualistic, and was dismissed for his refusal to carry out the orders of the Foreign Office. He died at Bonny in 1873 while on his way to England.

[3] F.O.84/1249, No. 1, Livingstone to Russell, 30 June 1865.

[4] F.O.84/1277, No. 13, Livingstone to Stanley, 13 July 1867.

[5] Whitford, op. cit., pp. 289–90. Cf. E. Lewis, *Alfred Aloysius Horn* (London, 1929), pp. 37–38.

Opposed to Oko Jumbo was Ja Ja, Head of the Anna Pepple House, a position which had fallen vacant with the death of the ex-regent Alali in 1861. As the history of Bonny from 1867 to 1873 was in all essentials the history of Ja Ja, his rapid rise from obscurity to prominence is worthy of note. He led the opposition against European penetration of the eastern Nigerian hinterland from 1879 until 1887 (the year of his deportation to the West Indies), and the part he played in eastern Nigerian history was more important than that of any African in the period. Ibos today regard him as the greatest man produced by their tribe in the last century.

Ja Ja was born at Amaigbo, in the heart of the Iboland, in 1821.[1] He was sold as a slave, probably at the age of 12, to Chief Iganipu-ghuma Allison of Bonny, who, finding him insubordinate and head-strong, made a gift of him to Madu, a chief of Anna Pepple House.[2] Thus began his connexion with the House he later came to lead. His rise from slavery to freedom, his exploits as a domestic slave of Madu, and his service under a British supercargo form interesting chapters in his exceptional career. It must suffice to record that during the king's exile in 1854 and the civil war of 1855, whereas his antagonist Oko Jumbo had become a public figure, Ja Ja was an unknown but rising young trader, apparently unconcerned with the political upheavals that had become a common feature of Bonny life. His energies were concentrated in extending his trade; but by 1861 he had risen to the rank of the first line of chiefs at Bonny and was soon to gain the leadership of his House.

An eyewitness described Ja Ja's election to the Headship. 'When Allaly died the Anna Pepple House was for some time left without a Head. The Chiefs held repeated meetings, and the generally coveted honour did not seem to tempt any of them; by right of seniority, a chief named Uranta was offered the place', but for reasons of his own he refused. After Uranta there were Annie Stuart, Black Foobra, and Warrasoo, all men of wealth and high standing. But they shirked the responsibility, for Alali had been a great trader and, it was said, owed the Europeans 1,000–1,500 puncheons of oil, equivalent to between £10,000 and £15,000 sterling. None of the chiefs felt able to tackle the settlement of such a debt, 'fearing that the late chief had

[1] An Opobo writer, Mr. E. M. T. Epelle, says Ja Ja was born at Umuduruoha, a village in Amaigbo, Orlu District, Owerri Province. The popular belief that he was born at Nkwerre has been disproved by Epelle's researches.
[2] This account of him was derived from Bonny sources.

not left sufficient to settle' the account. This might end in bankruptcy for Alali's successor and his 'final downfall from leadership. At this time there was in the House a young man who had not very long been made a chief, though he had, for a considerable number of years, been a very good trader, and was much respected by the white traders for his honesty and the dependence they could place in him to adhere strictly to any promise he made in trade matters. This young chief was Ja Ja, and although he was one of the youngest chiefs in the House, he was unanimously elected to fill the office. He, however, did not immediately accept, though his being unanimously elected amounted almost to his being forced to accept.' Ja Ja deliberated over the matter for some days, and 'at a public meeting of the Chiefs of Annie Pepple House'[1] accepted the Headship and solemnly pledged himself to maintain the high ideals of the founder and the great traditions of the House. The chiefs assembled unanimously promised him unstinted support and loyalty.

The British Consul, Sir Richard Burton, remarked on the exceptional character of the new man. 'In December 1863', he wrote, 'one Ja Ja, son of an unknown bushman, a common Negro', had been elected to head the Anna Pepple House. 'He is young, healthy, and powerful, and not less ambitious, energetic, and decided. He is the most influential man and the greatest trader in the River, and £50,000, it is said, may annually pass through his hands. He lives much with Europeans, and he rides rough shod over young hands coming into Bonny. In a short time he will either be shot or he will beat down all his rivals. At present he leads the party against King Pepple.'[2] Burton's prophecy was soon fulfilled.

Ja Ja was not unaware that in terms of Bonny laws and customs he was a parvenu; in one respect the stigma attached to his slave origins had been greater than that of the other ex-slaves, who were born in Bonny of free men and slave women. But for his genius and ability he would have been, like the first generation of slaves 'from the bush', on the lowest rung of the domestic slaves' hierarchy. This very disadvantage was, in a way, one of his greatest assets. He saw Bonny with the critical eye of the foreigner. He loathed its crippling politics, its sordid intrigues, and kept aloof until he was ready to act. Ja Ja was new to Bonny politics, but Bonny politics were not new to him. This conclusion stands clear from detailed investigation. He

---

[1] de Cardi, quoted by Kingsley, op. cit., pp. 526–7.
[2] F.O.2/45, Confidential, printed for F.O., Burton to Russell, 8 Aug. 1864.

knew the characters of the leading political figures, studied the Bonny scene, and made up his mind about his future line of action without disclosing his plans to anyone.

Realizing that the source of Delta wealth was in the oil markets, he made himself *persona grata* with the chiefs of the interior and spent more time with them than with the artificial society of the coast. Similarly he sought popularity with the supercargoes who were at the receiving end of the interior products. He perceived that Europe was determined to capture the hinterland trade and made his plans accordingly. It must not, therefore, be imagined that Ja Ja was idle because his name did not appear on the Bonny political scene until his dramatic election in 1863. Seven years later he was the greatest African living in the east of modern Nigeria.

With characteristic energy he set about putting his House in order. He had 'not been many months Head of the Annie Pepple House before he began to show the old chiefs what kind of metal he was made of'. During the first twelve months he had selected from the ex-regent's lieutenants no less than twenty young men of proven ability and elevated them to positions of trust. He helped them 'to trade on their own account, bought canoes for them, took them to the European traders' who gave them trusts, Ja Ja 'himself standing guarantee for them. This operation had the effect of making Ja Ja immediately popular amongst all classes of slaves.' In two years the debts owed by his predecessor to the supercargoes were paid. 'From this date Ja Ja never looked back, becoming the most popular chief in Bonny and the idol of his own people.'[1]

His successes aroused the jealousy of his opponents. The years 1864–7, between Ja Ja's rise to prominence and the death of King Pepple, represented a period of calm before a violent storm.[2] 'The demon of jealousy was at work,' said de Cardi, 'and in the private Councils of the Manilla House [the opposing faction] it was decided that Ja Ja must be pulled down, the only means of doing it was a civil war.' Both sides were openly engaged in an armaments' race, and Ja Ja's adversaries, suspecting that he had more wealth than weapons of war, did not intend to give him time to make good the deficiency. Though King George was supposed to rule the country, 'Oko Jumbo and Ja Ja were looked upon by everyone as the rulers of Bonny'.[3]

[1] de Cardi, op. cit., pp. 528–9.
[2] F.O.2/45, Confidential, printed for F.O., Burton to Russell, 8 Aug. 1864.
[3] de Cardi, op. cit., p. 529.

Between these two the parties in the city-state were equally divided. On the surface the king played the role of an impartial arbitrator, but there was evidence that his sympathy lay with the monarchist party of Oko Jumbo. In 1867 the first open rupture between the parties broke out. King George settled the two-day skirmish but informed the Court of Equity that he considered the presence of the Consul and a man-of-war necessary to prevent further disturbances.[1]

Consul Livingstone, who came to investigate the incident, refused to interfere in a purely domestic affair.[2] He noted that Ja Ja, like his predecessor the ex-regent, was quietly 'absorbing house after house', and thereby exciting the jealousy of his opponents. This was the origin of the quarrels. 'If we allow this to go on', said they, 'the whole of Bonny will soon belong to Annie Pepple.' The fear of the older chiefs was plain. To say, as did contemporaries, that they were jealous of Ja Ja does not adequately explain their disquietude. It was more than jealousy. Before the civil war of 1855 Alali had absorbed the small independent houses and with their aid supplanted the power of the king. In 1867 Ja Ja, his successor, was repeating the process. It was natural that his opponents should be alarmed by an ominous repetition of events. In spite of the supercargoes' fears that 'a civil war may break out at any moment', and that 'a display, or at least a threat, of force' was vital, the Consul consistently refused to intervene. He protested 'that Her Majesty's Government never desired to interfere in the internal affairs of any nation and that the King and Chiefs would be able to arrange these purely Bonny matters, which they understand better than anyone else, in a friendly and satisfactory manner'.[3]

On 22 December 1867, five months after the first incident, 'King George unaccompanied by his Chiefs called shortly after my arrival in Bonny', said Livingstone, 'and asked me to assist him in his government. The balance of power question was still exciting the fierce jealousy of his Chiefs, and he firmly believed that if I did not interfere, a terrible civil war would break out and the whole English trade would be stopped, perhaps for years.'[4] Consciousness of his lack of power drove the king to this extremity. At home and abroad he became the laughing-stock of contemporaries, yet he must be given credit for recognizing the *fait accompli*. He appealed to the only

[1] F.O.84/1277, No. 9, Encl. 3, King George to Court of Equity, 11 June 1867.
[2] F.O.84/1277, No. 13, Livingstone to Stanley, 13 July 1867.   [3] Ibid.
[4] F.O.84/1277, No. 28, Livingstone to Stanley, 24 Dec. 1867.

power he knew with the means of preserving peace. Livingstone still declined to interfere. Instead he reprimanded the king for not stopping the war which Brass and Okrika, allies of Bonny, were making against New Calabar at Bonny's instigation.[1]

Hostilities were delayed by the great fire which ravaged Bonny in 1868, when the House of Anna Pepple (Ja Ja) appeared to have been the greatest sufferer. Early in 1869, believing their antagonist to have been weakened by the disaster, Oko Jumbo and his supporters sought every means of precipitating a conflict. 'But Ja Ja was an astute diplomatist, and managed to steer clear of all his opponent's pitfalls. A most insulting message was sent to Ja Ja, intimating that the time had come when nothing but a fight could settle their differences. His reply was characteristic of the man; he reminded them that he had no wish to fight, was not prepared, and, furthermore, that neither he, nor they, had paid their debts to the Europeans. The latter part of the message was too much for an irascible, one-eyed old fighting chief named Jack Wilson Pepple',[2] the Commander-in-Chief of the Manilla Pepple forces, and through his influence hostilities commenced.[3]

In September 1869 the supercargoes informed the Consul that 'we are threatened with another civil war in Bonny Town between the two rival Houses of Annie and Manilla Pepple'. They had been given notice 'to remove our ships down the River in three days' time; but we cannot remove the valuable property on the beach in three or even thirty days' time. Extensive preparations are being made in Bonny Town for fighting: heavy guns are in position all around and about the town and all the war canoes are afloat heavily armed with cannon.'[4] Ja Ja had done everything to avoid the outbreak, but Oko Jumbo's eagerness to catch his powerful enemy unprepared prevailed.

Heavy fighting commenced on 13 September 1869 and within a

---

[1] Ibid.   [2] de Cardi, quoted from Kingsley, op. cit., pp. 529–30.

[3] In detail there are conflicting reports of the immediate cause of the civil war. At Bonny I was told that 'The Civil War of 1869 emanated from two traders' dispute at the Esseni Market [in the hinterland], Orudienga Jumbo and Oko Ja Ja Anna Pepple by names', members of the opposing parties, which, later, developed into a war between the Ja Ja and Oko Jumbo parties. This war, which involved Bonny in battle by land and by water, might have been provoked by various incidents occurring simultaneously; a situation of war had existed from 1867.

[4] F.O.84/1308, Encl. 1 in No. 24, Bonny, Court of Equity, to Livingstone, 11 Sept. 1869.

few days news was received that Ja Ja and his warriors had evacuated
Bonny Town 'after spiking all their guns'.[1] This was followed by a
letter from him to the chairman of the Court of Equity placing
himself under the 'protection of Her Majesty the Queen of England',
as well as the outlying settlements—Bonny 'colonies'—which he and
his men now occupied. Everyone knew that in terms of armaments
Ja Ja was outmatched. The last fire had wrought havoc in his store
of ammunition; but the suddenness of his collapse was unexpected
and startled contemporaries. Livingstone described his letter acknowledging defeat as 'sad'.[2] 'Gentlemen,' wrote Ja Ja to the Court of
Equity, 'I beg to inform [the] Court that I cannot fight any more,
because I have no house and no carriage and have [no] guns to fight
as all were burnt and now the small countries which [we] have in
hand [i.e. the outlying settlements his warriors occupied] belong to
the Queen.' In a sentence which is capable of many interpretations,
he implied a desire for mediation by the Consul and the Court of
Equity.[3] His opponents were jubilant with success. There was talk of
fining him 1,000 puncheons of oil, £10,000–£15,000, as a condition
of opening peace talks. In fairness to Oko Jumbo it must be admitted
that he did not desire vindictive terms. As a responsible statesman he
was bent on Bonny's recovery rather than Ja Ja's ruin. 'He be one of
ourselves', Oko Jumbo told Livingstone, 'we no want to crush him.'
His concern was for the uprooting of the cause of Bonny's troubles so
that 'the country may have lasting peace'.[4]

Following Ja Ja's letter to the Court of Equity a truce was arranged
through the good offices of the supercargoes, who tried to obtain for
Ja Ja as favourable terms as were possible. Innumerable meetings
were convened, yet 'after several weeks of palavering' no decision had
been reached. The Europeans interested themselves in the matter, but
'with the exception of one or two at the outside, they understood so
little of the occult workings of the native squabbles that they could
do little to smooth matters over'.[5]

Eight weeks after the outbreak of hostilities Consul Livingstone
returned to Bonny and, to his surprise, saw the situation entirely

---

[1] F.O.84/1308, Encl. 1 in No. 24, Bonny, Court of Equity, to Livingstone,
11 Sept. 1869.

[2] F.O.84/1308, No. 24, Livingstone to Clarendon, 26 Oct. 1869.

[3] F.O.84/1308, Encl. 2 in No. 24, Ja Ja to Court of Equity, Bonny, 14 Sept.
1869.

[4] F.O.84/1308, No. 24, Livingstone to Clarendon, 26 Oct. 1869.

[5] de Cardi, op. cit., pp. 531–2.

reversed. He 'found the Bonny Chiefs', that is Oko Jumbo and his party, 'in grave doubt whether they were the victors or the vanquished. The apparently defeated [Ja Ja] had only talked of peace in order to gain time. He has now established himself in the Andony Country, with the entire control of the creeks which lead to some of the best oil markets; all his people are with him, not one has deserted.' Oko Jumbo believed Ja Ja would return to Bonny if the supercargoes boycotted his settlement and refused him trade. Livingstone advised the Bonny authorities to offer liberal concessions to Ja Ja to induce him to return; 'otherwise Bonny would sink to the condition of a third or fourth rate African kingdom, instead of being a first rate'. The chiefs confessed that had they known 'what they do now, they would never have fought with Ja Ja'.[1]

That was precisely the point. Ja Ja had never intended to fight at Bonny. Within the city-state he knew he was outmatched both in guns and men, 'so he only kept up a semblance of fighting sufficiently long to allow him to make a retreat' to prepared positions.[2] He had carried out what Livingstone described as 'his masterly movements' unpursued and unharassed by the enemy. His diplomatic letter to the supercargoes declaring himself defeated, the envoys he sent to the Bonny chiefs 'informing them that he had been beaten' and was ready for a settlement, were merely devices to gain time.[4] While the peace negotiations kept his enemies talking, he had time to carry out a secret but orderly evacuation. The details of the preparation he had been making to facilitate his movements in 1869, his covenants with the interior chiefs, his choice of able commanders, all of them young, to take charge of his extensive schemes, lie outside the scope of this work.

When Ja Ja left Bonny in 1869 he had completed his plan to found a new state. Exactly four weeks after his evacuation he concluded the famous Minima Agreement with his principal chiefs on 13 October 1869, outlining the constitution of the new state, and he himself was chosen as king.[5] In doing this his aim was to occupy the strategic points on the main creeks leading to the oil markets and thereby cut off Bonny from the source of its supplies. The outposts he occupied

---

[1] F.O.84/1308, No. 37, Livingstone to Clarendon, 4 Dec. 1869.
[2] de Cardi, op. cit., p. 350.
[3] F.O.84/1326, Encl. 1 in No. 8, Livingstone to Clarendon, 17 Mar. 1870.
[4] F.O.84/1326, Encl. 1 in No. 7, Oko Jumbo, &c., to Livingstone, 7 Mar. 1870.
[5] See Appendix A. This agreement forms the basis of Opobo Constitution today.

on the way to his destination formed the Bonny trade routes to the Ibo and Qua markets. They were 'Tombo, Iya-Minima, Oloma, Eppelama and Elawma', all trading posts belonging to the kingdom of Bonny.[1]

His final objective was the occupation of the extensive area of land lying on the Ikomtoro river in the territory of the Andoni tribe. Once in this river, by fortifying two or three points, he could keep Bonny out of the oil markets. The faultless execution of a brilliant plan dazzled and confused his enemies. By the 15th of February 1870 he was master of the situation. Writing to the British Consul on this date he declared himself for ever separated from Bonny, signifying at the same time his willingness to enter into friendly relations with Great Britain.[2]

Consul Livingstone was in an unenviable position. He was faced with a grave threat to a trade worth to Britain about a million pounds annually. Naturally he was more interested in defending British interests than in welcoming the successes of Ja Ja. In December 1869, when the purpose of Ja Ja's movements became clear, Livingstone warned the supercargoes at Bonny that he 'could not guarantee protection to any who chose to go to Andony'.[3] This was a subtle method of prohibiting trade with the rebel chief.[4]

The Bonny chiefs had no option but to resume the war. They attributed their diplomatic defeat to the interference of the super-cargoes.[5] King George was entirely engrossed in legalistic arguments claiming that Ja Ja's forts which barred the way to the oil markets were in Bonny territory, and that the Andoni country which Ja Ja had now occupied was conquered by Bonny in 1846 and annexed by his father. These were valid claims so far as documents went. But the issue which faced Oko Jumbo and the Consul was the *de facto* negation of these legal rights by Ja Ja's achievements.[6]

King George's adherence to the party of Oko Jumbo, the latter a shrewd and practised politician, caused not a little embarrassment to that chief. The king was obsessed with issues of legality in a situation which demanded initiative and action. While Ja Ja acted, the king

[1] F.O.84/1326, Encl. 1 in No. 7, Oko Jumbo to Livingstone, 7 Mar. 1870.
[2] F.O.84/1326, Encl. in No. 8, Ja Ja to Livingstone, 15 Feb. 1870.
[3] F.O.84/1308, No. 38, Livingstone to Clarendon, 4 Dec. 1869.
[4] F.O.84/1326, Encl. 1 in No. 8, Livingstone to Clarendon, 17 Mar. 1870.
[5] F.O.84/1326, Encl. 1 in No. 7, Oko Jumbo to Livingstone, 7 Mar. 1870.
[6] F.O.84/1326, No. 12, F.P., Livingstone to Clarendon, 24 Mar. 1870, and its enclosures.

inundated the Consular Office at Fernando Po with letters that solved nothing. 'Again and again', the chiefs of Bonny told Livingstone, 'that George's big mouth was not their mouth.'[1] It must have been with some relief that they dispatched him to England in April 1870 to talk 'book' with the Foreign Office, and away from the scene of conflict.[2]

Ja Ja anticipated that the Bonny supercargoes might, as indeed happened, boycott his new settlement. He had, however, provided against that contingency. While still in retreat he had made an arrangement with a supercargo from the Brass city-state by the name of Charley,[3] 'who had been in the Bonny River some years before. At an interview with Ja Ja, that did not last half an hour, the whole plan of campaign was arranged.' Ja Ja was famous for his quick decisions. 'Charley returned to Brass and confided the scheme to his friend, Archie McEachan, who decided to join him.' Thus Ja Ja had the certainty of shipping his oil once he was established in the Ikomtoro river.[4] With success, other supercargoes, from several Delta ports, joined Ja Ja.

The appearance of Europeans on the Ikomtoro river angered the Bonny chiefs. They threatened that they would 'use every endeavour to stop all trade in Andony and Ekomtoro Rivers, and however much we might regret any injury to white men or their property, we will not hold ourselves accountable for same as by their assisting Ja Ja in the way they are doing they are ruining us in Bonny'.[5] In spite of these menaces white merchants flocked to Ja Ja. 'The large steamers lie outside the bar [as the narrow creek leading to the settlement proved too shallow for bigger vessels]. A small steamer, the *African*, belonging to Messrs. Taylor and Laughland of Glasgow' visited Ja Ja's port. 'Two other firms intend to go into these rivers. As the merchants seem determined on this the War between Bonny and Ja Ja is likely to continue.'[6]

The arrival of Europeans created complications, for Bonny war-canoes fired at British ships going to Ja Ja's territory. 'I visited Bonny to inquire into the matter and warned the chiefs that they must on no

[1] F.O.84/1326, No. 29, Livingstone to Clarendon, 9 July 1870.
[2] F.O.84/1326, No. 22, Clarendon to Livingstone, 23 May 1870.
[3] 'Charley', the supercargo in question, is de Cardi himself, who was close to Ja Ja in the first year of the latter's retreat from Bonny.
[4] de Cardi, op. cit., p. 532.
[5] F.O.84/1326, Encl. 2 in No. 7, King George to Livingstone, 19 Feb. 1870.
[6] F.O.84/1326, No. 14, Livingstone to Clarendon, 31 Mar. 1870.

account fire on English vessels there, as punishment would surely follow.'[1] The Bonny chiefs retorted that the Andoni (Ja Ja's new territory) was 'a battlefield' and that men who sought commerce in a field of war do so at their own risk. 'If the crows don't go near the windmill, the windmill would have no occasion to trouble or hurt them. If you the Consul are able to settle the fight between us and Ja Ja try and do so with all God's speed, if not, leave us natives' to fight it out among ourselves.[2]

Ja Ja was winning the war. Early in June 1870 when Livingstone visited Bonny he found Oko Jumbo and his chiefs 'anxious, apparently, to have the war ended, and Ja Ja restored to Bonny'. In order to have peace Bonny chiefs yielded to Ja Ja on every point in dispute. Had he chosen to accept their concessions, Ja Ja would have been virtually king of Bonny.[3] Livingstone himself decided that the time had come to act. The war was disastrous to all concerned; no one but Ja Ja had foreseen that it would reach such dimensions. Delta civil wars were usually over within a week or two. This one had dragged on for over nine months, involving not only the city-states but markets in the tribal hinterland.[4] On the 6th of June 1870 Livingstone paid his first visit to the Ikomtoro river.

He found that 'Ja Ja had hurried off to repel a rumoured attack' on one of his forts, 'but returned the following day'. The Consul's attitude during the interview was friendly, but when he stated 'the peace terms Oko Jumbo [and the Bonny chiefs] had proposed', Ja Ja 'instantly rejected [them] with scorn and derision. With intense savage bitterness he spoke of Oko and with contempt of "the Boy George" [King George]. He remarked that he had a fine rich country here, surpassing Bonny: could buy plenty of oil and fourteen of the native Chiefs of Bonny [i.e. heads of the principal Houses] had joined his House, while only four adhered to that of his opponents.' He would welcome British merchants, but 'would never allow the House of Manilla Pepple to enter the Oil Markets'.[5]

Although Livingstone threatened that 'Her Majesty's Government would insist on his opening those oil markets to the Bonny People',

---

[1] F.O.84/1326, No. 7, Livingstone to Clarendon, 16 Mar. 1870.

[2] F.O.84/1326, Encl. 1 in No. 7, Oko Jumbo to Livingstone, 7 Mar. 1870.

[3] F.O.84/1326, No. 20, Livingstone to Clarendon, 4 June 1870.

[4] F.O.84/1326, Encl. in Livingstone's No. 8, Oko Jumbo to Livingstone, 9 July 1870. According to Oko Jumbo, Ja Ja captured £30,000 worth of property in the interior markets.

[5] F.O.84/1326, No. 21, Livingstone to Clarendon, 6 June 1870.

Ja Ja remained obdurate.[1] Livingstone informed Lord Clarendon that only British interference would resolve the impasse. 'Peace can never be secured while the markets are shut to the Bonny Chiefs. Bonny must fight till they obtain access to their oil markets or sink to a mere fishing village. Ja Ja's blockade entirely cuts off the trade of seven English firms which can never go to Opobo', since their permanent shore establishments could not be easily moved. They must therefore sink or swim with the Bonny people.[2]

In August 1870 Livingstone paid a second visit to Ja Ja. 'I reminded him that he had stopped the trade of ten English firms in the Bonny for a year, and this could no longer be tolerated; he replied that he would never open the oil markets' to Bonny 'for a thousand years'.[3] The Consul then decided on force. 'I informed Ja Ja that as he declined any reasonable settlement, I shall now stop his trade, and place the matter in the hands of the Captain of the Man-of-War.' Commander Jones of H.M.S. *Pert* was called into the Ikomtoro river to take charge of operations. The Consul planned a show of force, not an actual bombardment of the settlement. His purpose was to bring Ja Ja's trade in the river to a standstill and thereby compel him to accept British arbitration in the dispute with Bonny. Commander Jones ordered the five English firms trading at the settlement 'to drop down the River' and assured the supercargoes 'that the stoppage of trade will be, to the [European] traders, but a temporary inconvenience which sensible men must surely prefer to constant danger from attacks of enraged cannibals'.[4] The Europeans viewed 'with deep concern the hostile measures adopted' against Ja Ja 'and regretted that H.M.S. *Pert* has already fired upon Qua Canoes [natives under Ja Ja's suzerainty], that the King of Encoro [Ja Ja's ally] was in the canoe turned back this morning. Should any of these people unfortunately be killed, the consequences of such will be very serious.'[5] Two people lost their lives in what was essentially 'a show of force'.[6]

Livingstone's intervention had the desired effect. He reported that 'Commander Jones stopped Trade so skilfully and thoroughly that Ja Ja yielded in 48 hours, and agreed to abide by the decision of two

[1] F.O.84/1326, No. 21, Livingstone to Clarendon, 6 June 1870.
[2] F.O.84/1326, No. 30, Livingstone to Clarendon, 11 July 1870.
[3] F.O.84/1326, No. 33, Livingstone to Granville, 23 Aug. 1870.
[4] Ibid. and its enclosures.
[5] F.O.84/1326, Encl. 3 in No. 34, Supercargoes to Livingstone, 19 Aug. 1870.
[6] F.O.84/1326, Encl. 8 in No. 44, Ja Ja to Livingstone, 16 Sept. 1870.

arbitrators, Amacree, King of New Calabar, and Fibia, King of Okrika. Meanwhile hostilities are suspended and the War Canoes recalled.'[1] But the truce did not last. Once again Ja Ja sought to win by diplomacy what he had lost by force. He put all sorts of difficulties in the way of negotiations and events worked in his favour. The Bonny supercargoes favoured the use of force against Ja Ja. They could not believe that a man so astute and energetic could be managed by the arbitrators and tried to influence Bonny chiefs against Livingstone's proposals.[2] Moreover, Amakiri, king of New Calabar, refused to play·the part assigned to him.[3] Livingstone believed this was also due to the influence of the Bonny supercargoes.[4] Hostilities were resumed, no doubt to Ja Ja's delight. He believed the prospects of maintaining his conquests were bright. A quick settlement might injure his chances of gaining the complete ascendancy he desired in the Niger Delta.

British traders were as involved in the conflict as were Africans and as equally divided. Lord Clarendon complained to Livingstone that from 'further correspondence' transmitted to the Foreign Office by African merchants it appeared that much assistance had 'been given by British Subjects to both parties. It appears that the War is as much promoted by rival British Agents as by the African Chiefs.'[5] The 'rival British interests' were supercargoes in Ja Ja's territory and those who were compelled by their investments to remain at Bonny. Lord Clarendon's successor, Earl Granville, came to the same conclusion after examining the mass of evidence at his disposal. 'It appears to me, as it did to Lord Clarendon, that the continuance of the present state of affairs is as much owing to the rivalry of British traders as to the quarrels of the natives, and that if it were not for the interference of Europeans the dispute might easily be settled.'[6]

Livingstone complained bitterly and repeatedly of the difficulties put in the way of peaceful settlement by European interests. 'English Traders have furnished the rival chiefs with guns, shot and powder, as required, until war materials are a drug' on the Delta market. 'Bonny

[1] F.O.84/1326, No. 34, Livingstone to Granville, 24 Aug. 1870.
[2] F.O.84/1326, No. 35, Livingstone to Granville, 25 Aug. 1870.
[3] F.O.84/1326, Encl. 12 in No. 44, Amakiri to Bonny, Court of Equity, 25 Sept. 1870.
[4] F.O.84/1326, No. 44, Livingstone to Granville, 15 Nov. 1870.
[5] F.O.84/1326, No. 25, Clarendon to Livingstone, 23 June 1870.
[6] F.O.84/1326, No. 27, Granville to Livingstone, 3 Aug. 1870.

Agents have wished Ja Ja smashed, and all trade brought back to
Bonny.' Ja Ja's allies favoured his blockade 'of the Bonny Oil
markets, because it brought oil to them: and white traders in both
rivers have sought only their own selfish interests reckless of all
others'. To show the extent to which the supercargoes could go, he
cited the instance of Mr. Cheetham, a Bonny supercargo 'who
actually bought the *Steady* [a gunboat] in England, but ordered it
to be sold on hearing that . . . I could only regard her English crew
as pirates should they fire on their own countrymen'.[1]

While Africans did the fighting, the opposing British interests
supplied their respective allies with the weapons of war. This armaments race intensified the struggle and widened the area of conflict
to the tribal interior. It was certainly the greatest war ever fought in
the Delta. Between September 1869 and May 1870 contemporary
estimates put the loss sustained by Bonny supercargoes following Ja
Ja's blockade at £100,000.[2] At the end of 1870 Livingstone, baffled
by an unprecedented situation, had come to the end of his resources.
He informed Granville that 'the Bonny Agents have prevented a
settlement by Arbitration'.[3]

The matter was reviewed by the Foreign Office with the aid of the
Administrator of Lagos, Captain John Hawley Glover.[4] He urged
'direct Government interference' and Wylde supported him. 'When
the Chiefs know that we are in earnest, it will take very little pressure
to compel them to agree to our terms.'[5] But the Foreign Minister had
grave doubts about the wisdom of 'much interference'. 'I confess',
he wrote, 'I am not in favour of our dictating terms of peace to these
rival Chiefs, for if so we make ourselves responsible for their being
observed. The utmost I think we should do is to tell them that if they
do not make peace, their interests will suffer, as merchants will not
resort to a country where there is no security for commerce.'[6]
Livingstone was told not to 'interfere any further except for the
protection of British life and property'.[7]

Judged by lessons learnt during forty years of improvisation the
Foreign Minister's instinct was right. Britain had arrived at a point

[1] F.O.84/1326, No. 35, Livingstone to Granville, 25 Aug. 1870.
[2] F.O.84/1326, No. 22, Livingstone to Clarendon, 7 June 1870.
[3] F.O.84/1326, No. 44, Livingstone to Granville, 15 Nov. 1870.
[4] F.O.84/1326, Memorandum prepared by C. Vivian, F.O., 29 Dec. 1870.
[5] F.O.84/1326, Minutes on Memorandum, W.H.W., F.O., 29 Dec. 1870.
[6] F.O.84/1326, Minutes on Memorandum, E.H. & G., F.O., 12 Jan. 1871.
[7] F.O.84/1343, No. 2, Granville to Livingstone, 25 Jan. 1871.

where what was needed in the Delta was not so much interference as
the assumption of governmental responsibilities. Intermittent interference, such as that which paralysed the Bonny Government, in the
long run profited no one. Meanwhile, on Christmas Day 1870, Ja Ja,
feeling his position secure, proclaimed the foundation of his new
kingdom and called it 'Opobo', after Opubu the Great, the illustrious
king of Bonny. The name Opobo was chosen by Ja Ja himself.[1]

It is characteristic of the man that he had not only a sense of the
occasion but of history. Settlements in the Delta were often named
after their founders: thus we have Aqua Town and Bell Town in the
Cameroons. But this clear-sighted statesman, by instinct a leader of
men, knew that his material victories were not sufficient to win the
loyalty of the masses who now adhered to his cause. It was necessary
to appeal to their imagination and to make them believe that he was
the heir of Opubu. Thus when Ja Ja named his territory Opobo he
was giving expression to the belief that the House he led was the
successor to the celebrated king. How widespread was that belief
may be estimated from the fact that out of the eighteen important
Houses in the city-state, fourteen followed him to Opobo. In the eyes
of Ja Ja, therefore, Opobo was Bonny in new surroundings. It is
a commentary on his genius that unlike his predecessor, Alali, he
did not essay to fight the Pepples in Bonny. His knowledge of the
political beliefs of the kingdom saved him from that error. Kingship
was impossible of attainment for anyone of slave origins in Bonny.
Instead he sought another land where he could give full scope to his
boundless energies.

Ja Ja of Opobo was regarded by contemporary Africans as the
successor to the Pepples. He was known to the interior Ibos as
'Jō Jō[2] na Ubani'. 'Ubani' is the Ibo term for Bonny. The phrase
conveys the same impression in the Ibo language as would 'Hitlerite
Germany', 'Napoleon's France', or 'Mussolini's Italy' to Europeans.
To the Ibos the word 'Opobo' became synonymous with 'Ubani' or
Bonny, and Ja Ja was from 1869 its leading figure. Since he was Ibo,
the predominant tribe in the east, Ja Ja had the goodwill of the
majority and was served by the best talents in Iboland.[3]

[1] de Cardi, op. cit., p. 532. It is not correct as de Cardi asserted here that Opubu
was the 'founder of the town of "Grand Bonny"'. He was its greatest king but
not its founder. Alagbariye, according to Bonny tradition, founded the town.

[2] Ja Ja's full name was JUBO JUBOGHA. This was abbreviated by Africans to
Jō Jō and by Europeans to Ja Ja.

[3] At Awka, in Onitsha Province, I met the grandchildren of a man who had

In 1871 the Acting Consul reported that the trade of Bonny river 'is paralysed, large trading establishments belonging to British merchants kept up at an enormous outlay, are doing nothing, the people must live—they have been able by going into the Okrikah Country to make a little trade and buy enough food to keep them from starving'.[1] This dramatic decline of the greatest Delta state within a period of two years emphasizes the completeness of Ja Ja's blockade. In 1873 it was reported that 'Liverpool trade with Bonny and Opobo had fallen off to the amount of £500,000 during the last two years'.[2] The Ja Ja revolution rendered bankrupt the greater number of English firms trading in Bonny. This Foreign Office estimate was confirmed by Consul Livingstone's dispatch of the previous year. 'Our merchants put their losses by this single war' at 'half a million pounds last year'.[3] It ruined the health of Livingstone himself. He was so broken in body and spirit that on 6 November 1873, while on his way to England, he died at Bonny.[4]

The disorders in the seventies were provoked in part by the challenge of the inland traders whose determined incursions into the interior everywhere threatened the economic organization of the Delta. To forestall these increasing European encroachments on the oil markets was one of Ja Ja's objectives in his movement away from the Atlantic coast to the Ikomtoro river. Events in the eighties proved that his calculations were correct.

As Ja Ja had hoped, time compelled Bonny to admit defeat and accept his terms. In July 1872 Livingstone reported that 'the Bonny–Opobo difficulty may now be considered, as in fact, practically settled. Ja Ja has now all the Ibo and Qua markets; and our five great English firms in the Opobo are doing immense trade.' Bonny, on the other hand, with its eight firms, was practically ruined, being only allowed to trade in the Okrika markets.[5]

Both sides were ready for a settlement; in January 1873 the British Government dispatched Commodore J. E. Commerell, V.C., C.B., with five warships to arbitrate between the two parties, assisted by the

been one of Ja Ja's medicine men. Accounts were given me of the great efforts he made to procure the services of this man, who was a famous doctor in his day. Ja Ja gathered round him at Opobo the illustrious Ibos of his generation.

[1] F.O.84/1343, No. 13, Hopkins to Granville, 7 July 1871.
[2] F.O.84/1377, Minutes on Livingstone's Nos. 1 and 11, 8 Feb. 1873.
[3] F.O.84/1343, 371, Consul Livingstone's Memorandum, 3 Dec. 1871.
[4] F.O.84/1377, No. 60, Hartley to Granville, 6 Nov. 1873.
[5] F.O.84/1356, No. 15, Livingstone to Granville, 9 July 1872.

Consul and neutral Delta chiefs. After three days' negotiations the peace treaty was concluded and Ja Ja's victories were, in all essentials, confirmed.[1] The concessions he made to Bonny were unimportant and the settlement gave the latter little satisfaction. In another treaty Britain recognized Ja Ja as king of Opobo.[2] This act signified the end of three centuries of Bonny supremacy in the Niger Delta.

In the seventies Ja Ja consolidated his power over the palm belt, occupied strategic points on the rivers leading to the interior markets, and barred the way not only to the Bonny middlemen but also to the invading Europeans. During the 'scramble for Africa' the latter found him the greatest impediment to their occupation of eastern Nigeria.

The advance of interior commerce although steady was slow; the Delta remained the centre of British trade and politics in the early seventies. In December 1871 Consul Livingstone showed, in a memorandum submitted to the Foreign Office, the extent of British property involved in the Bight of Biafra. There were sixty large trading establishments owned by some twenty Scottish and English firms. 'Their property in the Rivers in English manufactured goods, Hulks, Houses, River Steamers, Schooners, Lighters is not much short of a million pounds sterling, and is often estimated at a higher figure.' The carrying trade to and from the Bight of Biafra, he declared, was chiefly in the hands of two lines of steamers from Glasgow and Liverpool. 'Five Steamers leave Liverpool every month, and the Trade of the Oil Rivers being their principal support. About half-a-million pounds sterling is invested in these steamers.' He estimated that the palm oil then exported from the Delta was between 25,000 and 30,000 tons and that the price in England fluctuated between £34 and £44 per ton. 'Small quantities of Ivory, India Rubber, and bar wood are also exported.'[3] The permanent establishments in the Delta employed about 2,500 Europeans and Africans (British subjects) and these he described as 'men removed from all control'.

Since the development of the oil trade and the institution of the consulship, the constant problem of the British Government had been

[1] F.O.84/1377, No. 1, Livingstone to Granville, 7 Jan. 1873. Also Encl. 1.
[2] F.O.84/1377, No. 2, Livingstone to Granville, 8 Jan. 1873. See Appendix C.
[3] F.O.84/1356, 371, Consul Livingstone's Memorandum, Received F.O., 3 Dec. 1871.

how to check the lawlessness of its subjects in the Delta. The Courts of Equity had been instituted primarily for handling disputes between Africans and Europeans. The authority of these international courts had been flouted by supercargoes when it suited them, and although they were invariably established by treaty with native governments, experience had shown that competent British courts did not accept their decisions as binding. On several occasions their findings had been regarded as those of an unrecognized court by the colonial courts of the Gold Coast and Sierra Leone. In 1870 Lord Granville stated 'that a question has been raised as to the legal competency of the Courts of Equity on the West Coast of Africa in consequence of a decision given by the Chief Magistrate of the British Colonial Court at Cape Coast in a case which has previously been settled by the Court of Equity at Brass'.[1] Many natives of the Gold Coast employed as coopers and carpenters in the Delta by British firms were mal-treated by the supercargoes, and as the Courts of Equity were domin-ated by the latter they rarely got justice from that quarter. Hence Gold Coast natives were in the habit of appealing against its decisions in British courts in their own country. As a result supercargoes were sometimes arrested at Accra and Freetown on the homeward voyage and heavily fined for actions brought against them by Africans they had sentenced in the Delta. To avoid this unsatisfactory state of affairs attempts were made, albeit unsuccessfully, to endow the consuls with magisterial powers. British consuls had to face the fact that they had no means of punishing, or of bringing to justice, criminals among their countrymen residing within their consular jurisdiction. Because of this Consul Beecroft, in 1852, had to set free by order of the Foreign Office a British subject accused of murdering five Africans in the Cameroons.[2]

In 1856, when Hutchinson succeeded Beecroft, he found that although he could punish Africans and protect British property, he was powerless to check the violence and lawlessness of his country-men. In Old Calabar, for instance, when a supercargo, Cuthbertson, seized sixteen puncheons of oil belonging to an African, Hutchinson threatened to report the issue to Lord Clarendon, 'leaving to his Lordship the reference of the matter to a Court of Justice if neces-sary'. The Foreign Office in reply informed him that 'this brutum fulmen' could not be carried into effect. 'Neither H.M. Government

---

[1] F.O.84/1326, No. 28, Granville to Livingstone, 4 Aug. 1870.
[2] F.O.2/7, Malmesbury to Beecroft, F.O., 13 Oct. 1852.

nor H.M. Consul at Fernando Po have any legal power to oblige the
British supercargoes stationed in the rivers of the Bight of Biafra
to adopt or to obey any particular code of trading regulations.'[1]
When the Consul protested in 1857 'that my chief difficulty lies not
so much in arbitrating between the British supercargoes and the
native chiefs, as between the British supercargoes one with another',[2]
he was expressing the mind and experience of every British official
who had had to deal with the affairs of the oil rivers. The British
subject remained until 1872 a law unto himself.

As early as 1856 the 'expediency of regulating the trade of British
subjects in the Biafra Rivers by an Order-in-Council has been referred
to the Commodore on the African Station, to the African Association
of Liverpool, to Consul Campbell, to Consul Hutchinson, and to the
Governor of Sierra Leone; but the matter is not yet sufficiently
matured for the consideration of the Board of Trade'.[3] Every year
after this fresh efforts were made to bestow this much-needed power
on the consuls, but with little success. At each stage fresh difficulties
arose. In 1859 it was found necessary to obtain the permission of
Delta chiefs within whose territory the provisions of the proposed
Order in Council would operate. The Consul was therefore instructed
to approach them with a view to obtaining their concurrence with the
intentions of H.M. Government. Africans were frankly suspicious.
Men who knew what deadly political weapons 'treaties' could
become were afraid to put 'hand to book'. They had come to
recognize the Consul and the warship as the supreme political
force in the Bight of Biafra and were unable to perceive how they,
politically the inferiors of the Consul, could confer fresh powers
on him.

'King Amakree [of New Calabar] confessed to me', said Hutchinson, 'that he did not know how he could give me more power than
my Queen was fit to give: not being able to read the treaty, he
suspected its containing something insidious.'[4] Moreover, the chiefs
were advised against signing the treaty 'by the supercargoes who
feared that they will be the victims if such powers were granted'.[5]
They cited the instance of Gaboon, where the French got the natives

---

[1] F.O.84/1001, Minutes on Consul Hutchinson, No. 23, 12 Mar. 1856.

[2] F.O.2/19, F.P., Hutchinson to Clarendon, 30 Apr. 1857.

[3] F.O.84/1001, No. 30, Clarendon to Hutchinson, 23 Oct. 1856 and Minutes on
it by Thos. Ward, F.O., 19 Dec. 1856.

[4] Hutchinson, *Wanderings among the Ethiopians*, pp. 210–11.

[5] F.O.84/1176, Minutes on No. 16, F.P., Burton to Russell, 22 May 1862.

to sign a treaty they did not understand and then seized their country. At Bonny 'some of them [the chiefs] even went the length of stating their objections to be grounded on the dread that our government wanted to do with Bonny what the French had done at Gaboon'.[1] The inability of the Consul to obtain unanimous native support for the new measure meant its indefinite postponement from 1859, and, as Wylde admitted, 'Mr. Hutchinson, who was at the time Consul for the Bight of Biafra, was not thought to be a proper person to entrust with magisterial powers'.[2] For another twelve years the issue was shelved, and the European traders pursued their lawless course 'without let or hindrance'.

It was not till 1872 that the pressing question of the Order in Council and the legal status of the Courts of Equity were referred for solution to the Law Officers of the Crown. Lord Granville, the Foreign Minister, was 'advised that the judgments of these Courts are not entitled to the same respect in Law as the judgments of regularly constituted Tribunals of recognised and civilised communities', and that the way to have them placed on a proper footing was to invest the Consul with magisterial powers.[3] Recognition of the urgent need for this instrument in the Bight of Biafra enabled Livingstone to obtain the necessary permission and on 21 February 1872 the Order in Council was made. By this Order the Consul was given power to try and punish British subjects, under certain conditions, by fine up to £200 or by imprisonment up to twenty-one days or by banishment for twelve months, for breaches of the regulations which he should make under the powers given him, or by trade treaties with the natives. Of particular interest to the Delta was the fact that this Order recognized the Courts of Equity and provided for their co-operation with the Consul in dispensing justice. It was a tribute to the work which these irregularly constituted tribunals had done to bestow some sort of order on a disorderly community. Two or four members of the court were to sit as assessors with the Consul when the punishment was likely to exceed a fine of £40. The Court of Equity could deal with simpler cases, but had to submit its decision for the sanction of the Consul. All British subjects had to enrol as member of a court or forfeit their right to protection. British subjects and foreigners might also be tried if the latter consented and gave

---

[1] Hutchinson, *Wanderings among the Ethiopians*, p. 211.
[2] F.O.84/1176, Minutes by Wylde on Burton's No. 16, F.O., 14 July 1862.
[3] Ibid.

sufficient security that they would stand by the decision (clause 7). The courts were, in fact, granted full legal powers.[1] Everywhere British power was in the process of consolidation.

[1] Burns, op. cit. (see Appendix E for full copy of the Order in Council, Feb. 1872). Also *London Gazette*, 1872, i. 672, Scotter, op. cit., pp. 256–8, F.O.84/1356, No. 8, Encl. 1, Livingstone to Granville, 29 Apr. 1872.

CHAPTER XI

Inland Trade and the Niger Company

THE colonial policy of Great Britain and France in West Africa has been widely different. France from her basis on the Senegal coast has pursued steadily the aim of establishing herself on the Upper Niger and its affluents; this object she has attained by a large and constant expenditure, and by a succession of military expeditions. Great Britain, on the other hand, has adopted the policy of advance by commercial enterprise; she has not attempted to compete with the military operations of her neighbour.[1]

This dispatch, addressed to the British Ambassador in Paris, although a distortion of the French method of advance—France did not expand solely by means of military operations, witness the work of her brilliant explorers and traders—sums up adequately the British position in the Niger territories up to 1885. British trade with the Niger Delta was greater in volume and value when compared to those parts of West Africa such as the Gambia, the Gold Coast, and Sierra Leone where Crown Colony government operated.[2] In other words, half the trade of Britain was done outside the limits of her legal and constitutional empire in West Africa. As this study has demonstrated, in the half-century following 1830 Britain established and maintained an 'informal'[3] or commercial empire over the Delta states. In strict constitutional sense this region was foreign territory until the proclamation of the Protectorate and could not, *de jure*, be considered an integral part of the British empire. But British reluctance to annex the Delta formally was no evidence of her unwillingness to control the area politically. She achieved commercial supremacy over the coastal region through the medium of the African Squadron and from 1849 through the exertions of her consuls aided by the warships. Further, the unequal treaties concluded with the Delta states became her instruments of pressure and coercion in her dealings with native governments. Since these

[1] Parl. Pap., C 6701, 1892, quoted from Mary Kingsley, op. cit., pp. 307–8.
[2] See Chapters VI and IX.
[3] This term has been used by some writers to describe the economic expansion of Britain (or any great power for that matter) in territories not legally or strictly within their jurisdiction.

governments were strong enough to maintain the flow of trade between the hinterland and the coast, Britain tolerated and strengthened those city-states, such as Old Calabar and the Cameroons whose rulers collaborated in advancing her commercial interests. On the other hand, African rulers such as Pepple, king of Bonny, who refused to bend, were broken. In other words, so long as the existing native governments served her trade interests well Britain preferred the cheap informal dependency of the Delta type to the expensive formal colonies of the Gold Coast and Sierra Leone.

It has been shown that an important factor in the success of this informal empire was British sea power, which dominated the coastal communities in the bights of Benin and Biafra. As Palmerston reminded King Kosoko during the Lagos crisis of 1851, '. . . Lagos is near the sea, and . . . on the sea are the ships and cannon of England'.[1] No native power faced with the prospects of naval bombardment was ever known to defy the orders of the British Government. Until the necessity of defending her interests against the competing nations of Europe arose Britain held on to the cheap informal empire of the period 1830–84.[2]

In the Delta the transition from an informal to a formal empire was dictated, first, by the needs of a rapidly expanding hinterland trade. A survey of the position in 1878 will reveal the striking progress made since 1832. Four British companies were now operating in the Niger valley—The West African Company (Manchester); Messrs. Alexander Miller Brothers & Co. (Glasgow); The Central African Trading Company (London); and James Pinnock & Co. (Liverpool). This list does not include the several small firms and individual merchants pushing their way up the Delta rivers into the hinterland. Between them these companies employed fourteen steamers in the Niger trade. All maintained trading posts at Akassa, Abo, Ndoni, Abragada, Odogeri, Utchi, Osamari, Alenso, Lower Oko, Onitsha, Gbokem, Lokoja, Yimaha, Egga, and many other posts on the Niger and Benue. The approximate quantity of produce shipped from the Niger valley for the year 1878 was as follows:

---

[1] See Papers Relative to the Reduction of Lagos, 1852, p. 130, quoted from Burns, op. cit., p. 129.

[2] Lagos is a case in point. Britain attacked and occupied this island in 1851, partly to eject Portuguese slave-traders whose economic aims were opposed to her own and whom she could not eliminate other than by direct control. This to some extent explains why Lagos became part of the formal empire some twenty-five years before the Delta states were annexed.

	£
5,000 tons of palm oil at £39 a ton . . .	195,000
65 tons of ivory at £800 a ton . . .	52,000
1,500 tons of shea butter at £39 a ton. . .	58,000
150 tons of beri-seed at £24 a ton . . .	3,600
50 tons of ground nuts at £12 a ton . . .	600
	£309,200[1]

River navigation had been carried to a point 600 miles in the hinterland.[2] Laird's dreams had come true and the Nigerian hinterland had been opened to British commerce.

Once again the Foreign Office, in the hinterland as on the coast, had to face the fact that the invasion of the Niger basin by British traders had drawn the mother country irresistibly into the politics of the interior. 'Some years ago', wrote Wylde in 1876, 'the traders on the African coast were given to understand that if they chose to establish themselves up the Rivers where the natives were hostile they must do so at their own responsibility . . . they must . . . not expect to be protected by our cruisers.'[3] No one took this injunction seriously. The realization by the British Government that sea power was of little use hundreds of miles inland brought to the fore the issue of providing security for internal commerce. 'Where there is money to be made', continued Wylde, 'our merchants will be certain to intrude themselves, and . . . if they establish a lucrative trade public opinion in this country practically compels us to protect them.' Economic opportunity is dependent for its exploitation on political security; this security British merchants lacked in their trade with the interior. The Government recognized that to attain success, trade and political frontiers must march hand in hand.

Even in the sixties the consuls from Burton onwards emphasized that with the trade frontier moving fast into the hinterland the island of Fernando Po was no longer suited as the headquarters of their activities. In 1872 Lord Granville approved the transfer of the Consulate to Old Calabar on the mainland.[4] In this movement from the coast to the interior the inland traders did not always wait for the Government to protect them. As a rule they pushed their way

---

[1] F.O.84/1508, No. 40, Hopkins to F.O., 18 Nov. 1878.
[2] F.O.84/1508, Minutes on Consul Hopkins's No. 4, W.H.W., F.O., 21 Jan. 1879.
[3] F.O.84/1455, Minutes on Consul McKellar's No. 35, W.H.W., 6 Aug. 1876.
[4] F.O.84/1356, Separate, Granville to Livingstone, 2 Feb. 1872.

through the creeks and rivers of the Niger Delta, in armed boats, to the oil markets. The following description of one of these boats owned by a British company will illustrate the general trend: 'Messrs. Miller Brothers & Co. have a steamer out here the *Sultan of Socotoo* well armed and having iron screens for protection of those on board; she is . . . useful in establishing factories in unfrequented localities . . . .'[1] Using this steamer to fight their way through Delta opposition, Miller Brothers established factories on the Qua Eboe river, 'situated between Opobo and Old Calabar, where they diverted a portion of the Trade' from those two city-states. They were eventually driven off by Ja Ja and King Archibong of Old Calabar, the two most powerful chiefs in the area.[2] As the Liverpool coast traders accepted the inevitability of inland trade, the hostility which used to exist between them and the inland traders gradually disappeared. It now became a fight between the European merchants, on the one hand, and the Niger Delta middlemen on the other. In the seventies the word 'tapping' was frequently used to describe the activities of the trading steamers which passed above the Delta and intercepted the produce that used to pass through the hands of the middlemen. By 1876 'tapping' had become a regular feature of the Delta trade and with it British 'factories' sprang up like mushrooms in the Delta oil markets, formerly a preserve of the middlemen.

From time to time the British Government made efforts to provide protection for the expanding commerce of the Niger valley. When native hostility necessitated the evacuation of the interior consulate at Lokoja in 1869, Britain depended partly on her friendship with Masaba, king of Bida, and partly on the warships that ascended the river in the rainy season for the protection of the life and property of her subjects. In 1870 Lieutenant Molyneux went up the Niger in H.M.S. *Pioneer* accompanied by the Lagos government steamer *Eyo*, and paid a visit to King Masaba, who annually received presents and ammunition from the British Government for his services. In 1871 a diplomatic agent, Mr. W. H. Simpson, was dispatched by the Foreign Office to report on hinterland trade. He was at Lokoja (centre of this trade) from August to October and paid many visits to Masaba, reporting very favourably on the support of this chief for the British cause:

I was indeed much struck by the evident loyalty and reverence with which he [Masaba] treated any matter relating to Her Majesty and I am satisfied

---

[1] F.O.84/1418, No. 14, Hartley to Derby, 27 Mar. 1875.   [2] Ibid.

that the continued maintenance of friendly relations with the British Government and of commercial intercourse with Her Majesty's subjects is the principal object of his desires, as it is the mainstay of his policy at home and the foundation upon which his position and his influence amongst his neighbours unquestionably rests. But his great object is the obtaining of guns and ammunition from the expeditions and thereby maintaining a military superiority over his neighbours.[1]

Between the years 1871–9 military expeditions visited the Niger basin annually, destroying Delta and hinterland towns that had attacked British life and property. So long as the warships remained in the vicinity of the trading posts a thriving trade was done; during the seven months of the dry season, when the ships could not ascend the river, Africans resumed their attacks on the invaders. War and trade alternated with the seasons. In some localities, Onitsha for instance, the sustained attack on trading posts and the pillaging of British goods, even in the presence of warships, made trade impossible. In 1879 H.M.S. *Pioneer* removed the £50,000 worth of British trade goods at Onitsha and then subjected the town to naval bombardment for three days. Not content with destroying the section of the town situated on the river bank the British forces 'the following day . . . marched to the inner town about 3 miles distant, and burned it; and on the next day we levelled all the walls left standing in the lower town'. Consul Easton, who led the operations, concluded: 'Our proceedings at Onitsha will have a most salutary effect up and down the Niger, and the Missionaries and Traders unanimously gave us their thanks for our promptness and decision.'[2] The Onitsha affair was not an isolated incident. Yamaha on the Benue, another important inland trading station, was destroyed in the same year for attacking British traders.[3] Idah and Aboh were bombarded and at the latter 'several hundreds were killed and the streets were strewn with corpses'.[4] British newspapers, especially *The Times*, condemned these atrocities.[5] The Foreign Office, baffled by an unprecedented situation, complained that 'it would be impossible for Her Majesty's Government to undertake to protect [British] merchants in every quarter of the globe'. They admitted, however, that the economic opportunity offered by the Niger valley was great. 'We have opened' the Niger to trade 'and the result is a thriving business in many

[1] Geary, op. cit., pp. 170–1.
[2] F.O.84/1541, No. 31, Easton to F.O., 3rd Nov. 1879.
[3] F.O.84/1541, Lokoja No. 19, Encl. 4, King to McIntosh, 10 June 1879.
[4] Geary, op. cit., p. 175.   [5] See *The Times*, 21 Apr. 1880, p. 5.

portions of that river.' Although no specific plan for imposing its authority on the vast hinterland was devised, the Government laboured to introduce an 'Amended Order-in-Council . . . enabling our Consuls on the West African Coast to act magisterially up the different Rivers'.[1] The political unsettlement which accompanied commercial expansion in the Delta, Iboland, and the Hausa country made trade not only insecure but at times impossible. In 1879, therefore, the problem that confronted the British merchant and official was clear. Trade up the Niger had been proved large and profitable: its peaceful exploitation demanded some form of political security. Without peace and security, trade could not flourish.

In 1877 Mr. Goldie Taubman,[2] an officer of the Royal Engineers, who had some interest in the Central African Company, arrived in the Niger Delta. He was a keen explorer and had travelled in the regions of the upper Nile. In company with his brother he planned to ascend the River Benue and strike across the continent to the valleys of the upper Nile. For this purpose he brought out a steam launch, the *Benue*, 90 feet in length.[3] But this voyage was cut short because his brother 'got fever badly when we were half-way up the river and I had to bring him home. On the journey back I conceived the ambition of adding the region of the Niger to the British Empire.' From then on Goldie never looked back. 'My dream as a child', this masterful empire builder once said, 'was to colour the map red.'[4]

He found his opportunity in the Niger valley where, as he himself observed, 'there was no foreigner . . . in the entire basins of the Niger and Lake Chad, between the French Colony of Senegal on the extreme West Coast of Africa and the valley of the Nile on the extreme east, or between the seaboard factories on the Gulf of Guinea to the south and the Algerian and Tunisian frontiers on the north.'[5] Perceiving the ultimate results of French ambitions, he believed that British trading interests in the Niger basin could be saved and strengthened by the consolidation of her power in the hinterland. His energy and vision transformed the whole situation.

From 1877 to 1879 he strove to achieve an amalgamation of the

[1] F.O.84/1541, Wylde's minutes on No. 19, 30 Sept. 1879.
[2] He was later Sir George Dashwood Taubman Goldie (1846–1925).
[3] A. F. Mockler-Ferryman, *British West Africa* (London, 1900), p. 192.
[4] C. H. Currey, *The British Commonwealth Since 1815* (Sydney, 1951), p. 49.
[5] Wellesley, op. cit., pp. 17–20.

rival British interests in the river. Consul Hopkins, who visited the interior trading posts in 1878, reported that cut-throat competition, such as characterized the coast trade, had appeared in the interior. 'It is almost impossible to describe the constant bickerings between these rival factories . . . In one instance as many as five companies established trading posts in one town on the Niger.'[1]

By his energy and diplomatic skill Goldie succeeded in welding the British trading interests into the United African Company in 1879. The chairman of this new venture was Lord Aberdare, a former Cabinet Minister. Almost all the directors of the company were heads of Delta firms who had begun to extend their trading operations in the interior following the opening of the hinterland to trade.[2] They included James A. Croft, C. B. Edgar, James F. Hutton, George Miller, James Pinnock, Alexander Miller, and David McIntosh, the last-named holding the post of Agent-General of the company in Africa. Goldie himself was the vice-chairman and certainly the leading spirit.[3]

In the first four years of its life the subscribed capital of the company was 'between £100,000 to £200,000'. At first the shares were not open to the public and were held 'amongst some 70 to 80 persons'. International competition followed this amalgamation. From their base in the upper Niger the French now planned to encroach on this British preserve and under Gambetta's patronage two commercial associations were formed, the Compagnie française de l'Afrique équatorial of Paris, and the Compagnie du Senegal et de la Côte Occidentale d'Afrique of Marseilles.[4] According to Goldie himself one of these French firms 'had avowedly political aims and was supported in high quarters'. He recognized the danger of French competitors and sought to absorb them into his organization, now known as the National African Company. 'Six months of strenuous efforts resulted in failure owing to the patriotic scruples of the French

---

[1] F.O./1508, No. 40, Hopkins to F.O., 18 Nov. 1878.
[2] Mr. Pinnock, for instance, had been trading in the Delta for more than thirty-five years, mainly in the Warri and Benin rivers. See his Benin, The Surrounding Country and Trade (Liverpool, 1897). Messrs. Miller Bros. were a Glasgow firm established at Opobo and elsewhere in the Delta. At his death in 1922 Alexander Miller left £2,000,000. See Harry Johnston, The Story of My Life (London, 1923), p. 216.
[3] F.O.84/1879, Special Report on the National African Company, 8 Dec. 1885.
[4] W. E. C. de Wiarte, Les Grandes compagnies coloniales anglais au XIX Siècle (Paris, 1899), p. 50, quoted by A. N. Cook, British Enterprise in Nigeria (Pennsylvania, 1943), p. 83.

Directors.' When negotiations failed the two national groups entered into 'severe competition', and after fifteen months Goldie practically compelled the French to request 'fresh interviews which resulted in the National African Company buying both of the French companies on most satisfactory terms'. To meet the French menace Goldie had raised the subscribed capital of the company to £1,000,000 by 'the offering of the shares to the general public'.[1] He had other reasons for increasing the capital of the company. In 1881, when they applied to the Government for a charter, the demand was refused on the grounds that the company's capital was too small.[2]

With foreign competition eliminated Goldie had the field clear for planting British power in the Niger territories. Since it is not the main purpose of this study to trace the history of the Niger Company but to analyse its strategy with regard to the Delta and its hinterland, it will suffice here merely to sketch Goldie's main line of policy.[3] With the foundation of the National African Company he saved British enterprise in the hinterland from the cut-throat competition so typical of Delta trade; above all he conferred unity and cohesion on British activity in the Niger valley at a critical period in West African history, when the rivalry among the great powers was about to engulf the entire continent in the aggressive politics and expanding economy of western Europe.

But Goldie never looked on the unification of British trading interests as the main object of his ambition; to him amalgamation was merely a means to an end. 'If I believed the present state of things to be the final outcome', he wrote to the Foreign Office after his victories in the economic sphere, 'I would not waste another year of my life over the Niger.' He affirmed on several occasions that his company was not 'actuated by purely commercial motives' and that they were 'Englishmen first and investors afterwards'.[4] Goldie's over-riding urge was to secure for Britain political dominion over the Niger basin, an area he considered the most dazzling prize in West Africa. 'With old-established markets closing to our manufactures,

---

[1] F.O.80/1879, Goldie to Lord Salisbury, 15 Aug. 1885. In the economic war with the French, Goldie's tactics were to undersell the enemy: 'prices were cut about twenty-five per cent. in the districts where the French were established'. Cook, op. cit., p. 83.   [2] Crowe, op. cit., p. 124.

[3] The history of the Niger Company has been discussed elsewhere. See, for example, C. W. J. Orr, *The Making of Northern Nigeria*, (London 1911), pp. 17–50, Geary, op. cit., Cook, op. cit., pp. 79–148, &c.

[4] F.O.84/1879, Printed Paper . . . The Lower Niger, 15 May 1885.

with India producing cotton fabrics not only for her own use but for export, it would be suicidal to abandon to a rival power the only great remaining undeveloped opening for British goods.'[1] He assured the Foreign Office that 'it is in this healthy, but as yet unsettled region, that lie the rich resources of industrial wealth'. With political control 'light railways, tramways and telegraphs' would provide 'rapid communication' linking Britain's industrial power with the resources of the '30 to 60 millions [African] of the Niger and Chad Basins'. There was besides the highway of the Niger. 'Trade', he said pithily, 'seeks the sea by the shortest route'. For the West African hinterland that route was the River Niger. Goldie pursued the task of acquiring this vital region for Britain with a single-mindedness that amounted at times to an obsession.

As early as 1881, soon after he had dealt with the French danger, he began unofficially to make detailed inquiries 'as to the necessity of a charter' for his company. With the expansion of trade he 'fully recognized that the political situation in the Niger was growing too vast and too complex . . . to be safely administered in the previous haphazard and irregular manner'. Goldie sought a charter partly to bestow sovereign power on his company and partly to bring peace and stability over the Niger territories and gain supremacy in the political sphere as he had done in the economic.

In this his grasp of the situation was equally firm. The 'Niger Districts', he wrote, 'consist of two distinct territories'. The Delta or the seaboard region 'accessible at all seasons to ocean-going steamers, and to Her Majesty's gunboats', formed a separate political unit. Here the presence of consuls aided by British sea power was adequate for the maintenance of law and order. Then there was the 'essentially Central African territory', which he termed the 'Niger Benue' region, beyond the reach of warships, a territory governed by several hundred sovereign states. These two regions 'are as distinct commercially as they are politically'. Goldie believed that the Delta was already under control, and, in any case, 'a strong power holding the interior could cut off the entire commerce of the seaboard'.[2] It was therefore in the hinterland that he directed his boundless energy.

'Legitimate trade' and 'civilization' he often contended cannot prosper in an unsettled interior. A pre-requisite of commercial development was the 'pacification' of the Niger–Benue region.

[1] Ibid.   [2] Ibid.

Characteristically he relied on his own resources and that of the company in gaining the power he desired. His tactics were to assume practical control over the entire waterway and then present the British Government with a *fait accompli*. After the formation of the National African Company he established over a hundred trading posts on the banks of these rivers, employing more than 1,500 men.[1] Then he initiated treaty-making with the native states. Up to 1884 the company concluded thirty-seven treaties with African chiefs.[2] In 1886 the number had risen to 237.[3] These treaties, negotiated by the company's agents, notably David McIntosh, invariably ceded to the National African Company 'the whole of the territories of the signatories', conferring in addition the right to exclude foreigners and to monopolize the trade of the area.[4] Twenty gunboats, 'vessels of light draft', capable of navigating the Niger all the year round, were specially constructed for the service of the company. These were invaluable for police duties and for 'pacifying' 'robber chiefs . . . who were ever-ready to plunder our factories'.[5]

As was to be expected opposition to the company's rule by the indigenous people was widespread. In both the Delta and the upper Niger its crippling monopoly was bitterly resisted. In 1882, for instance, the company's factories at Akassa, Patani, and Brass (in the Delta), and at Asaba and Idah (in the middle and upper Niger), were attacked by the natives. In every case the towns responsible were subjected to naval bombardment. 'Rewards of three puncheons worth of cargo were offered for the capture' of the principal native leaders such as 'Opabi of Asaba and Abuderkama and Manimuma of Abari'.[6] In spite of these uprisings the company's superior arms kept the natives quiet but sullen.

In its bid for supremacy the company attacked not only Africans but all rivals and competitors, whether black or white. In 1885 a small English trader in the Brass city-state forwarded to Lord Salisbury copies of correspondence in proof of the arbitrary dealings of the National African Company and of their agent Mr. McIntosh against the established interests in the river.[7] On the other hand,

[1] F.O.84/1879, London, Aberdare to Granville, 13 Feb. 1885.
[2] Geary, op. cit., p. 179.
[3] F.O.84/1748, Goldie to Pauncefote, 20 Dec. 1886. The lists of the treaties are appended.
[4] F.O.84/1879, op. cit.   [5] Geary, op. cit., p. 179.
[6] F.O.84/1617, No. 16 and its enclosures, Hewett to Granville, 8 Nov. 1882.
[7] F.O.84/1879, Young to Salisbury, 26 Aug. 1885, and its enclosures.

traders and African rulers who co-operated with the company were treated as allies and became instruments of Goldie's policy. In 1881 and 1882 the Emir of Nupe, traditional friend of the British traders, was given help to fight the rebels in his dominions. In the international field Goldie successfully defended British interests against French and German encroachment. The attempt to secure northern Nigeria for Germany in 1885 failed because Herr Edward Flegel, who was commissioned by his Government to obtain treaties of cession from the Sultans of Sokoto and Gando, was forestalled in the same business by Joseph Thomson, a representative of the National African Company.[1] Thus even before it secured a royal charter the company had become, to a limited extent, the *de facto* government of the Nigerian hinterland.

Sir George Goldie has been called the 'Founder of Nigeria'.[2] But the making of modern Nigeria was not the work of one man. Before Goldie other giants had been in the field. They included John Beecroft, Dr. Andrew Baikie, Sir John Glover, and Macgregor Laird—to name but a few and the most important. It was Laird who literally dragged the Government into the hinterland and brought them to recognize the prize which the extensive Niger basin held for its conquerors. When he died in 1861 the foundation of British ascendancy in Nigeria had been laid. Neither the merchant nor the Government had any intentions of going back.

The apostles of inland trade were lucky in their leadership. At each stage in the development of interior commerce, the hour found the man. Under Goldie the exertions of fifty years of legitimate trade came to maturity. The companies he welded together had their foundations in Laird's day. The trading posts he multiplied were initiated by Laird in 1857. Like Laird, Goldie had a high sense of his mission; neither man was the victim of the selfish lust for personal gain. When Laird died Lord John Russell reported that the 'total loss sustained by Mr. Laird's Estate since the year 1859 in the spirited endeavours of that gentleman to open a trade with Central Africa by the River Niger amounts to no less than £26,000'.[3] Undoubtedly Goldie's achievements in the Niger valley from 1879 to 1884 enabled the British representatives at the Berlin West African Conference of

---

[1] Cook, op. cit., pp. 84–85. Cook's chapter on 'International Rivalry' in *West Africa*, pp. 115–48, is the best general treatment of the subject available.

[2] Wellesley, op. cit.

[3] F.O.97/434, Niger Expedition, Russell to Treasury, 3 Jan. 1863.

1885 to claim successfully that British interests were supreme in the Niger basin; but his contributions, along with those of Lord Lugard, must be viewed as the culminating point of the work of the pioneers.

The informal control which Britain exercised in the Niger Delta flourished as long as she remained the undisputed master in the Bight of Biafra. There is evidence that the Foreign Office had become suspicious of French activities in the Gulf of Guinea in the period 1880–5 and was planning to assume more direct and effective control of that part of West Africa. In fact Consul Hewett had been charged with the task of securing a protectorate over the Delta region in 1883. But it took twelve months to give effect to this decision and in the meantime Hewett found himself forestalled at the Cameroons by Bismarck's agent.[1] One is forced to the conclusion that the Consul and the Foreign Office could not have believed the French danger to be imminent. French competition, directed from the base at Porto Novo, was of course always watched, especially in the vicinity of Lagos. From time to time British merchants sent information about French intrigues on the coast to the Foreign Office.[2] But there was little evidence of a concerted move by France to displace the British on the coast of Biafra. In the Cameroons German merchants from Hamburg had always worked on friendly terms with British traders. Not a few became useful members of the Courts of Equity. International rivalry was therefore never acute in the Delta as it was in the hinterland until the unexpected German annexation of the Cameroons in 1884. This brief episode has been the subject of much comment.[3]

On 11 July 1884 the German gunboat *Mowe* anchored off the Cameroons river. It had on board Gustav Nachtigal, the German Commissioner for West Africa. Bismarck had notified the British Foreign Office of Nachtigal's mission, stating that he was 'authorized to conduct, on behalf of the Imperial Government, negotiations connected with certain questions'. The Commissioner sailed for

[1] Crowe, op. cit., pp. 124–5. See also Appendix XIII, pp. 221–2, of the same book.
[2] F.O.84/1630, Lister to Cust (of Royal Asiatic Company), 3 Feb. 1882, acknowledging information on French intrigues at Timbo on the Niger.
[3] A. J. P. Taylor, *Germany's Bid for Colonies* (New York, 1938), and Harry R. Rudin, *Germans in the Cameroons* (New Haven, 1938), are the best accounts available on the subject of German colonization. Rudin is particularly relevant on Anglo–German rivalry in the Cameroons. See also Evans Lewin, *The German and Africa* (New York, 1915); Crowe, op. cit.

Africa ostensibly to investigate 'the state of German commerce on the coast' and no one realized that Bismarck was about to launch Germany on her career of empire building. This mission had been a closely guarded secret, and Nachtigal, acting under careful instructions from Bismarck, avoided areas of the continent claimed by France. Before his arrival in the Cameroons the ground had been prepared by German traders there aided by the German Consul from Gaboon. As a result of their work, on 14 July 1884 the occupation of the Cameroons became official and German flags were raised in most towns of the new protectorate.[1]

It is usual to cite Britain's loss of the Cameroons to Germany as the perfect example of her indifference to the acquisition of African territories. In actual fact the Foreign Office had no good reason to suppose that her position in the Cameroons would be suddenly challenged by Germany in 1884. Edward Hyde Hewett, the Consul in the critical years 1879–85, had, it is true, repeatedly advocated the formal annexation of the coastal region from the Cameroons to the Benin river. But this demand was prompted not solely by the fear of a possible French intervention but even more by the considerations of interior trade. One danger which the Consul sought to stem by advocating annexation was that of the African middlemen who had begun to penetrate the hinterland in order to safeguard their markets from the encroaching Europeans. The British merchants feared that if the Delta middlemen led by Ja Ja were allowed to consolidate their power and authority over the tribal producers they might prove formidable antagonists in the inevitable struggle for the interior.

It has been shown that in the chaos which accompanied the collapse of the old order in Bonny Ja Ja had carved out a kingdom for himself at Opobo. Britain recognized him as king of this undefined territory in a treaty of 1873.[2] In 1881 Ja Ja occupied and annexed the Qua Eboe territory, an important oil-producing area to the Opobo hinterland; he was formally proclaimed king of this place on 8 June 1881.[3] As he conquered the interior countries Ja Ja barred the way to British traders. He resisted every demand from the Consul to open the markets to British merchants. 'My first and last words', said Ja Ja, 'are that the country [Qua Eboe] belongs to me and I do not want white traders . . . there. Any one who wants to trade . . . with me'

---

[1] Cook, op. cit., pp. 115–20.
[2] See Chapter X.
[3] F.O.84/1630, Opobo Town, Ja Ja to Lord Granville, 3 Apr. 1882.

was free to do so at the port of Opobo.[1] The consular dispatches for the years 1880–4 amply demonstrate that the British viewed Ja Ja's progress with alarm and that they were more concerned with the task of eliminating Ja Ja than of stemming possible French and German intervention.[2] A study of some of the requests for annexation prior to 1884 will show that they were directed mainly against the Delta middlemen.

In February 1882 John Holt appealed to the Foreign Office to protect Mr. Watts, a British trader in the Qua Eboe river, whom he claimed was a victim of Ja Ja's persecution. He suggested the annexation of the coast 'from Lagos to the Cameroons' as the only safeguard for the British merchant.[3] In June 1883 Hewett, writing to Granville, stated that his reason for urging the annexation of the Cameroons was to enable Britain to 'obtain the great influence in the interior now exercised by the Kings and Chiefs of Cameroon', i.e. the coast middlemen. He added that annexation would enable 'the white traders . . . [to] push into the interior and [so] get rid of the services of the Cameroon people as middlemen'.[4] 'These requests for annexation', commented a Foreign Office official, 'are becoming frequent', and they came almost entirely from merchants and the Consul who needed direct government intervention 'to break down the middlemen system of which Ja Ja is the champion'.[5] To attribute the demand for annexation solely to the fear of French competition leaves these requests unexplained.

Much has been made of the strange letters written in 1879 and 1881 and addressed to the British Government by kings Acquah and Bell of the Cameroons; both offered their country to the queen of England.[6] Letters of this type, so characteristic of the period,[7] were sometimes inspired and instigated by the British traders and were designed to influence the Foreign Office in favour of the merchants' requests. These documents must be read with great discrimination. What is clear, however, is that the petty kings of the Cameroons river were perhaps unable to distinguish between informal control and outright annexation. The consuls were governors in all but name and

---

[1] F.O. 84/1630, Obopo Town, Ja Ja to Lord Granville, 3 Apr. 1882.
[2] See F.O.84/1630, F.O.84/1617, F.O.84/1634, &c.
[3] F.O.84/1630, Holt to Granville, 16 Feb. 1882.
[4] F.O.84/1634, No. 4, Hewett to Granville, 7 June 1883.
[5] F.O.84/1750, Minutes on Vice-Consul Johnston to Salisbury, No. 1, 15 Jan. 1886.
[6] Geary, op. cit., pp. 92–93.   [7] See Chapter IV.

could with little inducement obtain the letters they desired from some of the corrupt minor chieftains on the coast. In 1884, when the Germans bribed these chiefs, they soon changed sides and transferred their allegiance from England to Germany.[1]

Undoubtedly international rivalry was a factor in some of the requests for annexation, but it was certainly not the most important in the two or three years immediately preceding the German adventure to the Cameroons. Further, in the eighties the energetic drive by Goldie to subjugate the hinterland had won the admiration of the coast community. Consul Hewett was himself in sympathy with the company's policy and had on several occasions aided them actively.[2] He even suggested that the coastal region should be made over to a chartered company.[3] It was natural that the coast traders should urge annexation in order to replace the haphazard development in the Delta with an energetic and clear-cut policy. They desired above all a government on the seaboard willing and able to control the African opposition.

The acquisition of the Cameroons by Germany, a district then dominated by British consular power, soon revealed the inadequacies of the informal methods of control which had served Britain well in the years before 1884. With the emergence of international rivalry it became clear that nothing short of formal annexation would meet the need. The German occupation of the Cameroons therefore marked a definite break in British policy in the Niger Delta.

Armed with the instructions which he received from the Foreign Office on 16 May 1884 and which charged him to secure a British protectorate over the Niger territories, Consul Hewett proceeded with great speed and efficiency to conclude treaties of protection with African states in the bights of Benin and Biafra. Treaty-making on the coast occupied him from 14 July to the end of August 1884. He ascended the rivers Niger and Benue in September and concluded further treaties with chiefs of the interior, most of whom were already under the protection of the National African Company. Before the end of October the countries in the Delta and lower Niger were brought under British protection.[4] It was due to Hewett's work and to the exertions of Sir George Goldie that the British delegates at the

[1] Cook, op. cit., pp. 119–20.
[2] F.O.84/1617, Hewett to Granville, No. 16, 8 Nov. 1882, and its enclosures. See also No. 17 and its enclosures.
[3] Rudin, op. cit., p. 21, cited by Cook, op. cit., p. 17.
[4] Crowe, op. cit., pp. 124–9.

Berlin West African Conference of 1885 were able to claim for their country ascendancy over the Delta and the lower Niger.

On the 5th of June 1885 Great Britain declared a Protectorate over the Niger districts which comprised 'the territories on the line of coast between the British Protectorate of Lagos and the right or western bank of the Rio del Rey', and the 'territories on both banks of the Niger, from its confluence with the River Benue at Lokoja to the sea, as well as territories on both banks of the River Benue, from the confluence up to and including Ibi'.[1] The Niger Coast Protectorate was designed to keep out European rivals. As Vice-Consul Johnston observed: 'So long as we keep other European nations out, we need not be in a hurry to go in.'[2]

After 1885 British policy in the Delta gradually became more coherent and consistent. But the 'paper protectorate' proclaimed in the Niger territories had yet to be converted into 'effective occupation'. The vague sovereignty bestowed on the great powers over West Africa by the Berlin Conference was based almost entirely on treaty rights. The greater number of these treaties were obtained in a questionable manner. Native chiefs were coerced into signing agreements the provisions of which they never understood. In this way they signed away their rights, the rights of their people, and their lands, acts which in strict West African customary law were beyond their competence. As events were to prove, however, these treaties became inadequate for the purposes of 'effective occupation'. Since the chiefs had not voluntarily surrendered their territories they resisted the encroachment of the foreigner with every means in their power to the bitter end. At best the treaties enabled the competing and invading Europeans to demarcate their spheres of activity in the scramble for African territory. But it was force that decided the issue. 'In the last analysis', said Cook, 'the position of every power in Africa rested on "effective occupation" backed by force.'[3] The critical years 1885–1900 witnessed the subjugation and 'pacification' of Nigeria by British forces. During these years the impact of European industrialism, hitherto restricted to the Atlantic seaboard, rapidly spread to the tribal interior. The events of this crucial period, of which this study is merely an introduction, will form the subject of another work.

[1] See the *London Gazette*, 5 June 1885.
[2] F.O.84/1750, Confidential, Johnston to Anderson, 13 Nov. 1885.
[3] Cook, op. cit., p. 127.

The Minima Agreement

AGREEMENT signed by the Chiefs of Opooboo Connections, otherwise known as the Founders of Opobo, before the outbreak of the Civil War in Grand Bonny in 1869

BY virtue of the powers and authority we vested upon Chief Jack Ja Ja Annie Pepple as Successor of Opooboo House, we, the undersigned comrade-Chiefs, comprising the political representatives of the said House, this day, hereby declare our voluntary engagement to elude Grand Bonny with a view to settle elsewhere in Andoni territory, and that the said Chief Jack Ja Ja Annie Pepple and ourselves, parties hereto, have agreed between us and concluded the following Articles:—

Article i

For the better carrying on of the war with the Manilla House people we hereby jointly engage to provide men, arms, ammunition, and to contribute money and property towards all expenses incurred in maintaining the war-men with the necessary stores.

Article ii

It is understood herein that, for our losses in men and property as the result of the Civil War, each of us and each of our successors or persons representing our interests, from time to time, shall have the indefinite title to a share of the revenues from Comey, Work-Bar, Custom-Bar, and such other imposts and levies after twenty-five per centum of the whole has been reserved as income for the Big House.

Article iii

It is also agreed among us that the executive authority for the government of the settlement shall be solely reserved to each of us and to each of our successors or persons representing our interests, from time to time, as lawfully qualified for election and installation as successor to the Big House.

MADE at Minima, Grand Bonny, the 13th October, 1869

Signed		Their Marks
,,	Jack Ja ja Annie Pepple	X
,,	Black Foobra	X
,,	Jim Wariso	X

Signed   Their Marks
    ,,   Wogo Dappa   X
    ,,   John Africa   X
    ,,   Annie Steward   X
    ,,   George Darriar   X
    ,,   Captain Uranta   X
    ,,   How Strongface   X
    ,,   John Tom Brown   X
    ,,   Obarney   X
    ,,   Fine Bone   X
    ,,   Deerie Tulefare   X
    ,,   Manilla   X
    ,,   Jack Tulefare   X

Witnesses for the 15 marks:—

Signed D. Taylor
    ,,   J. Hemingway
    ..   D. C. Williams.

Treaty between King Pepple of Bonny and the Chiefs of Andony

FROM the date of this document the natives of Andony shall be considered as subjects of King Pepple, and shall be entitled to the same rights and privileges as the Bonny men.

2nd. The Andony men bind themselves not to have any communication whatever with Young Calabar or Creeka country; if on the contrary such communication is held, the person or persons so offending shall be subject to such punishment as King Pepple shall choose to inflict. But should Young Calabar or Creeka men bring provisions to Andony for sale, the Andony men shall be allowed to buy the same; but under no circumstances or pretence whatever shall Young Calabar or Creeka men *retail* spirits in the Andony.

3rd. No marriage between Andony, Young Calabar, and Creeka country will be allowed.

4th. When the Andony men make their great Jewjew, the natives of Bonny promise to give them hip-cloths, caps, rum, &c.; and when the Andony men come to receive the above, they promise to present the Bonny men with some dried fish.

5th. The Andony men further promise, that when desired by the King of Bonny to catch fish for the public feasts, they will do it.

6th. They, the Andony men, also promise not to destroy the Guano, but allow the animal liberty the same as in Bonny.

7th. Should there be war between Bonny and any other power, The Andony men promise to supply war-canoes, well fitted out and ready-manned, in order to assist the Bonny men. If the Andony men should be short of canoes, guns, or ammunition, the Bonny men will supply them with the same.

Further, if any other country should in any wise molest the Andony men, the Bonny men bind themselves to interfere and act in the same manner as they would were it their own country.

9th. The Andony men also promise to supply Bonny canoes with men to assist in pulling to the fair.

10th. That in case of any dispute arising between any two parties, natives of Andony, King Pepple is to be informed of the same, and that he (the King) will send a competent person (without charge) to settle the matter.

12th. Should the Andony men kill any elephants, they are to present the teeth thereof to King Pepple; and should the Andony men at any time be short of muskets or powder, King Pepple will supply them.

13th. In case of any shipwrecks, and should any white men, under whatever circumstances, get into the power of the Andony men, they (the Andony men) are immediately to transfer them over to King Pepple without injury.

(Signed) PEPPLE REX and the Chiefs of Bonny.

(Signed) The Chiefs of Andony or their Representatives.

WITNESSES.

John Angus Ward.	Princess Royal.
Chas. Calvert.	William Batsford.
Wm. Kelly.	Huskison.
G. W. S. Witt.	Swiftsure.
G. W. W. Bond.	Fanny.
Wm. Owens.	B. Packet.
Arthur J. P. Cutting.	Warwick.
Peter Jacobson.	

Dated this 22nd December, 1846, in the Jewjew House, or Parliament House, Grand Bonny.

British Treaty with Opobo.
4 January 1873

1. In the name of Her Britannic Majesty's Government, we hereby acknowledge Ja Ja King of the Opobo, and fully entitled to all consideration as such.

2. The British traders in the River Opobo shall pay the same amount of 'comey' as British traders in Bonny. No other tax or impost shall be placed on them. Any disputes which may occur with JaJa's people are to be referred to Her Britannic Majesty's Consul for settlement.

3. After April 5, 1873, the King of Opobo shall allow no trading establishment or hulk in or off Opobo Town, or any trading vessel to come higher up the river than the white man's beach opposite Hippopotamus Creek. If any trading ship or steamer proceeds further up the river than the creek above mentioned, after having been fully warned to the contrary, the said trading ship or steamer may be seized by King JaJa, and detained until a fine of 100 puncheons be paid by the owners to King Ja Ja.

Signed on board Her Britannic Majesty's ship Pioneer, off Opobo town, on the 4th day of January, 1873.

> J. E. COMMERELL, Commodore, Commanding-in-chief Her Britannic Majesty's Naval Forces on the Cape of Good Hope and West Coast of Africa Station. CHARLES LIVINGSTONE, Her Britannic Majesty's Consul for the Bights of Biafra and Benin.

Note on the Sources

I. PRIMARY SOURCES

1. *Nigerian* (including oral traditions, historical remains, and manuscripts).

Little use has been made of the material collected from tribal or oral sources except in the writing of Chapters I and II. These sources have been checked, where possible, with early Portuguese records, as given in the footnotes.

(a) Benin

Benin City in Nigeria (the capital of the Old Benin empire) contains significant historical remains. In spite of the lootings of the 1897 expedition which led to the transfer of some of the priceless art treasures to Britain and to Germany, historical evidence can be seen in the Benin Museum and in the Oba's (King's) Palace. The pictorial representations on the bronzes can be explained by some of the local historians, members of ancient families who have acted as the repositories of tribal memory for generations. I was shown the Palace collection by the Oba Akenzua II; I also spent four days in the local museum and discussed the Benin origin of the Delta states with Chief Jacob Egharevba, the Curator. Chief Egharevba is the author of a number of tracts on Benin history, of which his *Short History of Benin* (Ibadan University Press, 1953) is the best known.

(b) The Niger Delta

(i) *Government sources*

Manuscripts in the possession of the Nigerian Government are not catalogued or classified. A survey of the historical records of Nigeria has now been completed, and a report, published under the title of *The Preservation and Administration of Historical Records and the Establishment of a Public Record Office in Nigeria* (Lagos, 1954), is now being implemented by the Government.

The most important Government source dealing with the history of the Niger Delta is the Consular Papers dating from the fifties, which are housed at the Nigerian Record Office, Ibadan. The Minutes of the Courts of Equity, dating from 1853, are also important. The subjects they cover range from disputes between European and African traders, to the wars and rivalries between the city-states for the control of the hinterland markets.

Another important Government source is the series of *Confidential Intelligence Reports*. These contain a great deal of historical material. The merit of these reports is that some were written by British political officers with wide local knowledge. They contain, therefore, much valuable material that is not available elsewhere. I found them most useful in checking information derived from rival native sources.

(ii) *Native sources*

By far the most important materials on the internal politics and trade organization of the Delta are in the city-states themselves. Nineteenth-century history is very much alive in the Delta. The descendants of the leading personalities of this period possess papers dealing with every phase of their past. The main problem is the pulling together of these scattered but valuable historical manuscripts. Each family guards its own possessions jealously.

I had access to valuable papers and many people were ready to proffer information on problems of internal politics. At each community there was usually an acknowledged local historian; and in the Delta, where contact with Europe has been continuous for over 400 years, these historians are nearly all literate. Some of them are in fact engaged in the writing of their local histories or have actually completed them. Many of the conclusions I have reached on questions of internal politics have been based on a study of papers owned by different families, some of which varied in important particulars. Because they are unclassified it has not been easy to cite these in footnotes.

Bonny. Thus at Bonny I found that the account given me of the Ja Ja revolution varied greatly from that which I received from Opobo sources. While Ja Ja remains the national hero of Opobo, at Bonny he is spoken of as a rebel and a traitor. This being the case it is important to discover the origin of one's information and the community to which the informers belong.

The great-grandson of King William Dappa Pepple showed me manu-scripts and historical relics dealing with the history of the royal family and various articles dug up from the site of the old king's House which was destroyed in the civil war of 1855. The trade routes which linked Bonny with the old oil markets are not only known but most of them are still used; the investigator has no difficulty in seeing for himself, or having explained to him, the nineteenth-century trade organization, the House System, and how they worked. Historical relics abound—war-canoes, various sizes of trading canoes, guns, large and small; in fact almost all the items of European manufacture used in the barter trade of the eighteenth and nineteenth centuries have been preserved. Bonny in its present state of decline is like one vast museum and is still dominated by the shadow of its historic past. I owe my best information on Bonny history to Mr. Adadonye Fombo, a retired civil servant.

Opobo. Mr. E. M. T. Epelle of Opobo Town is working on a biography of Ja Ja and gave me valuable information about his early life. In addition I discussed every aspect of his reign with the chiefs in several meetings. Just as Bonny forms the best source for the study of the Pepple monarchy so is Opobo the centre for any studies connected with Ja Ja. In the centre of the town there is a dominating statue of him in marble, and the three-story prefabricated house imported from Liverpool in which he lived is still standing.

At Old Calabar (now Calabar), New Calabar (now divided into the three towns of Abonnema, Degema, and Buguma) I held meetings with the chiefs and examined sources such as those at Bonny and Opobo.

There is little need to emphasize that without the use of Nigerian sources it would not have been easy to follow the internal politics of the Delta states. For instance, there is no reference to the famous 'Minima Agreement' of 1869 in Foreign Office Archives (see Appendix A), a copy of which was easily obtained at Opobo. Events such as the Bonny-Andoni war of 1846, by which Andoni became a vassal of Bonny (see Appendix B) are hardly ever mentioned in British sources. Hence the two kinds of source supplement each other.

2. *British*

(*a*) *Manuscript sources*

(i) *Colonial office*

C.O.82 (Fernando Po): Original correspondence and entry books. This series covers the period of the British occupation of Fernando Po. It is concerned almost exclusively with the Bight of Biafra; and because Fernando Po was dependent on Old Calabar for its provisions, it contains much information on Old Calabar's trade and politics at · this time. It is an important source for the period 1830–7 in Delta history. The series starts in 1828 and ends in 1842.

(ii) *Foreign Office*

F.O.2 (Fernando Po): Africa Consular. This series starts with the appointment of the consuls to the Bights of Benin and Biafra, and is concerned almost exclusively with the consuls in the Bights. It covers the whole of the Niger Delta.

Many volumes are devoted to the Niger expeditions, starting with that of Baikie in 1854. It contains also much administrative correspondence and finishes in 1872.

F.O.84: Slave trade. So far as the Niger Delta is concerned this is by far the most important of the whole series. It includes not only consular dispatches to the Foreign Office, but also papers relevant to the Delta from the Board of Trade, the Admiralty, the Treasury, and the Colonial Office. The Slave Trade Department dealt, in fact, with all questions concerned with Africa. As an example of the detailed nature of this series with regard to events in the Delta the following volumes were devoted almost entirely to King Pepple's exile:

    (i) F.O.84, 1161, 1855–1856: Case of King Pepple.
    (ii) F.O.84, 1162, 1857:   ,,   ,,
    (iii) F.O.84, 1163, 1858–1859:   ,,   ,,
    (iv) F.O.84, 1164, 1860–1861:   ,,   ,,

This series, which runs into many volumes, was done away with and the dispatches were marked 'AFRICAN' from 1883. (See F.O. to Hewett, 1 March 1883. F.O.84/1634.)

F.O.97, 432. Treaties concluded with native chiefs 1818–66. (Details of these treaties were covered in the F.O.84/S from 1830 to 1856.)

F.O.97. Almost exclusively devoted to the Niger expeditions in the sixties.

(b) *Parliamentary Papers*

1830, X (661). Report of Select Committee on Sierra Leone and Fernando Po.

1840, XXXIII (57). Correspondence relating to the Niger expedition.

1842, XI; XII (551). Report of Select Committee on British Possessions on West Coast of Africa.

1842, XXVI (494). Cost of the Niger expedition.

1843, XXXI (83). Mortality, in the Niger expedition.

1843, XLVIII (472). Papers relative to Niger expedition.

1847–8, XXII (272), (366), (536), (623). Four reports from the Select Com-
'mittee on Slave Trade.

1849, XIX (309), (410). Two reports, following session.

1850, IX (53), (590). Reports of Select Committee of House of Lords on Slave Trade.

1854, LXV (296). Quantities of palm oil imported into U.K. 1844–53.

1865, V (412). Report of Select Committee on State of British Settlements on the West Coast of Africa.

II. SECONDARY SOURCES

1. *Unpublished theses*

N. H. STILLIARD: 'The Rise and Development of Legitimate Trade in Palm Oil With West Africa.' (Thesis submitted in 1938 for the degree of M.A. in History at the University of Birmingham.) This work is important for the study of the *origins* of the Delta palm-oil trade with Liverpool, particularly for the period before 1830.

W. H. SCOTTER: 'International Rivalry in the Bights of Benin and Biafra 1815–1885.' (Thesis submitted in 1933 in the University of London for the degree of Ph.D.) It is important for this study because of its full treatment of Anglo-Spanish negotiations over the island of Fernando Po.

G. R. MELLOR: 'British Policy in relation to Sierra Leone.' (Thesis submitted in 1935 for the degree of M.A. in the University of London.) Relevant to this study for the controversy over Sierra Leone and Fernando Po as bases for the suppression of the slave trade.

SIDNEY R. SMITH: 'The Ibo People, A Study of Religion and Customs of a Tribe in the Southern Provinces of Nigeria' (unpublished manuscript, written in May 1929). Seen by kind permission of the widow of the author. Good for a study of the Aro Settlements and the migration from north to south following the slave trade.

2. Semi-official publications

JAMES BANDINEL: *Some Account of the Trade in Slaves from Africa.*
E. HERTSLET: *Commercial Treaties,* 22 vols.
Map of Africa by Treaty (London, 1894).

3. Contemporary material

The contemporary material is voluminous. But it is necessary to be very discriminating in the choice of one's authorities; it appeared that the ambition of every nineteenth-century traveller or trader to the River Niger and its Delta was to produce a book on this little-known region. Among this crowd of writers there are, undoubtedly, a number of outstanding authors whose works are of great importance to the investigator.

CAPTAIN HUGH GOW: *Memoirs* . . . (Liverpool, 1830). A valuable source on Bonny trade at the time of the abolition of the slave trade. The author was very intimate with the reigning Pepple and was for many years engaged in the Bonny trade. His ship, the *Kitty's Amelia,* was the last English slaver to sail from the port of Liverpool, on 27 July 1807.

JAMES MACQUEEN: *A Geographical and Commercial View of Northern and Central Africa* . . . (Edinburgh, 1821). Reflects perhaps more than any other work the popular interest in the Niger at the time.

T. F. BUXTON: *The African Slave Trade and Its Remedy* (London, 1839).

J. F. JOHNSON: *Proceedings of the General Anti-Slavery Convention* . . . (London, 1843). Important as illustrating the state of opinion about the West African slave trade in the forties. Contains Laird's views on 'free emigration'.

CAPTAIN JOHN ADAMS: *Sketches Taken During Ten Years Voyages to Africa between the years 1786–1800* . . . (London, 1822). Undoubtedly the best account of the Delta trade at the abolition of the slave trade and the rise of the oil trade in the early years of the nineteenth century. A reliable and scientific treatise.

RICHARD AND JOHN LANDER: *Journal of an Expedition to Explore the Course and Termination of the Niger,* 3 vols. (London, 1832).

MACGREGOR LAIRD AND R. A. K. OLDFIELD: *Narrative of an Expedition into the Interior of Africa* . . . 2 vols. (London, 1837). It is superfluous to comment on the works of these Niger pioneers. They are indispensable to this study.

CAPTAIN W. ALLEN AND T. R. H. THOMSON: *A Narrative of the Expedition to the Niger River in 1841,* 2 vols. (London, 1848). Easily the best of the various books and pamphlets produced by the members of the Niger expedition of 1841.

SAMUEL CROWTHER AND J. F. SCHÖN: *Journals of the Revd. James Frederick Schön and Mr. Samuel Crowther* (London, 1842). A good account of the first missionary enterprise in the Niger valley.

J. O. McWILLIAM: *Medical History of the Niger Expedition of 1841* (London, 1843). A good account of the battle against malaria.

H. M. WADDELL: *Twenty-nine Years in the West Indies and Central Africa* (London, 1863). A lucid and honest account of contemporary life at Old Calabar, and to some extent at Bonny, by a distinguished missionary.

HUGH GOLDIE: *Calabar and Its Mission* (Edinburgh, 1890). First four chapters devoted to a study of Old Calabar institutions, political and religious.

D. C. CROWTHER: *The Establishment of the Niger Delta Pastorate Church, 1864–1892* (Liverpool, 1907). An authoritative account of the work of the Church of England in the Niger Delta by the son of Bishop Crowther, founder of the Niger Mission.

W. B. BAIKIE: *Narrative of an Exploring Voyage . . .* (London, 1856). An account of the first successful Niger expedition of 1854. It is the best informed of all contemporary writings so far as Ibo institutions were concerned.

MARY KINGSLEY: *West African Studies* (London, 1899). It is the Appendixes to this book, written by C. N. de Cardi and others and running to about 150 pages, that are of importance to Delta history. They contain eyewitness accounts by English traders who had many years' experience of trade in the Delta.

T. J. HUTCHINSON: (i) *Narrative of the Niger, Tchadda, and Benue Exploration . . .* (London, 1855). (ii) *Impressions of Western Africa* (London, 1858). (iii) *Ten Years Wandering Among the Ethiopians* (London, 1861). All three written by a former Consul, and important for all aspects of Delta trade and politics in the period under survey.

J. AFRICANUS B. HORTON: *West African Countries and Peoples* (London, 1868). This work is important as representing the nineteenth-century 'educated African' view of the 1865 Parliamentary Select Committee Report recommending self-government for West African peoples. The author was an M.D. of Edinburgh University and an Associate of King's College, London.

A. C. G. HASTINGS: *The Voyage of the Day Spring . . .* (London, 1926). A useful journal written by Lieutenant (later Sir) John Hawley Glover during the 1857 Niger expedition.

S. WHITFORD: *Trading Life in West and Central Africa* (Liverpool, 1877). Contains some information on the social life of the traders.

The following give a general impression of the period:

W. COLE: *Life in the Niger, Or Journal of an African Trader* (London, 1862).

J. SMITH: *Trade and Travels in the Gulf of Guinea* (1851).

J. A. CARNES: *Journal of a Voyage from Boston to the West Coast of Africa: with full description of the manner of trading with the natives on the coast* (Boston, 1852).

SIR RICHARD F. BURTON: *Wanderings in West Africa: from Liverpool to Fernando Po* (London, 1863).

A. P. CROUCH: *Glimpses of Feverland* (London, 1889).

A. J. DAWSON: *In the Bight of Benin* (London, 1897).

ADOLPHE BURDO: *The Niger and the Benue* (London, 1880). A French traveller's views on the trade of the Niger and its future possibilities.

W. WINWOOD READE: *Savage Africa* (London, 1864). Impressions of the first English journalist to visit West Africa.

HAROLD BINDLOSS: *In The Niger Country* (London, 1898). Describes the lives of inland traders in the Niger valley.

HENRY ROE: *West African Scenes* (London, 1874). A graphic description by a missionary of life at Fernando Po in the sixties and seventies.

Index

Aba: landing port for Ngwa palm-oil market, 41.

Abam: professional Iboland warriors, 28, 39.

Abari, 212.

Abeokuta, 96, 117, 131.

Abeona, palm-oil ship, 119.

Aberdare, 1st baron, 209.

Aberdeen, 4th earl of, 85, 87–88.

Abiriba: professional Iboland warriors, 39.

Abo: Benin migrants at, 25–26; Ossai, king of, 26, 48; trade monopoly, 26–27; distance from Aro Oracle, 40; Brazilian rum in, 53; factory erected by Laird in, 171; destruction of, 174; British companies' trading post at, 204; government attack on, 207.

Abragada: trading post at, 204.

Abuderkama of Abari, native leader, 212.

Accra, 20, 199.

Acoona-Coona and Omun dispute, 129.

Actaeon, H.M. frigate, 94.

Ada: Ibo professional warrior, 28.

Ada, *see* Edda.

Adams, Capt. John: salt from sea-water, 22; Bonny trade and traders, 29, 67, 102, 104; power of the king of Bonny, 32; education at Old Calabar, 111.

Adawai: mixed migrants at, 26.

Adderley, Mr.: chairman of Parliamentary Select Committee (1865), 167.

Adelaide islet: British guns on, 55.

Ado na Idu: Ibo term for kingdom of Benin, q.v.

Africa: British trade with, 1 n. 1; native opposition to internal penetration by whites, 7–10; regeneration of, through African agency, 116, 170.

Africa, palm-oil ship, 119.

African, S.S., 191.

African Association (London Society Instituted for Exploring the Interior of Africa), 13–14.

African Association of Liverpool, 91, 200.

African Company, 53, 108.

African Institution, 58.

African Merchants, Company of, 178–80.

African Steamship Company, 61 n. 2, 114–15.

Africans: differences between those of West Africa and the Cape of Good Hope, 9–10; alleged sloth of, 63–64; emancipated and educated, 111, 116, 119.

Agballa Oracle, 40.

Agberi: 'Hostile Village', 173.

agriculture, African, 13.

Akassa: distance from Abo, 26; old Portuguese houses in, 47; trading post at, 204; Niger Company's factory attacked by natives, 212.

Akitoye, king of Lagos, 130–1.

Akrai: mixed migrants at, 26.

Akwete: palm-oil market, 41.

Alagbariya: chief and hunter, 24.

Alali (Anna Pepple), son of Madu, head of the Opubu royal house and regent of Bonny: account of, 69–72; supports slave traders, 74; traders' views on him, 75; visited by Craigie, 76–77; his downfall, 78, 98; usurps kingly powers, 98; opposition to king Dappa, 134–8, 140–2, 147–8, 163–4; and the cause of Dappa's death, 149; after the Bonny civil war, 150–2; head of the Regency Council, 152, 160; his death, 161; and Oko Jumbo, 182; and Ja Ja, 182–3, 186, 196; his debts, 183.

Alburkah, steamship, 62.

alcohol: unchanging item of barter trade, 105.

Alenso: trading post at, 204.

Algerian frontier, 208.

Allen, Capt. William: on size of Abo, 27; and slave smuggling, 52.

Croft, James A., 209.
Cross river, 19, 33.
Crow, Capt. Hugh, 13.
crown colony government in West Africa, 203.
Crowther, Samuel Adjai, negro bishop, 161-2.
Cuba: African slaves in, 51, 82.
culture contacts, 5.
Cumberland, slaver, 49.
Cummins, Richard: on French slave traders, 54.
Curaçao, 2.
curlews, 24.
currency, 104-8.
Cuthbertson, Capt., 119-21, 199.

Dahomey, 13, 20, 95; king of, 131; importance of guns in, 107; opposition to consular power, 130.
Dalzel, Archibald: governor of Cape Coast, 7.
Danish, the: in the West Indies, 2.
Danish guns, 107.
Dappa, William (Pepple), king of Bonny: of Ibo descent, 29; and slave trade, 48; a minor on his accession, 69-70; his actions after the fall of the regent, 74-80, 128; and slave-trade treaties, 83-89, 131; and the 'trust' system, 90-93, 112-13; and the palm-oil trade, 99; and consul Beecroft, 132-52; fall of his monarchy, 134 sqq.; exiled to Fernando Po and elsewhere, 142-4; his debts and his wealth, 142-3; his own version of events leading to his deposition and exile, 144; account of him in exile, 145-6; his income, 146; place in history of his exile and downfall,146-7; effect of his downfall on the Court of Equity, 147-8; events following the death of king Dappo, 149-52; on the position of ex-slaves, 153; agitation for his reinstatement, 160, 162-3; his return and death, 163-4, 182.
Dappo, Prince, puppet king of Bonny, 143-5, 147; his death, 148-9.
Davies, Capt., 119.
Dawson, Ralph, master of palm-oil ship, 74.
Dayspring, S.S., 169-70, 175.

Deane, Capt. E., slave trader: pioneer in palm-oil trade, 49; on ivory, 49.
Delphic Oracle, 38.
Delta states, see Niger Delta.
Denham, Major Dixon, 15; on seizure of slave ships, 98.
Denmark: and the slave trade, 2.
Dillon, Richard, palm-oil merchant: protests against the government's abandonment of Fernando Po, 57.
diplomatists, 28.
Docemo, king of Lagos, 176.
doctors, 28.
dollars, Spanish, 108.
Donnan, E., 3.
double trust, 109.
doubloons, Spanish, 108.
Douglass, Commander, 178.
drugs, trade in, 14.
Dubois, W. E. B., 3.
Duke Ephraim, African chief of Old Calabar, 59, 67, 119-20, 129.
Duke Town, Old Calabar, 33-34, 87, 118-20, 157-9.
Dupleix, Joseph François, 7.
Dutch, the: in the west Indies, 2; number of slaves exported (c. 1798), 47 n. 1.

East Africa: slave-trade treaties with, 81.
East India Company, 7.
Easton, —, consul: attacks on Onitsha and Yamaha, 207.
Ebi-nya, 24 n. 2.
Ebony, 101.
economics: 19th-century changes, 11-12.
Edda (or Ada): professional Iboland warriors, 39.
Edgar, C. B., 209.
Edmonstone, Commodore, 124, 174.
education and schools, 112-13, 129.
Edwards, Bryan: and the slave trade, 3, 47 n. 1.
Eendragi, Dutch palm-oil ship, 119.
Efik, Nigerian tribe, 20, 24, 68; in Niger Delta, 30; social organization, 33, 43; adaptability and genius for trade, 45-56.
Efik territory, 156.
Egba tribe, 96.

Latin American states: African slaves in, 51–52.

La Vigie, French man-of-war, 68.

Ledyard, John, 14.

Leeward Islands, 2.

legitimate traders, 49.

Leonard, A. G., 23–24, 44.

Levinge, Lieut., 48.

Liberia, 96.

Lisbon, 2.

Liverpool: and the cotton trade, 12, 51; slave traders become pioneers in palm-oil trade, 49; Macgregor Laird and, 61 n. 2, 62; supercargoes, 86, 88, 117–19, 170 sqq.; Delta palm-oil trade largely done through Liverpool houses, 102; monopolies of pioneers in palm-oil trade, 108–27 *passim*; coast monopolies, 179–80.

Liverpool Association of Merchants of the Board of Trade, 124.

Liverpool, 3rd earl of, 58.

Livingstone Charles, consul; on Delta middlemen, 103, 110; and Liverpool monopolists, 115; consul at Bonny, 182; account of him, 182 n. 2; on Ja Ja and fears of civil war, 186; and Ja Ja's defeat, 188; visits Ja Ja, 190–3; naval force against Ja Ja, 193–4; on trade losses in Bonny, 197; his death, 197; on Ja Ja's position after the revolution, 197; on the extent of British property in the Bight of Biafra in the early seventies, 198; receives Order-in-Council for regulating British trade in the Bight of Biafra, 201.

Livingstone, David, 172.

Lokoja, 61 n. 2; government post at, 169 n. 1; factory erected at, 171; Baikie unauthorized consul at, 175–6; closing of the consulate (1869), 177; companies' trading posts at, 204; government protection during evacuation of the consulate, 206.

London: king Dappa of Bonny exiled to, 144; merchants of, 179.

London Society Instituted for Exploring the Interior of Africa (African Association), 13–14.

Long Ju Ju, Aro Oracle, 38 n. 4.

Lower Oko: trading post at, 204.

Luiz d'Aubuquerque, French schooner, 68.

Lynslager, I. W. B., consul: and palm-oil trade dispute, 117–18; report on Alali, 147; and the death of king Dappo, 148; after the Bonny civil war, 150–2.

Macaulay, Zachary, governor of Sierra Leone, 59.

machinery: development of, causes rise in demand for palm oil as a lubricant, 50.

McEachan, Archie, 191.

McIntosh, David, 209, 212.

McLeod, Lieut., consul at Lokoja, 175.

Macmillan, W. M., 28.

McQueen, James, 14, 61.

Madagascar, eastern: king Radama of, 81.

Madden, Dr.: on West African trade, 51, 97–98.

Madjine, Spanish slave trader, 100.

Madras, 7.

Madu (Maduka), ex-slave, head of the Opubu royal house and regent of Bonny, 69–70, 183.

Al-Maghili, Arabian missionary and teacher, 5.

mail-carrying steamships: effect on West African trade, 114 sqq.

Malaguetta Coast, 6.

malaguetta trade: decline in, 2.

malaria, 8, 10, 169, 172.

Malaya: British trade with, 1 n. 1.

Malimba: treaty with chiefs against slavers and pirates, 66.

Malimba river: palm-oil trade, 101.

manilla: a copper currency, 43, 107.

Manimuma of Abari: native leader, 212.

Mansell, Capt., 94.

man-stealers, 49.

Marie Galante, 2.

market governments: take the place of the Aro Oracle, 45.

market laws in the Niger Delta, 42–43.

Martinique, 2.

Masaba, king of Bida, 169 n. 1, 175, 177, 206–7.

'masked men', 88, 92.

materialism and religion, 161–2.

ℓ

CPSIA information can be obtained at www.ICGtesting.com
Printed in the USA
BVOW06s1502200915

418762BV00010B/214/P